America's Post-Truth Phenomenon

Library of Congress Cataloging-in-Publication Data

Names: Prado, C. G., editor.
Title: America's post-truth phenomenon : when feelings and opinions trump facts and evidence / C. G. Prado, editor.
Description: Santa Barbara : Praeger, [2018] | Includes bibliographical references and index.
Identifiers: LCCN 2018001372 (print) | LCCN 2018003854 (ebook) | ISBN 9781440862731 (ebook) | ISBN 9781440862724 (alk. paper)
Subjects: LCSH: Political culture—United States. | Truth. | Emotions.
Classification: LCC JA75.7 (ebook) | LCC JA75.7 .A48 2018 (print) | DDC 306.20973—dc23
LC record available at https://lccn.loc.gov/2018001372

ISBN: 978-1-4408-6272-4 (print)
     978-1-4408-6273-1 (ebook)

22 21 20 19 18   1 2 3 4 5

This book is also available as an eBook.

Praeger
An Imprint of ABC-CLIO, LLC

ABC-CLIO, LLC
130 Cremona Drive, P.O. Box 1911
Santa Barbara, California 93116-1911
www.abc-clio.com

This book is printed on acid-free paper ∞

Manufactured in the United States of America

America's Post-Truth Phenomenon

When Feelings and Opinions Trump Facts and Evidence

C. G. Prado, Editor

PRAEGER™

An Imprint of ABC-CLIO, LLC

Santa Barbara, California • Denver, Colorado

Contents

Preface

Often in 2017, the online version of the *New York Times* opened with a pop-up that boldly asserted: "TRUTH. It's grounded in facts."[1] As one might expect, the pop-up led to an invitation to online viewers to subscribe to the website or the hardcopy newspaper, but what is notable about the pop-up is that it reflects how the *New York Times* views, and especially how it is responding to, a current phenomenon that has attained a surprisingly extensive scope and which is sociopolitically disquieting. That phenomenon is the growing use and acceptance of *post-truth*: what the *Economist* described as "assertions that 'feel true' but have no basis in fact."[2]

Despite the common association of post-truth with Donald Trump, its use antedates him. But its newly widespread use and remarkably broad acceptance were lent significant stimulus and momentum by Trump's speeches in his presidential campaign and even more so by his presidential speeches and his persistent postings or tweets on Twitter. Trump's claims, though invariably eccentric and never substantiated, apparently served to justify and legitimize the use of post-truth for many people. In addition, Trump's refusal to offer relevant responses to challenges to assertions and claims made in his speeches and tweets has served to make adopters of post-truth feel impervious or simply indifferent to challenges directed at their own post-true contentions.

Acceptance and use of post-truth have serious implications for social and political activities and interactions. An editorial published in February 2017 captured the basic problem as concisely as any statement of it that I have found. The editorial maintained, "It has become commonplace to say that we live in a 'post-truth' world. That one person's opinion is as good as another's. That when we come right down to it, *everything is subjective*."[3]

The scariest and unfortunately most probable political consequence of wholesale adoption of subjectivism through use and acceptance of post-truth was caught in another editorial. That editorial maintained that "if the post-truth era starts by blowing up current knowledge structures," if factual bases for assertions are abandoned or ignored, then use and acceptance of post-truth "most likely leads to authoritarianism."⁴ This is a crucial point regarding wholesale adoption of subjectivism through espousal and even tolerance of post-truth, especially in sociopolitical contexts. As the *New York Times* pop-up implicitly emphasizes, the press relies on facticity in collating and publishing news stories. An initial major step toward despotic rule, then, is the discrediting of the press. The objective is to establish the dictatorial government as the sole source of supposedly trustworthy information.

A crucial aspect of the discrediting of the press was perceptively articulated by the *Economist,* which said of post-truth: "The lies of men like Mr. Trump . . . are not intended to convince the elites, whom their target voters neither trust nor like, but to reinforce prejudices."⁵ Employment of post-truth by politicians is not intended to convince voters of the truth or falsity of anything; it is intended to cater to their biases and prejudgments and in that way to make them feel as one with the politicians using post-truth. Recent developments regarding activity by white supremacists and other racist groups support the *Economist's* contention that prejudices are being reinforced—or perhaps, better, both reinforced and validated in the minds of those holding them.

Contrary to various newspapers that are actively resisting the use of post-truth, as in the case of the *New York Times* and the *Washington Post,* online news media have actually fostered use and acceptance of post-truth. Promulgation of post-truth has been "abetted by the evolution of the media." This is due to how "fragmentation of news sources has created an atomised world in which lies, rumour and gossip spread with alarming speed."⁶ In addition, the secondary but important effect of the evolution of the news media is what I have for some time considered a misconceived and ultimately counterproductive practice. This is the well-intentioned "pursuit of 'fairness' in reporting," a practice that "often creates phony balance at the expense of truth."⁷ If every expressed opinion is given equal coverage by the press in an effort not to discriminate against individuals interviewed or quoted or otherwise referred to, then opinions based on good evidence and sound reasoning are buried in chatter.

This last point brings up the fact that if the news media have knowingly or unknowingly encouraged the use and acceptance of post-truth, the significance of their doing so pales in comparison to how social media have fostered both its use and acceptance. This is a point I pursue in my contribution, "The New Subjectivism," but two vital points need to be briefly made here.

The first point is that social media enable individuals to voice their opinions to hundreds of thousands, if not millions, of people. The problem is that the voicing is effectively indiscriminate, in that social media sites censor only flagrantly racist and obscene postings. Moreover, the minimal censoring that does take place is invariably reactive, which means that the questionable postings at issue will have been available to a vast audience for hours and even days before they are removed. As a consequence, postings that run the gamut from deep, productive, and insightful to empty, misrepresentative, and simply inane are available for all to see. The second point is that misguided efforts at fairness on the part of social media sites pose a basic problem, in that it is in the name of impartiality that social media sites allow people to post pretty much whatever they want, barring blatantly lewd and discriminatory remarks. As is the case with online news reporting, a phony impartiality is achieved at the expense of acknowledging some measure of authority.

The chapters that follow are intended to discuss post-truth from different perspectives in order to bring out issues and problems that need to be addressed, as well as some that might not otherwise occur to one. The objective is to provide as full a picture of the post-truth phenomenon as is practically possible. We are facing a complex development with highly significant and largely negative implications. It is crucial to understand as many of this development's aspects as presently can be discerned. Unlike most collections, therefore, the following chapters neither do intend nor were intended to cohere with one another on the topic at issue. Rather, they do intend and were intended to approach post-truth from diverse angles and with different priorities.

I want to close this preface by expressing my thanks to Ms. Debbie Carvalko, my editor at Praeger, for all of her efforts and help regarding the production of both this collection and my previous one, *Social Media and Your Brain*.

Notes

1. www.nytimes.com.

2. *Economist,* Editorial, September 10, 2016, Vol. 420, No. 9006, p. 9.

3. Lawrie McFarlane, Editorial, *Anahin/Nimpo Lake Messenger,* February 2017, Vol. 13, No. 12, p. 4. The *Messenger* is a small monthly newspaper published in British Columbia, and its editorial illustrates the extent of the press's concern with the post-truth phenomenon. My emphasis.

4. Sergio Sismondo, "Post-truth?" *Social Studies of Science* 47, no. 1 (2017): 3–6.

5. *Economist,* 2016.

6. Ibid.

7. Ibid.

CHAPTER ONE

Introduction: The New Subjectivism

C. G. Prado

Theorizing about the nature of truth is no longer an abstract philosophical exercise due to the increasingly commonplace use and acceptance of post-truth. There is need to understand the nature of post-truth, and of its rapid popularization, in order to better resist and discourage use and acceptance of post-truth because of their negative sociopolitical consequences. There is also need to consider and assess the extensive discussion of post-truth in the news media. The bulk of such discussion is critical, and often sharply negative, and the danger this discussion poses is that we may end up not with a better understanding of post-truth but with persistent discord between the news media and a large percentage of the population. The most obvious sign of such discord is the dismissive attitude many are taking toward the news media's criticism of the assertions Donald Trump makes in his speeches and the impulsive tweets he posts on Twitter.

The Economist described use of post-truth as the making of "assertions that 'feel true' but have no basis in fact."[1] This disregard for facticity is why acceptance and use of post-truth have serious implications for social and political activity and interaction. What makes things worse is that the disregard for facticity is not just a matter of individuals expressing what they think to be the case. What is worrying is that users of post-truth are not simply voicing their views or beliefs. An editorial published in February 2017 captured the basic problem as concisely as any statement of it I have found: "It has become commonplace to say that we live in a 'post-truth' world. That one person's opinion is as good as another's. That when we come right down to it, everything is subjective."[2] Users of post-truth see themselves as expressing their opinions, but opinions that call for no verification, and in being their opinions, are on a par with anyone else's opinions. Once facticity is abandoned, opinions lose the authority some may have regardless of their sources.

The central point that must be appreciated is that post-truth relocates the grounds and authority of assertions or propositions from facticity to personal conviction. Many fail to see the misconceived nature of this relocation, or see it as a positive development, not realizing that post-truth is the terminus of a conceptual degradation of objective truth. Post-truth is the final step in the misguided move away from objective truth to relativization of truth. If truth is objective, assertions or propositions are true depending on how things *are*. If truth is relative, assertions or propositions are true depending on how people *take* things to be. Post-truth is an extreme form of relative truth because in being subjective, it makes assertions or propositions true depending only on how *individuals* take things to be. This is why use and acceptance of post-truth allow no recourse to how things actually are or to how others take things to be. Individuals' post-truth assertions may be accepted, or they may be rejected by others, but those assertions cannot be rated for truth value because they are grounded only on individuals' own perceptions and judgments, and perceptions and judgments of the moment, at that.

Unfortunately, many people who use, accept, or simply tolerate post-truth see use of post-truth as a fresh self-assertiveness and fail to see it for what it is: a negative sociopolitical development. There is need for deeper consideration of what use and acceptance of post-truth involve, and how its use and acceptance attained their contemporary currency. Only then will it be clear that we are not dealing with a positive development but rather with a socially perilous one.

A clear illustration of the perilous nature of use and acceptance of post-truth is that one consequence is loss of accountability. As noted, post-truth assertions admit only three responses by others: agreement, disagreement, or indifference. Post-true assertions are not open to calls for substantiation or assessment of correctness or, for that matter, even requests for explanation. Once truth is rendered subjective, once truth is made entirely personal, post-truth users cannot be held accountable for whatever they say. This is an untenable situation, generally, but it is both untenable and socially very dangerous when post-truth users are individuals with political power.

This point is echoed in another editorial focusing on the leveling of opinions and adoption of the view that everything is relative to individuals' perspectives. The editorial warns that "the post-truth era starts by blowing up current knowledge structures" and that if factual bases for assertions offered as true are abandoned or ignored, then adoption of post-truth "most likely leads to authoritarianism."[3] The way this happens is what we are witnessing in Donald Trump's treatment of the news media. Briefly put, accepted political use of post-truth discredits the news media, thereby making it look as if the government is the only source of reliable information.

A central aspect of this press-discrediting tactic was captured by *The Economist,* which said of post-truth that "lies of men like Mr. Trump . . . are not intended to convince the elites, whom their target voters neither trust nor like, but to reinforce prejudices."[4] When post-truth assertions, directed at supportive voters, are criticized and challenged by the news media, politicians like Trump ignore or ridicule the criticism and disregard the challenges. The politicians then charge the news media with being biased. The targeted supportive voters, hearing what they want to hear from the politicians, then see the news media as unfairly critical and agree with the charge of bias. This greatly strengthens the politicians' positions, in effect precluding news-media revelation of their deceptions and wrongdoings.

Consideration of post-truth needs to begin with a review of how post-truth, as an understanding of truth, has an enabling history in the form of the relativization of objective truth. Despite this history, post-truth, as the phenomenon we are seeing today, is new in significant ways. For one thing, most of its adopters know little or nothing about post-truth's enabling history. For another, post-truth is diversely understood despite—or perhaps because of—the extent of its use and acceptance. To sort things out, we need to briefly review objectivist and relativist conceptions of truth. We then need to consider the more prominent current definitions of post-truth.

Conception of truth as objective is likely best represented by the correspondence theory of truth, which holds that true propositions are true when they accurately correspond to states of affairs: when they faithfully mirror the relevant aspects of so-called external reality—that is, reality independent of the mind.[5] Conceiving of truth as objective, then, is holding that if what we think, write, or say is true, it is so in virtue of our accurate propositional replication of matters of fact that are wholly independent of human perception and interpretation. Propositions "are assessed as true when . . . the way they represent things as being is the way that things really are."[6] This is essentially a restatement of Aristotle's definition of truth, which was that truth is "to say of what is that it is, and of what is not that it is not."[7]

The central point underlying truth as correspondence is that propositions, whether ideationally or propositionally formed or expressed, are "made true by how things are in the world."[8] When the content of propositions matches mind-independent states of affairs, the propositions correspond to what is the case independently of the minds forming the propositions and the propositions are true.[9]

Brief review of truth conceived as relative is trickier because of the diversity of interpretations. Most philosophers consider objective truth to be integral to realism and see relativist truth as deriving from tacit or explicit adoption of idealism. But there are two forms of idealism, both of which support relativization of truth: "epistemological idealism (the view that the contents of human knowledge are ineluctably determined by the structure of human thought), and ontological idealism (the view that epistemological idealism delivers truth because reality itself is a form of thought and human thought participates in it)."[10]

Complicating things further is that those holding the form of relativist truth most prevalent today have no time for epistemology or ontology and are indifferent to claims about relative truth's conceptual origins, other than occasionally acknowledging Friedrich Nietzsche's major contribution to its promulgation. This current form of relativistically conceived truth is definitive of postmodernism and is paradigmed in the writings of Michel Foucault and Jacques Derrida.[11] Taking their cue from Nietzsche's rejection of Cartesian/Kantian objectively conceived truth, philosophers like Foucault and Derrida rejected objective truth and relativized truth to consensus among groups. Relativization of truth was the predominant factor in the transition in philosophy's historical development from modern to postmodern.

Postmodern relativistically conceived truth essentially has it that propositions are true when they are sanctioned by established discursive practices and are generally accepted as true. Being true is held to be a function of the communal construals and practices of the members of a society or culture, construals and practices sanctioned by those individuals respected as authoritative figures in those cultures and societies. The particular version of postmodern relativistic conception of truth that is most relevant in the present context is Foucault's, and its core description merits restatement. Stressing the discursive nature of truth, Foucault tells us that

> truth is a thing of this world: it is produced only by virtue of multiple forms of constraint. . . . Each society has its regime of truth, its "general politics" of truth: that is, the types of discourse which it accepts and makes function as true; the mechanisms and instances which enable one to distinguish true and false statements, the means by which each is sanctioned; the techniques and procedures accorded value in the acquisition of truth; the status of those who are charged with saying what counts as true.[12]

Stressing the communal aspect of truth so defined, Foucault finds it necessary to add that while it "is always possible one could speak the truth in a void; one would only be in the true (*dans le vrai*), however, if one obeyed the rules of some discursive 'policy.'"[13]

"True," then, is a description that applies only to propositions articulated in a rule-bound, communicative context. This essential point precludes conception of truth as wholly subjective. That is, it rules out propositions being true when held or voiced only by individuals and regardless of others' responses or indifference. "True" is applicable to propositions only when uttered or otherwise expressed by one individual to one or more other individuals in a communal communicative context.

The key idea here is that Foucault's relativization of truth is to groups, not individuals, and his conception is characteristic of postmodern relativization of truth. Postmodern conception of truth as relative, therefore, is not consistent with conception of truth as wholly relative to individuals. Postmodern relativization of truth at most only enables the extreme relativization of truth to individuals; it is not itself relative to individuals. The force of this point is that efforts to portray post-truth as the evolutionary product of postmodern conception of truth are misconceived. These efforts muddle what we can best describe as an enabling precedent with what many wrongly see as a causally active prior stage in a continuous intellectual progression. The importance of this point about post-truth not being an aspect or product of postmodernism emerges when we consider definitions of post-truth. When we do so, we appreciate that post-truth is a long-standing, though currently more used and accepted, phenomenon and not a final stage in an intellectual development. Attempts to connect post-truth to postmodernism, even when critical, effectively lend post-truth something of a philosophical history that is, in fact, bogus. But to better understand the point, we need to consider some authoritative definitions of post-truth.

The aim of the foregoing discussion is to establish two key points prerequisite to consideration of definitions of post-truth. The first point has to do with the difference between objectively and relativistically conceived truth. The second has to do with how post-truth is not, as many think, the product of postmodernist thought about truth. Postmodern conception of truth is categorically relative, but it is relative to groups, not individuals as is post-truth. With these two points in mind, we can now turn to how post-truth is currently defined.

The first point to note about definitions of post-truth is that provision of the definitions has been prompted mainly by current political events. In particular, they have been prompted by efforts to deal with Donald Trump's various pronouncements and especially his impulsive tweets. The definitions, then, are not philosophical definitions of truth; they are efforts to articulate the essence of a worrying contemporary phenomenon. Central here is that though varied in nature, the definitions invariably contrast post-truth with facticity, so are grounded on conception of truth as objective and characterize use of post-truth as violation of factual veracity.

Perhaps the most authoritative definition of post-truth was produced by the *Oxford English Dictionary* committee that was responsible for choosing "post-truth" as Word of the Year for 2016. The committee defined post-truth as "*relating to or denoting circumstances in which objective facts are less influential in shaping public opinion than appeals to emotion and personal belief.*"[14]

One point to note about this definition is that the definition mainly applies to political usage of post-truth. A second point to note is that the definition strongly implies that post-truth users are prevaricators presenting emotively loaded views and ideas to serve their own ends. What the definition fails to acknowledge, though, is that political usage of post-truth need not be knowing and deliberate prevarication. For example, the best way to understand some of Donald Trump's post-truth claims and remarks is to appreciate that when he addresses an audience, he impulsively embellishes in response to how his audiences react to his speeches and to the nature of questions raised by journalists.

While most proffered definitions of post-truth also rely on objectivist conception of truth, one exception is a definition of post-truth that does not explicitly refer to facticity and could accommodate a moderate form of relativistic understanding of truth. This definition characterizes post-truth as "describing debate that is based on passion and emotion rather than reason and evidence."[15] More typical definitions preclude such accommodation. One example is definition of post-truth as "relating to a situation or system in which facts are neglected in favour of emotions and beliefs."[16] A similar definition is of post-truth as "relating to a situation in which people are more likely to accept an argument on their emotions and beliefs, rather than one based on facts."[17]

A definition of post-truth that merits special mention is one that notes the importance of repetition: "Post-truth politics (also called post-factual politics) is a political culture in which debate is framed largely by appeals to emotion disconnected from the details of policy, and by the repeated assertion of talking points to which factual rebuttals are ignored."[18] The importance of repetition is often missed. Repetition lends a false legitimacy to talking points by making them familiar. This last-quoted definition also refers explicitly to an essential characteristic of post-true assertions, which is that they are presented as indifferent to challenges and demands for substantiation. However, while this definition of post-truth makes explicit reference to the ignoring of factual rebuttals to post-truth assertions, what the definition does not specify is that the standard response to persistent factual rebuttals is to attack those making them.[19] This is a marked characteristic of Donald Trump's way of dealing with news-media criticism of his speeches and tweets. Trump strives to portray the news media as biased and maliciously antagonistic, thereby making himself look justified in ignoring demands for substantiation of his assertions. This tactic has proven surprisingly successful with his supporters, and given what is evident about his character and inclinations, Trump may well believe the demands for substantiation and factual rebuttals are genuinely antagonistic and biased.

The foregoing definitions of post-truth are those I thought most merited inclusion here. There are other definitions, and all vary to some extent regarding what they emphasize, what they mention explicitly, and their degree of generality. To proceed, what I offer now is an amalgamation of the major points of the aforementioned definitions of post-truth and of some others I have examined. My amalgamation goes as follows: *post-truth pronouncements prioritize personal beliefs and feelings, spurn consistency, disregard objective facts, and disdain factual rebuttals and demands for substantiation.*

Central to the foregoing definitions and my amalgamation is that use of post-truth effectively disallows applicable criteria for distinguishing between the truth and falsity of assertions made. Post-truth usage allows only what it courts, which is acceptance, and what it cannot prevent, which is outright rejection of assertions made. Post-truth usage precludes any form of assessment of what is said and systematically refuses to recognize the need for corroboration or substantiation of the content of what is said. Post-truth assertions simply are true so long as the individual making the assertions holds them true. Use of post-truth is personal appropriation of truth.

Post-truth, then, does look like the inevitable consequence of the relativization of truth because relativization is a slippery slope. Once being true is relativized to group, societal, or cultural communal determination, once objective facticity is abandoned, the next step, misconceived though it may be, is to further relativize truth to individual determination. If this step is taken, the result is subjective truth, where what is true becomes a function of wholly personal perception and judgment. When that occurs, communal mechanisms for distinguishing truth from falsity are rendered inapplicable and immaterial. This idea is what underlies the inclination to see post-truth as a final stage in a philosophical evolution. But political and personal use of post-truth is as old as the use of language. We must keep in mind that while *communal* use and acceptance of post-truth do appear to be the final stage in an intellectual progression, *individual* use of post-truth has been with us since we began to communicate with one another. Put differently, what we are seeing today, particularly in the conduct of some politicians, is what we can describe as the institutionalization of what was previously personal.

Perhaps the most ironic aspect of the shift from communal or group-relative truth to subjective or individual-relative truth is also the most elusive. Both critics and supporters of post-truth fail to comprehend the coincidental nature of agreement on post-truth assertions. They do not fully fathom the profound singularity, the total subjectivity, of truth relativized to individuals. The consequence is that agreement prompts assumption of a communality that is totally artificial. The assumption of communality is enabled by nothing more than ignorance of how some individual-determined truths may merely coincide with other individual-determined truths without in any way ceasing to be entirely subjective. Chance concurrence is not communality.

Chance concurrence does not strengthen or support or validate what is believed or asserted by any two or more individuals because the concurrence is fortuitous. Coincidental concurrence of belief may be due to similarities in backgrounds, life experience, and the like. But such similarities do not alter the fact that once truth is conceived as subjective, once it is individual-determined, truth is wholly fragmented and cannot be unified by what then can only be fortuitous agreement.

The key point here is that an assertion's truth is neither corroborated nor generalized by the occurrence of one or more individuals happening to hold the same thing true as the individual making the assertion. Objective truth originates in external states of affairs; truth relativized to groups or cultures originates in communal practices; post-truth originates in individuals' beliefs. In the case of objective truth and truth relativized to groups or cultures, individuals accept or reject truths that originate outside of themselves. In the case of post-truth, individuals project truths outward that originate within themselves. Commonality of post-truth assertions, therefore, has nothing to do with their truth. What such commonality does do is manifest that many individuals may hold similar views, often prejudicial ones. This is what *The Economist* put so clearly in saying that Trump's speeches and tweets are primarily intended to reinforce his supporters' prejudices.[20]

Our speaking of post-truth as being truth relativized to individuals, as truth understood to be wholly subjective, may prove useful, but it does little to counter present-day use and growing acceptance of post-truth. Post-truth needs to be recognized for what it is: the voicing of personal views, exaggeration, embellishment, impulsive expression, and straightforward prevarication. In particular, it is necessary to defeat the misconceived idea that post-truth assertions, being expressions of personal opinion, are thereby inviolate. The proper response to expression of this idea is to point out that there are right and wrong opinions, informed and uninformed opinions, impartial and biased opinions, reasonable and unreasonable opinions. Currently, the counterresponse is usually angry dismissal: dismissal heavily laden with the implicit contention that how an individual sees a situation is immune to criticism or correction. But while it is reasonable enough to respect statements of personal opinion, what is not reasonable is expanding that respect to an irrational level by holding all such statements equally viable and inviolate regardless of content.

The ingenuous insularity of post-truth was evident in the context of Steve Tesich's coining of the term. Tesich used the phrase "post-truth" in an article titled "A Government of Lies."[21] In his article, Tesich was very hard on the Nixon and Reagan administrations for deceptiveness, by both omission and outright falsehoods. He then went on to offer an explanation as to why the deceptiveness at issue succeeded to the degree it did succeed. Tesich maintained that the electorate had come to prefer hearing pleasant lies from elected officials rather than having to listen to the harsh realities facing governments. Specifically, Tesich observed that "dictators up to now have had to work hard at suppressing the truth. We, by our actions, are saying that this is no longer necessary. . . . In a very fundamental way we . . . have freely decided that we want to live in some post-truth world."[22]

Tesich's use of "post-truth" is contrary to what a number of journalists are presently maintaining. For instance, Russell Smith is one who argues that use and acceptance of post-truth are how postmodernism is imposing itself on "public life and policy."[23] He paints post-truth as the intellectual evolutionary result of postmodern relativization of truth, rather than recognizing what I considered earlier, which is that postmodern relativization of truth only enabled subjectivism or the further relativization of truth to individuals. Another example is Casey Williams, who argues that Trump's speeches and tweets indicate he is availing himself of postmodern philosophical ideas or tools.[24] Williams even goes some way toward justifying acceptance of post-truth by maintaining that "alternative facts" may "reflect the view that language itself distorts reality" and thereby relativizes what is expressed. Unfortunately, like other, similar ones, both of these articles inadvertently lend a measure of legitimacy to post-truth. What such articles do is give users of post-truth the impression that there is something deep underlying their practice, even if they have little or no idea of what it might be.

Attributing use and acceptance of post-truth to the intellectual consequences of postmodernism is a mistake. As indicated earlier, postmodern relativization of truth to groups and practices did open the door to the final relativization of truth to individuals, to the rendering of truth as wholly subjective. But opening the door to that final relativization is not the same as causing that relativization. What journalists and academics trying to ground post-truth on postmodernism should be doing is tracing what social developments led to the exaltation of personal opinion. They should, above all, be focusing on and assessing what I next consider: the role of social media in the shaping of present attitudes. Unfortunately, though, it is not only that some journalists and academics are making more of post-truth than they should, and so contributing to its use and acceptance. There are at least two other crucial factors.

We live in a time when social media are an inescapable influence operant in the shaping of people's views and inclinations. Of special importance is that, thanks to social media, everyone now has a voice. A consequence of this is that influences on individuals have multiplied a thousand-fold. Social media inundates individuals with other peoples' views and concerns. We also live in a time when the news media have become far more concerned with capturing and entertaining consumers than with conveying the news. One consequence of this shift in priorities is that whereas before there were liberal and conservative television news programs, newspapers, and magazines, there now are many gradations of these leanings evident in how material is presented to audiences. Moreover, winning and keeping audience loyalty prompts continuing efforts on the part of the news media to please their audiences by slanting coverage of newsworthy events and doing so in ways that often are inconsistent from hour to hour and day to day. The combined result of social media and the change in news reporting is a population, a body politic, that is intentionally but more often unintentionally manipulated to a degree never seen before.

A different but equally crucial element in the role social media play regarding use and acceptance of post-truth is the overemphasized commitment of social media sites to complete neutrality with respect to users' postings. Social media sites are uncritical of the postings they accept in the name of fairness and impartiality. The only exception to this commitment to impartiality is the censoring of flagrantly obscene and equally flagrant racist postings. Even then, many such postings must await complaints to be censored and so remain available on the affected sites for hours or days. These very narrow assessment standards ensure that a great deal of misconceived, ignorant, prejudicial, and flatly erroneous postings are available to impressionable and undiscriminating members of a very large audience.[25] Nor are misinformation and distortion the only issues. Misconceived, ignorant, prejudicial, and erroneous postings strongly tend to validate the equally wrong-headed views of those who read the postings and agree with them. The result is the reinforcing of misconceptions, ignorance, prejudices, and mistaken views.

The overemphasized commitment to impartiality operates in a somewhat similar manner in the news media. As *The Economist* puts it, the news media now engage in leveling practices that supposedly support the "pursuit of 'fairness' in reporting," but which are practices that go too far and actually manufacture a false reportage balance "at the expense of truth." This happens most notably when the press relies on the personal-opinion-prioritizing attitude we have been considering. *The Economist* illustrates this exaltation of personal opinion with a generic example of how newspapers and television news programs present incompatible elements of a news report as if their incompatibility is a matter of perception and not of facticity: "NASA scientist says Mars is probably uninhabited; Professor Snooks says it is teeming with aliens. It's really a matter of opinion."[26] Added to this sanctification of opinion is the mind-numbing repetition of television news programs. Newsworthy events are incessantly discussed by "talking heads" who offer audiences diverse analyses of whatever is at issue, though with moderators making points and raising questions to balance the analyses offered. We have, then, an electorate overwhelmed, not by information but by diverse points of view all presented as if equally worthy of consideration.

Because of the extent of its promulgation, post-truth poses a serious contemporary problem, and it is a problem that goes well beyond concern with what immediately comes to mind when post-truth is mentioned, namely, Donald Trump's pronouncements and the persistent media coverage of those pronouncements. Serious though the implications of Trump's pronouncements may be, the larger difficulty is that people are increasingly basing their personal and political decisions and actions on what the courts would call hearsay: unsubstantiated claims and assertions that gain unmerited force from sheer reiteration and presentation as all on a par with respect to their worth. The issue of truth decidedly has escaped seminar rooms and philosophy texts. It is now a pressing practical problem.

We very much need to keep clearly in mind what is fundamentally at issue when post-truth is used and accepted. We cannot allow ourselves to forget or overlook that unlike expressions of emotions, desires, or fears, all assertions capable of being true or false have truth conditions that must be satisfied for the assertions to be true and to be rightly taken as true. Those truth conditions are satisfied only when mind-independent reality is so disposed that it contains delineable states of affairs that satisfy what the assertions say is the case. When the assertions correspond to how things are, to those delineated states of affairs, they are true.

Admittedly, there are complications. These mainly have to do with two areas of ambiguity. The first area of ambiguity involves assertions about the past. In these cases, assertions about some events and states of affairs cannot be conclusively confirmed. The second area of ambiguity has to do with descriptions of events and states of affairs from different points of view and prompted by different interests. The same state of affairs or event may be described in ways that differ from one another regarding details, significance, causes and effects, or scope. This second area of ambiguity is the sole grain of truth in talk by Trump supporters about so-called alternative facts.

With respect to assertions about the past, it is crucial to differentiate between a claim to the effect that Abraham Lincoln was assassinated and a claim such as that economic problems were the main cause of the U.S. Civil War rather than slavery. In the former case, there is abundant, relevant evidence; in the latter case, interpretations of social and economic conditions will vary, and though there is reasonable evidence for each of the two different causes, it is not possible to say that one is true and the other false. The truth of many assertions about the past calls for special assessment of evidence and some measure of compromise in drawing conclusions about which description is preferable. But the reality of this undeniable ambiguity does not mean that the fact that there is such ambiguity regarding assertions about past events and states of affairs precludes that any assertions about the past can be judged true or false.

Ambiguity due to diversity of descriptions of events and states of affairs is more complicated. The reasons descriptions may vary usually have to do with interests prompting the descriptions and with attribution of consequences.

For instance, description of the Civil War as primarily caused by economic factors, rather than slavery, may be due to interest prompted by work on the political consequences of economic trends. It is certainly true that interests differ and result in dissimilar descriptions of the same events and states of affairs. There is also the undeniable fact that some individuals are more perceptive than others, and may discern factors that others miss. What matters here, though, is that even if sorting out the diversity of descriptions of a given event or state of affairs is complicated, that is insufficient reason to simply accept the diverse descriptions as so many sundry opinions.

The current phenomenon of post-truth is, in the end, the result of a combination of two disquieting developments. One development is people's growing disposition to take everything anyone says, from well-founded assertions to impulsive outpourings, and reduce it to expressions of opinion. The other development is politicians' increasing preparedness to hoodwink the electorate. In the first case, whatever is said is leveled; in the second case, whatever is said is contrived. In both cases, facticity is forgotten.

Reduction of assertions to expressions of opinion levels the assertions because expertise, experience, perceptiveness, and knowledge all cease to be factors strengthening or supporting assertions when those assertions are taken as voiced opinions. A term used with increasing frequency in posted comments is "opinionator." The term, now archaic, was originally used to refer to an opinionated person or one given to conjecture.[27] Currently, it is used to refer to individuals posting comments on Internet articles, but mainly to whoever wrote the article commented on. This use effectively reduces the contents of the article commented on, an article no doubt researched before being published, to the level of the comments made about it because someone presenting an article on the Internet is seen as simply expressing an opinion.

As points of view, opinions are as much products of emotional factors as of intellectual ones. More important is that the intellectual factors involved in the production of opinions function causally, not inferentially or deductively as with conclusions drawn. This is how an opinion differs most from a conclusion drawn on the basis of evidence, background knowledge, and expertise. Opinions are essentially products, results of feelings and inclinations, not conclusions drawn, which is why opinions are not challengeable the way conclusions are challengeable. Lumping all assertions as expressions of opinion, then, renders them unassessable.

Politicians misleading their electorates is nothing new. What is new with the spread of post-truth are two recently developed features of political talk that together have changed things quite considerably. One feature is what we can think of as the significant broadening of the range or scope of acceptability of questionable assertions. Prior to the post-truth phenomenon, what politicians said was judged to be either true or false. Now, what politicians say is judged to be perspectival and so is not so much judged or assessed as it is taken more or less seriously depending on one's own perspective on the issue in question.

The other feature is that since political claims or assertions are now deemed to be perspectival, to be expressions of personal points of view, and therefore not assessable as factually right or wrong, agreement or disagreement with them is no longer straightforward acceptance or rejection. Agreement or disagreement with political assertions and claims now is either endorsement of them as expressing one's own views or denunciation of them as misguided or pernicious. Abandonment of facticity regarding evaluation of political claims and assertions results in agreement or disagreement with them being on the basis of what can only be described as moral grounds.[28] This is because, as expressions of held opinions, they are judged to be good or bad, even though not right or wrong on the basis of their grounds or lack thereof.

One of the clearest indications of how posting on social media has been rethought as supportive or offensive, rather than as correct or incorrect, is how the word "troll" has been redefined through different use. A troll is no longer a fictional cave-dwelling dwarf. A troll now is a person who authors offensive postings on social media. And trolling no longer has anything to do with fishing. "Trolling" is now a general descriptive term for offensive posting on social media. This is the sense Jason Hannan had in mind when he made a point with which I will close:

> Twitter is a schoolyard run by bullies. . . . Although originally designed as a social tool, Twitter soon devolved into an anti-social hellscape. The 140 characters are hardly conducive to civil disagreement. They do, however, lend themselves to . . . vicious insults. . . . Whoever insults hardest wins. The problem is that trolling has gone mainstream. It is no longer confined to the darker corners of the internet. The president of the United States is a troll.[29]

Notes

1. *Economist,* Editorial, September 10, 2016, Vol. 420, No. 9006, p. 9.

2. Lawrie McFarlane, *Anahim/Nimpo Lake Messenger,* February 2017, Vol. 13, No. 12, p. 4. The *Messenger* is a small monthly newspaper published in British Columbia, and its editorial illustrates the extent of the press's concern with the post-truth phenomenon.

3. Sergio Sismondo, "Post-Truth?" *Social Studies of Science* 47, no. 1 (2017): 3–6.

4. *Economist,* 2016.

5. Marian David, https://plato.stanford.edu/entries/truth-correspondence/.

6. John Searle, *The Construction of Social Reality* (New York: The Free Press, 1995), p. 219.

7. Aristotle, *Metaphysics,* 1011. A. J. Ayer and Jane O'Grady, *A Dictionary of Philosophical Quotations* (Oxford: Blackwell's, 1992), p. 18.

8. Searle, *The Construction of Social Reality.*

9. For discussion of some problems that arise from the correspondence theory, see my treatment of John Searle on truth in C. G. Prado, *Searle and Foucault on Truth* (Cambridge: Cambridge University Press, 2006).

10. Paul Guyer and Rolf-Peter Horstmann, https://plato.stanford.edu/entries/idealism/.

11. Gary Aylesworth, https://plato.stanford.edu/entries/postmodernism/.

12. Michel Foucault, "Truth and Power," in *Power/Knowledge: Selected Interviews and Other Writings 1972–1977,* ed. Colin Gordon (New York: Pantheon Books, 1980), p. 131.

13. Michel Foucault, *Discourse on Language,* trans. R. Sawyer (New York: Pantheon Books, 1971), p. 224.

14. Alain Tolhurst and staff writers, http://www.news.com.au/lifestyle/real-life/news-life/posttruth-named-oxford-dictionaries-word-of-the-year/news-story/da07b64694db8960397c70b124c094e8, emphasis in original.

15. Austin Allegro, https://www.collinsdictionary.com/submission/17496/post-truth.

16. http://www.macmillandictionary.com/dictionary/british/post-truth.

17. http://dictionary.cambridge.org/us/dictionary/english/post-truth#translations.

18. https://en.wikipedia.org/wiki/Post-truth_politics.

19. Tom Fiedler, "Trump vs. the Media: The War over Facts," March 11, 2017, http://www.csmonitor.com/USA/Politics/2017/0311/Trump-vs.-the-media-the-war-over-facts.

20. *Economist,* 2016.

21. Steve Tesich, "A Government of Lies," *Nation,* January 6, 1992, Vol. 254, No. 1, p. 12. Note that the *Economist* attributes first use of "post-truth" to David Roberts but gives no date. *Economist,* 2016, see pp. 17–20.

22. Tesich, "A Government of Lies."

23. Russell Smith, "How Postmodernism Is Infiltrating Public Life and Policy," *Globe and Mail,* April 18, 2017. See also Matthew d'Ancona, *Post-Truth: The New War on Truth and How to Fight Back* (London: Ebury Press, 2017) (Penguin Books), and Evan Davis, *Post-Truth: Why We Have Reached Peak Bullshit and What We Can Do about It* (London: Little, Brown, 2017).

24. Casey Williams, "Has Trump Stolen Philosophy's Critical Tools?" *New York Times,* April 17, 2017.

25. It is tempting to devote some space to consideration of the effect on audiences of the atrocious spelling, terrible grammar, and misuse of words so prevalent in postings and comments.

26. *Economist,* 2016.

27. http://en.academic.ru/dic.nsf/cide/122763/Opinionator.

28. My thanks to Lawrie McFarlane, who made this point to me.

29. Jason Hannan, "Trolling Ourselves to Death in the Age of Trump," *MacLean's,* July 20, 2017.

CHAPTER TWO

Truth Claims, Interpretation, and Addiction to Conviction

Mark Kingwell[1]

Everyone knows that campsite disputes can escalate, especially if brewed liquids are involved, but a 2016 dustup near the Ontario town of Brockville struck even seasoned campers as a little, uh, stupid. An argument over whether the Earth is round or flat prompted an angry man to toss various items, including a propane tank, into a fire. He left the scene before firefighters arrived.

It turned out the outdoorsy Flat-Earther is the girlfriend of the tank-tosser's son—so, you know, family dynamics. Still, despite the existence of a whimsical society for people like her, we don't expect otherwise sane people to dispute centuries of scientific knowledge founded securely on the work of Pythagoras, Galileo, and Giordano Bruno. Or do we? It can seem as if we are living in a world where fact, truth, and evidence no longer exert the rational pull they once did. Our landscape of fake news sites, junk science, politicians blithely dismissive of fact-checks, and Google searches that appear to make us dumber renders truth redundant. We are rudderless on a dark sea where, as Nietzsche said, there are no facts, only interpretations.

We have been here before, of course, if not so comprehensively. Misinformation, rhetorical deceit, bogus belief systems, and plain ignorance are the norm, not the exception, in human affairs. But in most ages there has been a sense that this is a bad thing, something to be combated actively. Plato acknowledged the sad dominance of *doxa,* or opinion, in everyday life. He countered with a stout defense of *episteme,* true knowledge, which philosophers alone could discern. Even philosophers no longer believe in that kind of philosopher, and the less modest notions of truth we have offered instead—pragmatic, empirical, falsifiable—can't halt cascades into skepticism and relativism. If it isn't divinely ordained or metaphysically copper-bottomed, truth looks like a sick joke or power grab, an epistemic check-kiting scam. Maybe Pontius Pilate was right to mock the idea rhetorically—"What is truth?"—and not even tarry for an answer.

The costs of giving up on truth are pretty severe, though. In the perfervid summer of 2016, when this incident took place, it was hard to address any issue of public life without mentioning the presumptive Republican candidate for president of the United States, but Mr. Trump really does represent a new stage of post-rational campaigning. The cynical, political-realist aides of George W. Bush argued that they created reality out of power. That position was doctoral quality compared to the haphazard, say-anything approach of the new Republican regime. The shooter is an Afghan even if born in New York! The president is a Manchurian-Candidate ISIS mole! Muslims and Mexicans are—*you know*! What is significant is that rational pushback on this dangerous nonsense has so little traction. Correction used to cause shame and confusion; now it just prompts a rhetorical double-down. *A lot of people are saying this!* Actually important things—climate change, foreign policy—get dragged along for the moronic ride. For the record, yes, Mrs. Clinton has lied pretty widely too, albeit with more consistency.

Claims for the authority of reason have always been more hopeful than stable. There is, we want to say, a basic regard for truth in making any claim, however bizarre or unproven. Watching the nightly pundit parade, or the scroll of toxic opinionating on Twitter and discussion boards, we have cause to doubt it. This is the carapace of reason, a shell of discourse preserved in debate-club tactics and the collective delusion that this constitutes discourse. We must distinguish, as Martin Luther did, two kinds of reason (though he got the priority wrong). Ministerial reason deploys argument forms in the service of existing belief, convincing someone else that I will not be convinced otherwise. Magisterial reason, by contrast, is autonomous: it engages in dispute openly to pursue—if not always find—the truth. If evidence and argument are contrary to my preexisting beliefs, reason demands that I change them.

Meanwhile, for those tracking these things, Google itself seems to be getting smarter; it might even constitute a new form of artificial intelligence. Maybe we should stop worrying and welcome our new search-engine overlords! Or maybe we should recall that rational thought really just means this: an ongoing agreement to take each other seriously. In the age of (alleged) post-truth conviction and "alternative facts," let us frame the fundamental question this way: in what way is truth dependent on interpretation?

An orthodoxy of a certain brand of hermeneutics and critical theory is this: truth claims are context dependent; indeed, the contours of a given interpretive frame or method act to generate the sorts of truth claims that will count as valid within a given discourse. This view, not in fact postmodern but rather high modern, is what people often attack as a "relativism" or "subjectivism" concerning truth. It is, of course, no such thing, since context dependence forbids the comparison of truths from different contexts that would make them equally and compatibly true (what most people mean by relativism), while also ruling out accounts of the world based entirely on a single point of view (what most people mean by subjectivism).

The ethical and political implications of this epistemological dispute have long been noted. Are there standards of action and judgment that are true, or are there just conventions that vary between cultures? Can we decide matters of behavior and evaluation according to a reliable objective standard, or will we always find ourselves mired in endless irresolvable disputes?

So stated, this is a false dichotomy concerning the issue of normative evaluation. There can be standards of judgment that are action guiding and reliable, even as they forebear from pretending to universal or extra-human status. We need not purchase ethical life at the cost of committing to an objectivist position. Contextualism offers one promising route away from this otherwise-crippling dichotomy, and I will explore and defend a version of it in what follows. The subjective–objective bind proves to be a self-imposed imprisonment, one from which we can free ourselves without courting incoherence or anarchy.

Even more interesting in the present moment, however, are the political implications of context dependence. If the "postmodern" left was accused of making truth subservient to political ends in an overt ideological fashion, it has been in fact the political right that has achieved this spectral triumph. Postmodern right-wing political *realpolitik* creates "realities," "facts," and (crucially) perverse accusations of "fakeness" in pursuit of a specific political agenda. Perhaps the most surprising thing about this for many people today is that it by no means began with Donald Trump, unlikely 45th president of the United States. This chapter explains why.

Is There a Text in This Debate?

The most basic, and most erroneous, assumption of untutored discourse about discourse, especially of the political kind, is that there is a firm distinction between "the facts" or "the fact of the matter," on the one hand, and the various, perhaps competing interpretations of those facts on the other. The assumption represents a mistake of presumption, namely that interpretations supervene on a baseline reality which, at best, can be discerned through effort and methodology, perhaps via triangulation among competing interpretations; and further that the baseline reality, once so discerned, will prove decisive in whatever matter is at hand. Consider, for example, the experience of watching Akira Kurosawa's classic 1950 film *Rashomon*. Here, in chilling near-repetition, we are exposed to rival and contradictory versions of the "same" series of events, involving a rape and murder in the Japanese countryside. But the four accounts, given in turn, prove self-serving, strange, and inconclusive.

What are we to make of this? Is the truth of what happened something that matches none of the narratives perfectly but has elements of truth from each? Or is there a further *ur*-narrative that none of the individuals can recount but which, from a God's-eye (or viewer's or director's) perspective, can be made out? Maybe, most disturbingly, there is no truth here at all, in the sense of a stable array of actions and reactions, motives and consequences. Naturally the last possibility is both the most probable and the most important: human affairs, especially extreme ones, do not surrender to our assumptions about "making sense" of "what happened." The film works to both highlight and undermine the assumption, and its critical logic is of a piece with what we might call the *unveiling* function of modern critical theory. What is unveiled is not the truth but instead our fervent but doomed wish for there to be such a thing as the truth.

I align this aesthetic intervention with contemporaneous critical theory for several reasons. First, we can see here how, in the mid-20th century, there operated a widespread intellectual consensus about what we might call the duty of exposure. By this I mean the impulse shared by Nietzschean-Marxist-Freudian hermeneutics of suspicion—in very broad terms, thoughts are never innocent, ideology functions everywhere, and we suppress awareness of our own suppressions. The critical intervention then takes the form of showing what has been hidden, exposing comforting social conventions, political self-deception, and psychological repression, respectively. Everyday society and psychology alike work to maintain illusions that are conciliatory and serving the interests of the current arrangement. The duty of exposure meets this shell game of falsity by leveraging penetrating insight and an unwillingness to take the taken-for-granted for granted.

I label this impulse high modern because it is fundamentally implicated in a larger project of Late Enlightenment. In fact, though, this implication has a long and complicated pedigree, especially in politics and philosophy. We can certainly trace it back to Kant's well-known injunction in "What Is Enlightenment?"—sapere aude, "have the courage to think for yourself"— but we could equally follow a longer and somewhat crooked line that would trace its way to Socratic elenchus and the exposure of false consciousness in the words and concepts of everyday life, philosophy in its basic critical mode, in short.

But the ground here is, not surprisingly, unstable, and that generates a second reason to implicate the so-called Rashomon Effect in our account of post-truth. According to communications theorist Robert Anderson, whose work has popularized the term, "The Rashomon effect is not only about differences in perspective. It occurs particularly where such differences arise in combination with the absence of evidence to elevate or disqualify any version of the truth, plus the social pressure for closure on the question."[2] The last qualification is essential, since it illustrates how the multiple-interpretation experience is *both* destabilizing *and* driven toward a new moment of new stability. This "closure" can no longer claim the mantle of baseline reality associated with the untutored or naive view of "what happened," but it, nevertheless, exerts a normative force of consensual order.

Thus, the very same impulse that forces us to confront our hidden assumptions and ideological precommitments must recognize, sooner or later, the second-order problem of its own assumptions and precommitments. At its most obvious, insufficiently self-reflexive critical theory generates a performative contradiction, whereby the exposure of what lies hidden results in a reification of the exposure. In crude terms, the work of showing "what is really going on" simply falls into a trap of reactionary ontological conviction. Instead of the naive realist view of the world as we find it, we adopt an "enlightened" view of the world as self-deceived. But that latter is as much committed to the notion of baseline reality as the former.

Less obviously, the status of the exposure efforts may prove itself uncertain: what is gained, after all, by bringing to the surface ideas and commitments that were hitherto buried? (The images of surface and depth are rife in the literature, of course; Freud's famous image of the iceberg, with 85 percent of the psyche "underwater," is memorable here.)

Hence, as awareness of these tangles becomes more inescapable, theorists begin to make a genuine postmodern turn. By this I mean the traditional "incredulity towards metanarratives" that Lyotard identifies in his canonical work, but also those reversions to simulacral logic that are prompted by crisis of faith in the standard critical-theoretic project. One can observe the problem already in the late work of Adorno and even (though less vividly) in Barthes: if the work of theory is to reveal by way of denaturalizing assumptions and power relations, how do we avoid simply valorizing the revealed condition as *more true*?[3] Adorno labeled the basic project one of "seeing-through," and he was rightly troubled by its potential tangles and endgames. That is, the logic of revelation seems to carry with it an *implicit reification of the (now) seen* that is impossible to evade. Only a principled refusal of this logic can suffice in maintaining a critical attitude. And, notably, the function of criticism must now shift, because there is no longer any possible claim to authoritative interpretation nor indeed to the assumed hierarchical relation of interpretation to thing interpreted. It is, we might say, interpretation all the way down.

Of course, Nietzsche himself had glimpsed this insight in the much-quoted passage concerning facts and interpretations ("There are no facts, only interpretations"). But in a crucial sense Nietzsche did not take his own insight seriously enough, or perhaps he was too addicted to the pleasure of the intellectual reveal to commit to it completely. By the middle of the following century, Barthes and others had added the structuralist apparatus of linguistics to their cultural-critical toolkit but still without abandoning a project of penetrative insight. Of his groundbreaking work in the study of popular culture, *Mythologies* (1957), Barthes wrote the following:

> This book has two determinants: on the one hand, an ideological critique of the language of so-called mass culture; on the other, an initial semiological dismantling of that language: I had just read Saussure and emerged with the conviction that by treating "collective representations" as sign systems one might hope to transcend pious denunciation and instead account in detail for the mystification which transforms petit bourgeois culture into a universal nature.[4]

We see here a standard (and persuasive) account of the reveal project. Barthes always wishes us to see what has been encached in the "mystifications" of cultural production and consumption, thus the demystification project, which will presumptively reverse the transformation of particular (petit bourgeois) interests into universal (natural) norms by showing precisely their origins, limits, and political tendencies. We are still in the realm of Socrates.

As mentioned, Adorno had struggled with the same commitments, though he is considerably less consistent in avoiding the "pious denunciation" that Barthes sees as unhelpful in this quarter. Adorno knew that his dyspeptic critiques of camping, sunbathing, television, radio, jazz, and movies (among other things) were reactionary. He also came to know, rather more reluctantly, that these critiques were pointless. If Barthes senses that denunciation is not the point, understanding is, Adorno simply abandons any stance other than the "get off my lawn" crankiness of a man out of joint with his time and place.

Only Debord and Baudrillard, it seems to me, really see the extent of the difficulty here.[5] We must take seriously the idea that there are no facts of the matter, that culture is not a shell game working to prop up articulable bourgeois interests but instead a free play of empty signifiers and random spectacles that—yes—tend to reinforce current interests, but not by hiding a discoverable truth. Indeed, the basic truth is there for all to see: *there is no definitive truth in play*! There really are only interpretations and semi-random arrangements of cultural properties that suggest or provoke but never—can never—speak plainly. The people who understand this are the true post-modernists, those who do not subconsciously revert to a truth-revealing logic of emancipation but instead accept that the distinction between reality and fantasy is not stable, perhaps does not exist at all.

What this means politically, of course, is that the comprehensive triumph of spectacle renders moot all other scales of evaluation. The advent of the "reality television" chief executive is a predictable symptom of an epistemological system in which truth and falsity are indistinguishable. One may tarry on the structural conditions that make these erasures possible—erosion of traditional authority, wide dissemination of social media, encroachments on the phenomenology of "real life"—but they all point to the same conclusion. We can no longer reliably separate truth from falsity, reality from appearance. The long-standing Western philosophical project has reached its endgame, and its results are in: not only can anyone say anything, but the anyone saying anything can be the highest elected official in the most powerful nation on Earth. Welcome to the postmodern condition!

Interlude: Premodern or Postmodern?

Of course, nothing is quite that simple in the realm of human affairs—or, indeed, in the realm of epistemology. Many people see in President Trump a primitive mendacity that is more primordial, appealing to the reptile brain of those who find pleasure in the basic logic of us versus them. (This can be, to be sure, a more sophisticated political force too: compare Carl Schmitt's nuanced realist political philosophy of friend and enemy.)[6]

"Where do Donald Trump and other world authoritarians fit into the history of facts?" one critic asked. "It's fashionable these days to claim that Mr. Trump and his ilk are super-sophisticated 'post-truth' types, that they have expropriated the terrain of postmodernism and seized the handy high ground where everything is relative, where the truth is simply what you can convince people of." The writer begged to differ: "Within the history of facts, the 45th president is actually a throwback, an atavist of a more primitive consciousness. And it is digital-information technology that has allowed him to be that way."[7] The writer feels the need to repeat the claim, saying that "it's important to understand Donald Trump within the context of the history of facts. He's not a sophisticated post-factual postmodernist. He's a throwback, not just beyond the rationality of Voltaire to the emotionalism of Rousseau, but way, way, waaaaaay back, to pre-Enlightenment mystical shamanism, to the credulous world of shadows inside Plato's cave, to abracadabra and the wowza flash of fire."

I haven't the room here, given what else I wish to argue, to perform the needed McLuhanite analysis of information technology, particularly on Twitter, the president's favorite medium. I can argue, here, that the *apparent* premodernism of Trump is in fact a property emerging from right-wing post-modern conditions. Granted, Trump is more the unwitting beneficiary of these conditions than the conscious creator thereof. But his ability *not to regard facts,* or to rely on *alternative* ones, is essential to his success. Perhaps the premodern media-age avatar is just the logical extension of the new post-modern condition?

Because postmodernism has traditionally been associated with the left, we must consider two singular moments in recent American political history, one an apparently minor but telling remark from a functionary in the George W. Bush administration and the other a landmark U.S. Supreme Court deci-sion whose influence is still not entirely understood.[8]

In October 2004, *New York Times Magazine* journalist Ron Suskind quoted a then-unnamed source from Bush's inner circle who dismissed those still mired "in what we call the reality-based community," defined as people who "believe that solutions emerge from your judicious study of discernible real-ity." He continued: "We're an empire now, and when we act, we create our own reality. And while you're studying that reality—judiciously, as you will—we'll act again, creating other new realities, which you can study too, and that's how things will sort out. We're history's actors . . . and you, all of you, will be left to just study what we do."

The quotation was later attributed to Karl Rove, who was then a senior political advisor to Bush and became White House deputy chief of staff the following February, serving in that office until August 2007.

One might be tempted to dismiss this statement as typical Rovean bluster, and indeed the defeat of the Republicans in the 2008 presidential election gave many people hope that the imperial "Mission Accomplished" posturing of the Bush administration was a thing of the past, an aberration. But I tend to credit Rove with a deeper insight here, namely that his diagnosis is cor-rect, even in the absence of an American imperial mission. Rove understood, in other words, that the new millennium had generated new norms of politi-cal discourse and behavior. The old pieties of Enlightenment thought, includ-ing the essential premises that there is such a thing as "reality" penetrable by reason and that such penetration has the power to alter behavior, were in the dustbin of history. In their place was something we might call *postmodern right-wing realpolitik,* the conviction that power ("action" in Rove's formula-tion) creates its own rules and (temporary) realities. Those of us still trapped in the norms and methods of the "reality-based community" can now only stand by and watch, no doubt wringing our hands all the while. Our sharp tools of the mind, the honed chisels of evidence and logic, are just so many parlor tricks—and worse, ones whose unexamined exercise results only in pulling the wool over our own eyes.

The landmark court decision is, of course, *Citizens United v. Federal Elec-tion Commission,* decided in January 2010. In it, the Court held that restrictions on independent corporate expenditures in political campaigns, as opposed to direct political contributions, are unconstitutional restrictions on the freedom of speech. This decision at once inhibits democracy by quantifying (and then hiking) the opportunity costs of participation, even as it reduces the idea of such participation to money itself. To be sure, corporations have been granted some of the rights of citizens in American law for some decades. But *Citizens United* does more than extend such rights. By means of a spectral metaphysics of plutocracy, it effectively delivers the electoral process over to the moneyed interests whose pools of capital are now instantly transformed into pools of influence.

These two artifacts of recent political history might seem unrelated, and yet, in the context of standard liberal views on pluralism, civility, and integrity, they are not only related but matters of the utmost urgency. Alasdair MacIntyre, in his canonical book *After Virtue,* argued that a viable virtue ethic required not just an enumeration of desirable character traits, or dispositions to act, but also, crucially, two other features.[9] First, there must be a sense of a *role* that one could legitimately play, a virtuous identity, such as the Aristotelian *phronimos,* the Augustan gentleman, or the thrifty New Englander; and second, there must be a suitable background *context* for the exercise of the enumerated virtues, a set of shared assumptions that would assure the reinforcement cycle between action and character.

The presumption of virtually all philosophical argument concerning civility and pluralism, whether one takes an explicitly virtue-style account or not, is precisely that there is such a context: public reason, courts of reasonable appeal, individuals with preferences to articulate, and so on. But what if the context is in fact one where these presumptions are maintained only as fictions, where the real influence and even the notion of speech has been stealthily—and not so stealthily!—removed from the hands of individual citizens and placed, instead, in spectral agencies or pools of power in the form of money?

Philosophers cannot go on, it seems to me, without addressing these practical realities of civic life. Defenders of civility may need to abandon the optative, restraint-based accounts that have hitherto dominated and seek instead routes of argument that include analysis of systematic discursive distortions, once thought (e.g., by Habermas) to be the exclusive preserves of ideology or madness.

Perhaps the sad conclusion of our own moment is that what was once considered a declension from the norm—the norm being rational discourse of a more or less well-intentioned sort—is now the new normal, namely of presumptively ideological speech that all too often resembles the sort of madness that cannot be reasoned with. If this is so, or even partially accurate, then new lines of argument may be necessary, for example, ones that operate negatively, attempting to show not why civility is a good thing but, rather, why incivility is self-defeating. This sort of collective action problem argument will no doubt appear cynical to those of a more ideal persuasion, and they may risk a certain kind of self-envelopment, giving away the stakes in search of victory, as, for example, when we attempt to defend the value of humanistic education with reference to its ability to secure law-school admission or a higher median income at 40 years of age.

Conviction Addiction and the Scaffolds of Reason

The murderous Nazi hate-fest in Charlottesville during the summer of 2017, in addition to revealing the extreme moral vacuity of the current White House, prompted a call for more compassion and empathy when dealing with basic ideological differences. Pundits orated on National Public Radio about how to recognize the psychological damage of those given to right-wing rage. Classes were offered in tactics for engaging those on "the other side" of political debates. My impeccably Democratic New Hampshire in-laws set off to attend one of these sessions last week, earnest in their desire to find common ground with fellow Americans who voted Trump.

These efforts and sentiments are noble but doomed to fail. Even a minute of exposure to the views of Richard Spencer or David Duke—let alone the Twitter feed of POTUS 45—is enough to show that there is no rational engagement possible here. There is a moral baseline that Nazism is indefensible; we ought likewise to recognize that most people can't actually be reasoned with.

That's why, much as it pains me to say so as someone theoretically committed to the rule of reason, what we need in public debate is decisively not more efforts to understand. The utopia of a rational public sphere is an illusion, and exhortations to unearth it—in the form of core American values, Canadian tolerance, or some other political chimera—are fool's errands. What we need, instead, is what social scientists call scaffolding.

In simple forms, scaffolding means things like air traffic control, highway roundabouts, exit signage, and queuing conventions—small mechanisms that allow humans to coordinate action when their individual interests might otherwise generate chaos. In more subtle cases, we constrain our own desires in the form of, say, computer apps that time-out social media access (the enabler-in-chief could use one of these). Or else we impose limits on freedom in those suffering harmful addictions. Addicts can always try therapy or self-control, but we know that denying access to the drug or even inflicting benign behavioral modification is far more effective.

Why don't we acknowledge that political belief is also an aspect of human behavior in need of external control? Let's call it conviction addiction. Sure, some people can, like social drinkers, moderate their views and stay clear-headed over the course of the day. Others fall into a pattern of abusive behavior and acting out. They can't help themselves.

The gateway drug is interrupting, raising your voice over objections, and deliberately misunderstanding interlocutors—all standard moves of a CNN segment, in an instant obliterating any useful ethics of interpretation, even if there are agreed facts in play. Conviction addicts then move on to ranting at hidden forces, demonizing ethnic groups, and sounding dog whistles—all standard moves of Rebel Media or Sean Hannity. Finally, if unchecked, they order the fashy haircut, don the white polo shirt, and fire up a tiki torch. The fact that a slogan like "Jews will not replace us" literally *makes no sense* is, at this point, not a defect but a mark in its favor.

Classical liberals argue that bad speech should be met with more and better speech and that the marketplace of ideas will short bad stocks and return investment on good ones. Alas, not so. The mental market is far more irrational than the one governing wealth, which veers from high to low based on rumor, wisps of policy change, and random tweets, thus the need for market regulation, antitrust legislation, and the Securities Exchange Commission. These are hard-floor scaffolds on trading, meant to combat excesses at the margins. Consider, then, that individual consciousness is considerably less sane than even the most rapacious corporation. Mere existence is sufficient for each of us to form a limited company in the world of thought. That's frightening! There is no dialectic possible here. Haters gonna hate.

Research indicates, as we might expect in the post-truth condition, that facts, even amply demonstrated ones, have very little pull when it comes to our states of belief.[10] This is distressing to those committed to the idea of rational mind-changing, but it is only practical to accept the limitations of reason if we are not to commit, yet again, a performative error of self-delusion. It is no rap against reason as such to note that the degree to which it operates in human thought and action is limited. It follows that appeals to reason, especially on the level of firmly held belief (of which political belief is a prominent subset), are going to be very minimal in their power. There may be some agreeable souls who, shaken by some philosophical intervention in a debate or university classroom, find some of their core beliefs begin to crumble. This is wonderful, awe-inspiring, fearsome, and, of course, extremely rare. Does it happen? Yes, and any teacher feels the heavy weight of responsibility associated with such scenes. It is, after all, sometimes as easy to be a charlatan of reason as to be its devoted midwife. Socrates was reckoned a sleight-of-hand artist by some, only a divine presence by some others.

Therefore, let us likewise recognize the conviction-addictive quality in all of us and stop imagining that free public discourse will bend toward reason. Curbs on speech and strict rules of engagement—no interruptions, no slogans, no talking points—may be the right answer here. Governments already, in Canada and elsewhere, ban hateful speech. Let's go farther and insist on participant-accepted discourse norms, penalties on unhelpful public outrage, and aggressively regulated social media. We could even ban media panel discussions! (Probably not going to happen, though this proves a popular suggestion to those on both the Left and the Right.)

On these terms, we would still coexist, versions of Kant's notional "nation of devils" ruled by uneasy self-interest. But it will not be through talking things over, let alone hugging them out, that we maintain our modus vivendi. Limit indulgence in the cup of conviction; let's have more constraint, less conversation. When we can't agree on facts, or truth, we can perhaps at least agree on wanting to stick around and pursue our different life plans. That's your path to a stable future, friends—by not trying to be friends.

Now, many people seemed to find these gently proposed measures altogether too draconian and suspect. In the resulting reaction storm, I was called "next-level Orwellian," "totalitarian," a "leftist jackass" who had mastered "the political philosophy of the militant left" and offered "a pep rally to the anarchist Left." (The last correspondent was a little confused about the political philosophy of the militant Left, suggesting I move to a communist country if I didn't like it here—something no self-respecting anarchist would do. Read your Bakunin, frenemies!)[11]

Not coincidentally, these judgments came in tweets, blogs, Reddit posts, unsolicited e-mails, and an e-mail letter to the editor, respectively. On the long-standing advice of my editor, I never look at the hundreds of comments posted on the website where this argument was published, so I have no idea what went on there. That, as we all must accept, is nobody's idea of rational discourse. My favorite single comment, though, sent to my public university e-mail, was this: "You are a moron and fake professor. Your place is in North Korea. You are a shame to Humanity." I know, right? Another faithful correspondent suggested China as my proper home, which I suppose is no more (or less) appropriate.

Anyway, for the sake of those still-sane people who think an argument in favor of scaffolding is tantamount to an abandonment of discourse—when it is, of course, no such thing—allow me to expand the argument along the following rational lines.[12]

First, the abandonment of empathetic identification as the salve of public reason is not an endorsement of government coercion, censorship, "official" discourse, or other bugbears of the so-called Free Speech Movement—which is in fact code for the new right. Witness, for example, the dismal spectacle of "Free Speech Week" at the University of California, Berkeley, which an off-world observer might imagine as a celebration of that great institution's history of liberal dissent. But no: the week, boycotted by a number of professors and many students, most of them of color, was a platform for an ideologically obvious cluster of speakers, including Steven Bannon and Milo Yiannopoulos.

Meanwhile, speaking of *actual* proposed censorship, the president sent tweets in the wake of a September terrorist attack in London, first blaming

Scotland Yard for not preventing it and then suggesting six minutes later that what was needed was a "tougher" tactic against "loser terrorists": "The internet is their main recruitment tool which we must cut off & use better!" As one commentator said, "Cut off the Internet? How, and for whom? Might the Constitution prohibit such action? The President didn't seem to have time to linger on such details, because after another six minutes he tweeted, 'The travel ban into the United States should be far larger, tougher and more specific-but stupidly, that would not be politically correct!'"[13] Whatever that means.

More seriously, to note limits on empathy in the public square is not to abandon genuine freedom of speech at all. Constraint is not coercion—a conceptual elision that is itself extremely dangerous. And limits on hate are not, contrary to the view of the U.S. Supreme Court, limits on liberty. All speech is regulated in some fashion; there is no more an Edenic condition of unfettered freedom of expression than there is a notional free market where blind forces ever execute rational economic outcomes. All markets, whether of commodities or ideas, are likewise regulated in someone's favor. My suggestion here is that the so-called marketplace of ideas—itself a highly dubious metaphor, possibly a liberal fantasy—should be regulated in favor of pragmatic coexistence rather than chasing after an alleged rational legitimacy that is extremely unlikely to emerge even with the best intentions in the world.[14]

A word of clarification should also be entered on the systematic misuse, or misunderstanding, of the idea of empathy. This is a form of emotional identification which is, to my knowledge, literally impossible. One cannot, in fact, *actually feel the pain of another,* despite the political rhetoric of another, more charming POTUS (42 if you're keeping score at home). Human emotional attachment is limited by human physiognomy; we inhabit individual bodies, and there is no way to overcome this fact, even in the most intimate relations between us. One can, to be sure, be pained at the pain of another, and that is a great lever of political and ethical insight. But this is, to be precise, *sympathy* rather than *empathy.* It is what Hume and Adam Smith wisely identified as the linchpin of society even when our individual interests are so strong that, sometimes, we might (as Hume memorably said) view the destruction of half the world as of little moment compared to the pricking of our own little finger. This position, as Hume wryly accepted, is not at all "against reason" given the monstrous narcissism of most humans. Hume and Smith were realists: they, like Hobbes, took humans as they are and laws as they might be.

The main point should never be lost. Reason is extremely limited and contingent when it comes to fellow-feeling. Moreover, such fellow-feeling, as does obtain, is likewise extremely limited and contingent. Further, those who view sympathy as somehow lesser than, and maybe suspect compared to, norms of empathy should check their privilege. This linguistic-conceptual confusion is, I believe, a function of generalized therapeutic culture, which imagines that emotional identification is possible and desirable, and views the sympathetic attitude as somehow detached and inadequate. The hard fact is that sympathy is awfully good going when it comes to human-on-human interaction, and empathy is revealed, by contrast, as a shadow figure, a political nonstarter.

Second, there is nothing in these modest proposals that defies reason or even devalues its power when traction is possible. I'm all for rational changing of minds! And, of course, there are other uses of conversation besides rational conversion: creating intimacy, expanding one's own personal narrative, exchanging gossip, all the discursive analogues of simian or feline grooming in fact. But, contrary to Enlightenment conviction, there is no bright line between reason and its lack—we are far too cognitively complex for that to be so. Sure, rational persuasion is possible, as are moments of genuinely motivated self-reflection prompted by an incisive interlocutor (the last presumptively ourselves, of course). But it is extremely unlikely that humans will achieve these ends in any reliable fashion and almost equally unlikely that we will change our own minds—something we might have thought easier, or at least more within our control, than changing the minds of others. Once more, the hard fact is that minds do not, as a rule, tend toward change.[15] Assuming otherwise is supremely arrogant, not morally righteous, and is correctly viewed as one of the recurrent vices of the oblivious intellectual elite.

I can add, from vast and mostly unpleasant personal experience among the supposedly rational high reaches of academic life, that there is very little solace available to the pro-reason crowd. Even here, where argument is rated extremely highly, and consistency and noncontradiction are valued to a degree unknown in general discussion, any possible rational meeting of minds vanishes like so much morning mist. Sad but true. The exchanges are, in fact, dominated by ego, social and professional position, assumed gender markers, ageism, and a host of other factors that cannot be squared with—though, yes, sometimes mitigated by—reason as such. Critics of my notion of discursive constraint should be a little less sanguine about the practical prospects of generalized rationality as a guide to real-world conversation. Never going to happen.

Third, then, it must be emphasized that there is nothing in what I propose here that favors any ideological commitment over any other one. Though critics may try to discern here some larger strategy of social control, in fact the proposal is liberal in the classical sense. Think just what you like, but cooperate for the general peace, such that others may do the same. The view accepts that there may be no generally acceptable social beliefs, not even somewhat vague formulations such as "common decency" (a favorite offering) and certainly not inherently controversial foundations such as a benevolent divine creator (a minority but still popular view).

Many critics suggest that there is much more possible in the way of mind-change than I allow here. But this smacks of old-fashioned intellectual superiority, together with a large dollop of condescension: I see that your political views are offensive to me; I surmise that they arise from bad or false or ugly foundational beliefs. These can be changed! Allow me to put you into my program of discursive therapy, whereby our well-meaning, empathetic, and compassionate critiques of your basic worldview will break down the base (both senses) structure of your mind. Eventually you will emerge a better and more tolerant person!

Say what you will about scaffolding as social control or "coercion," it, in fact, takes far more seriously the independence of persons and their minds than this program of mind control and does not stoop to smugness when it comes to differences in political belief. Acknowledging that I cannot change your mind and, more important, *do not wish to* should be reckoned a compliment, not an insult. That an entailment of this lack of epistemological ambition is that I do not care what you believe, and have no special wish to understand why you do so, is merely the consequence of democracy. Nobody ever said, did they, that I have to *understand* and *empathize with* those with whom I am made to live side by side? That, surely, is asking far too much of us. When one can sometimes barely understand a roommate or a spouse of many years, supposing more with respect to random fellow citizens must be reckoned bizarre.

And so, finally, scaffolding is just that: external guidelines that help us cooperate and coexist as we pursue our various, and probably incompatible, individual projects. This is entirely consistent with my own earlier defenses of civility, for example, as a virtue of public life.[16] In early versions of that defense, I leaned on the Aristotelian notion of virtue as *disposition to act* and followed him in emphasizing imitation and habituation as the key aspects of cultivating socially positive character traits. This remains valid as a goal, but one must perforce recognize the limits of virtue cultivation just as one acknowledges the limits of reason. We need other, more Hobbesian arguments in favor of civility to make the entire program run, hence the identification of incivility as a collective action problem, with attendant self-interested reasons for avoiding it at the margins and hence, too, the current argument in favor of external mechanisms of discursive sense. Civility can be expressed as rules, but they are rules in the sense of those we might accept as we enter a game-space, prepared to play fairly and honestly.

There are limits here, too, of course. Regulation can be expensive, and it can be gamed. I'm fairly sure, despite my own desires, political panel shows and Twitter are not going anywhere fast. But to introduce the notion of scaffolding, whatever form it may take, is really a reminder that we cannot continue to maintain the fiction of the empathetic citizen motivated by sweet reason.

It strikes me, in sum, that reactions to proposals concerning discursive scaffolding are themselves almost invariably ideological, sometimes hilariously so. They are rooted in the convictions of the respondents, who see only what their blinkers allow. People who wish to find state coercion everywhere read the notion of "constraint" as inevitably statist, even though this does not follow—the queuing convention, for example, requires no state and no law. Likewise those who fear encroachment of regulation and the endgame (already noticed by Plato) that laws begetting laws is a recipe for paralysis, if not disaster. But no such program is proposed here: most relevant kinds of discursive constraint would be self-imposed. And the alleged threats to free speech are bêtes noires roused from slumber through selective misreading and deliberate excision of context, all masquerading as rational engagement. Ironically, these are among the very tactics that my position is meant to combat.[17]

Indeed, we can observe a series of typical contradictions in the attempted expressions of free-speech absolutism in the post-truth world. On the one hand, the views perceived to be under threat are typically labeled "unpopular," the targets of "political correctness." On the other hand, these same views are celebrated for being what *the majority of people actually believe,* namely, strict gender binarism, free-market true belief, and pro-police. If these views are indeed majority, surely they require no special protection? If they are not majority, they still deserve the same protections in law as other minority beliefs—but only on a liberal-democratic conception of the state, which is free to criticize them, even limit them if hateful or harmful. A local unpopularity, say on liberal university campuses, should surely be no more of an issue here than local unpopularity of ugly (but legally protected) views at a dinner party or community gathering. Free speech does not mean, and never has meant, the freedom to say anything at all without consequence.

Even a rights regime explicitly protecting speech does not offer the blanket protections some people imagine. The First Amendment of the U.S. Constitution does not apply, for example, to private companies or private universities, who may constrain speech in quite dramatic ways—as long as they are willing to shoulder the reputational consequences of doing so.[18] Individualism, meanwhile, and rights attached thereto are lauded, but individual decisions to favor more collective, progressive, or socialist agendas are dismissed as juvenile, impaired, infantilized, and so on.

By the same tortured logic of grievance, the free expression of ideas is celebrated as basic and sacrosanct *even as* expression of criticism of specific policies and actions is routinely met by personal insults, ad hominem attacks, and sarcasm. Instead of engaging the ideas, the status of the idea holder is challenged: "fake professor," "pseudo-philosopher," "charlatan," "pretentious," "superannuated cultural Marxist," and, of course, much, much worse. In a world where facts were respected, being an actual professor of philosophy, no matter what one's political views (for the record, not a Marxist, cultural or otherwise), ought to dismiss catcalls about fakery or pseudo-whatever. About pretentiousness—well, surely in the eye of the beholder. In any case, such slurs are the cries of those who cannot meet ideas with ideas but reflexively resort to personal attack. Whither the marketplace metaphors now, one wonders?

Let us accept a modestly pessimistic view on the chances of all this changing much any time soon. No single person, not even the current U.S. president, is responsible for such widespread confusion and irrational entanglements. We have a situation in which people utter what they know to be untrue (or should) *even as* other people pretend to take it seriously as truth claims *even as* the same people in some important sense don't believe it because *even as* their failure to believe suits their political purposes and sense of outrage. The question then becomes, what can reason offer here?

The advantages of the scaffolding proposal should now be more obvious than ever. Not least is its principled combination of optative rationalism (we assume our fellow citizens are rational enough to see the benefits of a scaffolded system) and pragmatic realism (we don't presume that they are, or need be, more rational than that). There is no assumption here of superiority in moral or political views implied here, which must be a better understanding of freedom of speech than mere open-season licensing. And the deep presumption that social cohesion is a goal both reasonable and viable suggests a modesty with respect to changing minds that is respectful as well as realistic concerning the prospect of agreement about what is or is not the case.

This is, in short, appropriate revamped liberalism for the post-truth era.

Conclusion: Reason within Reason

Traditional scientific method might be considered, with some justice, the ideal form of discursive scaffolding. In addition to providing essential curbs on bias and prejudice—falsifiability, reiterability, strict disinterest—the method acts as a gate for participants. If you do not accept the rules of the game, you are not a valid player in the game. If you attempt to fabricate studies or twist the rules, you (and your results) will be expelled from the game. You can't game the rules of this game, nor can you trump them, because any attempt to do so is an automatic disqualification in essence if not in (short-term) effect. There is no possible transactional corruption: you can't buy your way to validity, nor can you overpower the game with sheer force of wealth.

In other forms of discourses, all of these depredations are possible. It is, as it were, always an open chance that someone losing at the monopoly game of public discourse will attempt to overwhelm opponents with real-world money rather than the conventional money that operates within the game.

There are, further, no clear gates in public discourse: anyone can play who wants to. This is, of course, a huge positive and yet just as surely invites false trading, cheating, parasitic undermining, and all the other familiar pathogens of the public square. Most dangerously—and this is, after all, how we got here in the first place—there are precious few external constraints on such discourse. Factual claims and logical validity possess normative power, yes, but it is tenuous and variable at best, dangerously misleading at worst.

Now, it is easy to oversell this contrast. We know that scientific discourse is, like all human undertakings, shot through with social and psychological forces that mitigate against "pure" rational results. We know, too, that there is enduring disagreement within scientific subspecialties, something we might expect not to see if the results are as method driven as we sometimes desire. This is simply the nature of complexity in discursive practices, of course. There are no such disputes in logic; there are considerably more in law and even more in, say, literary criticism or art theory. Good interpretation becomes the essential goal, not knockdown correctness. Naturally, what counts as "good" in the realm of interpretation will itself be a matter open to interpretation. This is the best we can hope for, and it is a great deal. But even this multiplicity of dispute requires, at a minimum, some measure of good faith as interlocutors come together to compare and argue.

This last criterion of discourse in the public square can no longer be assumed—if it ever really could be. Social and technological factors have only worsened a problem that is as old as human society itself and found in everything from large-scale politics to the tiniest domestic dispute or argument between siblings. Scientific study of our rational practices holds the key to understanding why.

Two findings stand out here. The first, drawn from a series of studies at Stanford University, provides evidence for the claim made earlier that facts do not have clear motive power in mind-change. In several deceptive experiments, subjects were asked to make judgments—about firefighter competence, for example—and then later shown factual claims, which they accepted as valid, overturning their initial judgments. And yet, the subjects were tenacious in their hold on *what they now knew* to be faulty judgments. This may be viewed as a version of the familiar notion of confirmation bias but is more clearly operative than just the pleasure we get from having our prior judgments confirmed. (Other studies show that a definite endorphin boost occurs in human brains when our cherished notions are "proved right.") In these cases, the bias was in favor of judgments without confirmation. Psychologists prefer the term "myside bias" for this apparently hard-wired tendency to surrender any judgment, however erroneous, once it is made.

The other relevant scientific claim concerns the nature of rationality itself. Though we valorize it as the highest part of ourselves—a scaling of the psychic economy with us at least since Plato, indeed the foundation of the Western philosophical tradition—in fact our rational faculties are somewhat low minded. Not only is reasoning affected by emotional, psychological, and physiological forces that have no basis in rules of inference or validity, but rationality itself is also revealed as a kind of drug. Developed during the intense socialization periods of our species, when cooperation emerged as a social good, our rational faculties are good at problem-solving and distribution of labor. But they are also inordinately biased toward winning, as in outsmarting opponents in argument or tactics.

This tendency may still fulfill cooperative needs, as when one group goes to war with another: one thinks of the myriad examples of cleverness called forth by the demands of warfare. In general, though, it means that we are very adept at spotting weaknesses in the position of interlocutors but very clumsy in seeing them in our own views. We are also forever on the lookout for breaches of cooperation within the group—free-riding, for example. This last feature, according to one tart critic, reflects the task that reason evolved to perform, which is to prevent us from getting screwed by the other members of our group, living in small bands of hunter-gatherers. Our ancestors were primarily concerned with their social standing and with making sure that they weren't the ones risking their lives on the hunt while others loafed around in the cave. There was little advantage in reasoning clearly, while much was to be gained from winning arguments.[19]

Or, in the sharp words of a psychiatrist (Jack Gorman) and a public-health specialist (his daughter Sara Gorman), "It feels good to 'stick to our guns' even if we are wrong."[20] By the same token, two other researchers, Steven Sloman and Philip Fernbach, say this: "As a rule, strong feelings about issues do not emerge from deep understanding."[21] Sloman and Fernbach's findings show, in addition, that the foundational notion of the individual rational actor, weighing options and arguments in perfect isolation and clarity, is a philosophical chimera.

So what is the solution? Some psychologists suggest that we need to be made more aware of the depths of our ignorance, especially about those things that we think we understand. The currently favored example is the function of the common toilet, which most people can't correctly describe. Now, there is nothing disgraceful in such lack of knowledge; in fact, using tools and tricks devised by other humans, without being able to replicate or even describe them, is a perfect example of rational scaffolding. We get more things done more effectively if we don't each have to invent the crescent wrench—or the toilet, internal combustion engine, grammar, and parliamentary democracy—every single time we need them.

It ought to follow that we are individually modest in the face of this and willing to exercise ourselves a little when it comes to the tools of human cooperation. And yet, you are far more likely to encounter someone who admits ignorance about how to galvanize rubber or distill alcohol than to do the same about the Affordable Care Act, immigration policy, comparative religion, and the working of the global economy. More humility and more study will always prove chastening to our convictions.

But how likely is that? Regulation is a scaffold that works when self-motivation and individual discipline will not. Reason itself is more a scaffold ensuring (minimal) cooperation than it is a royal road to truth. If we were to accept that, and accept further that reason works only when there are social conventions and mechanisms to prop it up, we would achieve two essential goals. First, we would see that the threats of post-truth collapse are real but remediable: reason can still win. But, second, we would have appropriate wariness about the way this will happen and of the role simple expression of conviction has within the realm of reason.

We say that we should speak truth to power, but we must also acknowledge in these days how power speaks to, and limits, truth. *Reason within reason* is not a rallying cry to rival Kant's sapere aude, but it has two virtues that the generalized call for audacious rational self-guidance conspicuously lacks. It assumes rather than denies the social character of any rational undertaking. We are not individual heroes of reason, savvy shoppers in the marketplace of ideas. It also insists, firmly and necessarily, that reason is the only possible response to the lies, half-truth, provocations, and deceptions of the public square.

That is a conviction, not a fact. But I dare to believe it is true, and I further dare to believe that my belief will help make it so. "A great many people think they are thinking when they are merely rearranging their prejudices," William James said more than a century ago. We must all try not to be one of them.

And just as a parting irony, this quotation, attributed to James by restless anthologist Clifton Fadiman, remains unverified. Of course it does!

Notes

1. I thank Lauren Bialystok, Emma Planinc, Leah Bradshaw, Mark Migotti, and audiences at the University of Toronto, Ryerson University, and Queen's University for comments on early versions of this material. Some portions of the chapter were published previously as opinion articles in the *Globe and Mail* (Summer 2017).

2. Robert Anderson, "The Rashomon Effect and Communication," *Canadian Journal of Communication* 41, no. 2 (2016): 250–65.

3. The works collected in Adorno, *The Culture Industry*, ed. and trans. R. M. Bernstein (New York: Routledge, 2001), include both originary analysis about Adorno's landmark collaboration with Horkheimer, *Dialectic of Enlightenment* (Stanford, CA: Stanford University Press, 1944, rev. ed. 1947), and later specific—

and bilious—forays into television comedy, sunbathing, radio, and the idea of leisure.

4. Roland Barthes, *Mythologies,* trans. Annette Lavers (New York: Farrar, Straus & Giroux, 1972), Introduction.

5. Compare Jean Baudrillard, *Simulacra and Simulation* (orig. *Simulacres et Simulation,* Stanford, CA: Stanford University Press, 1981), trans. Sheila Faria Glaser (Michigan, 1994), and Guy Debord, *Society of the Spectacle* (orig. *La société du spectacle,* 1967), trans. anon. (Detroit: Black & Red, 1970/2002).

6. See, for example, Schmitt, *The Concept of the Political* (orig. *Der Begriff des Politischen,* 1932), trans. George Schwab (Chicago: University of Chicago Press, 1995; 2nd ed. 2007).

7. Ian Brown, "An Encyclopedia Brown Story: Bound and Determined to Fight for the Facts in the Time of Trump," *Globe and Mail,* July 7, 2017, https://www.theglobeandmail.com/arts/books-and-media/an-encyclopedia-ian-brown-story/article35586033/.

8. The following analysis is drawn from an earlier discussion, Kingwell, "Review of Ed Langerak, *Civil Disagreement: Personal Integrity in a Pluralistic Society,*" *Notre Dame Philosophical Reviews* (August 21, 2014), http://ndpr.nd.edu/news/civil-disagreement-personal-integrity-in-a-pluralistic-society/.

9. Alasdair MacIntyre, *After Virtue: A Study in Moral Theory* (London: Duckworth, 1981; 2nd ed., Notre Dame, 1984).

10. A recent study by psychologists Hugo Mercier and Dan Sperber explores the flimsiness of fact-based argument when it comes to influencing people's states of mind. See their work *The Enigma of Reason* (Cambridge, MA: Harvard, 2016), which counters a good deal of more pro-reason research. The issue was accessibly addressed by Elizabeth Kolbert in "Why Facts Don't Change Our Minds," *New Yorker,* February 27, 2017, http://www.newyorker.com/magazine/2017/02/27/why-facts-dont-change-our-minds. I have to say about this issue in the concluding section of this chapter.

11. http://hilobrow.com/2014/05/30/mikhail-bakunin/.

12. The scaffolding proposal was made in an opinion article for the *Globe and Mail* (August 29, 2017, p. A11). It draws on arguments made by, among others, my philosophy colleagues Juan Pablo Bermudèz-Rey and Joseph Heath. See especially Heath, *Enlightenment 2.0* (Toronto: Harper, 2014), which is considerably more optimistic about rationality than I am. I explore some of the relations between addiction and social media in Kingwell, "Boredom, Subjectivity, and the Interface," C. G. Prado, ed., *Social Media and Your Brain* (Santa Barbara, CA: Praeger, 2016). Regulating social media already happens, of course, and suggestions to extend regulation in scaffolded constraints are no different from any other mechanism we might adopt to control our own addictive behavior.

Among the febrile responses, which divined far more oppressive motives in my views than I can discern myself, was Burt Schoeppe, "University of Toronto Progressive Professor Wants to Limit Free Speech," *The Postmillennial,* August 30, 2017, https://thepostmillennial.com/university-toronto-progressive-professor-wants-limit-free-speech/.

Sample quotation: "With this article, Kingwell has accomplished a new betrayal, turning aside from reason and opting for the repression of ideas that we used to associate only with the enemies of democracy." As a friend of mine said in response: "Wow. You've been busy." I know, right? Some further details can be found in the following notes.

13. Amy Davidson Sorkin, "The Anatomy of a Trump Twitter Rant: From Scotland Yard to 'Chain Migration,'" *New Yorker,* September 15, 2017, https://www.newyorker.com/news/amy-davidson-sorkin/the-anatomy-of-a-trump-twitter-rant-from-scotland-yard-to-chain-migration.

14. See, for example, Stanley Fish, *There's No Such Thing as Free Speech . . . And It's a Good Thing, Too* (Oxford: Oxford University Press, 1994). As Fish argues there, "When someone observes, as someone surely will, that anti-harassment codes chill speech, one could reply that since speech only becomes intelligible against the background of what isn't being said, the background of what has already been silenced, the only question is the political one of which speech is going to be chilled, and, all things considered, it seems a good thing to chill speech like 'nigger,' 'cunt,' 'kike,' and 'faggot.' And if someone then says, 'But what happened to free-speech principles?' one could say . . . free-speech principles don't exist except as a component in a bad argument in which such principles are invoked to mask motives that would not withstand close scrutiny."

For a good overview of recent controversies, especially on university campuses, see Ira Wells, "The Age of Offence," *Literary Review of Canada*, April 2017, http://reviewcanada.ca/magazine/2017/04/the-age-of-offence/.

15. I explore the slight prospects of mind-change in Kingwell, "'It's Not Just a Good Idea, It's Law': Rationality, Force, and Changing Minds," Joshua Nichols and Amy Swiffen, eds., *Legal Violence and the Limits of Law* (New York: Routledge, 2016), pp. 1–16. This is, in turn, based on an initial foray, "Changing Minds: The Labyrinth of Decision," *Primer Stories* 4, no. 1 (August 29, 2016), http://primerstories.com/4/changingminds.

The cherished idea of the free expression "marketplace of ideas," meanwhile, is just as subject to failure as any market. In a landmark 1984 article, legal scholar Stanley Ingber called it a "legitimizing myth" (*Duke Law Journal,* February 1984); more recently, commentators have noted how the metaphor values provocation over rational discourse, enabling what Cass Sunstein calls "polarization entrepreneurs" in place of honest traders. A brief survey may be found in Aaron R. Hanlon, "The Myth of the 'Marketplace of Ideas' on Campus," *New Republic,* March 6, 2017, https://newrepublic.com/article/141150/myth-marketplace-ideas-campus-charles-murray-milo-yiannopoulos. Another recent examination of the metaphor's hollowness is David Shih, "Hate Speech and the Misnomer of the 'Marketplace of Ideas,'" *NPR,* May 3, 2017, http://www.npr.org/sections/codeswitch/2017/05/03/483264173/hate-speech-and-the-misnomer-of-the-marketplace-of-ideas.

16. Kingwell, *A Civil Tongue: Justice Dialogue and the Politics of Pluralism* (University Park, PA: Penn State, 1995). I offer a reverse, collective-action-problem critique of incivility in later iterations of the basic argument. See Kingwell,

"'Fuck You' and Other Salutations: Incivility as a Collective Action Problem," Deborah Mower and Wade Robison, eds., *Civility in Politics and Education* (New York: Routledge, 2012), pp. 44–61; reprinted in my essay collection *Unruly Voices* (Windsor: Biblioasis, 2012).

17. See, for example, these two outraged responses to the original published version of the argument. Both focus on one phrase from a 700-word, deliberately polemical article: Ezra Levant, "'We Could Even Ban Media Panel Discussions': Globe & Mail Columnist Calls for Censorship," *Rebel Media,* September 1, 2017, https://www.therebel.media/globe_mail_columnist_calls_for_censorship; and Gerry Bowler, "Putting a Muzzle on Those You Disagree With," *Troy Media,* September 1, 2017, http://troymedia.com/2017/09/01/putting-a-muzzle-on-those-you-disagree-with/.

Both of these media commentators seem particularly exercised by the idea that there might be rational curbs, executed by the people (not the state), on media panel discussions—as if those represent a form of rational debate. "They hate you, my friends," Levant's article concludes. "And they will want to silence you." Hide from the philosopher, friends! He has a muzzle!

An apparently more-considered response posted on *Alternative Right* (proudly listed as "The Founding Site of the Alt-Right") labored to deploy some philosophical reasoning but just couldn't resist resorting to insults instead of argument: "fraud," "simplistic and nihilistic," "adolescent," "half-clever," and (*per contra*) "some Harry Potter–reading cat lady writing for slate.com," whatever that means; and so on and on in the usual way, speaking of half-clever. There screed also included now-familiar deliberate misunderstandings of the original argument, and the presumed sense of grievance at being targeted by "postmodern" and "communist" thought police.

There is also systematic misreading of my positions on morality (I am not an objectivist), ideology (I certainly do not regard it as a settled matter—quite the contrary), and desire (of course, it often is irrational—that was my whole point). Anyway, the bottom line is that it's almost as if—and exactly as I argued—these people *actually can't help themselves*. If you are so inclined, see Ryan Andrews, "Free Speech Is Violence, and Its Might Makes Right," *Alternative Right,* September 5, 2017, https://alternativeright.blog/2017/09/05/free-speech-is-violence-and-its-might-makes-right/.

18. See, for example, A. J. Willingham, "The First Amendment Doesn't Guarantee You the Rights You Think It Does," *CNN.com,* August 8, 2017, http://www.cnn.com/2017/04/27/politics/first-amendment-explainer-trnd/index.html.

19. Kolbert, "Why Facts Don't Change Our Minds," summarizing Mercier and Sperber.

20. Jack Gorman and Sara Gorman, *Denying the Grave: Why We Ignore the Facts That Will Save Us* (Oxford: Oxford University Press, 2017), as quoted in Kolbert, "Why Facts Don't Change Our Minds."

21. Steven Sloman and Philip Fernbach, *The Knowledge Illusion: Why We Never Think Alone* (New York: Riverhead, 2017), as quoted in Kolbert, "Why Facts Don't Change Our Minds."

CHAPTER THREE

Because I Say So: Media Authenticity in the Age of Post-Truth and Fake News

Greg Kelly

Truth is just truth. You can't have opinions about truth.
—Peter Schickele[1]

Despite the near ubiquity of the term "post-truth era," there is still debate over what it means and whether it actually means anything at all. I think the term is meaningful. Because I can remember the moment when I felt we'd entered it. We'd been approaching it for a while, arguably for a century. But I first felt its tectonic rumblings during the lead-up to the 2016 U.S. presidential election. During that time, I lost count of how many predictions asserted that Donald Trump wouldn't win, not just the election but the Republican nomination—predictions not only that he wouldn't win but that he *couldn't* win. With each of his gaffes piling on top of one another, the prognostications would rain down harder, asserting that *this* time he'd really crossed the line and that what had been his growing support would evaporate.

Then he'd take another misstep. And we'd see the same hands-to-face shock and hear the same wrong predictions, and later go through the same rinse and repeat cycle. One source counted all the gaffes that Trump had made, any one of which would likely have killed a presidential candidacy in previous times.[2] They counted a total of 37 missteps.

Among these were demeaning a disabled person, insulting John McCain's war record, denigrating the natural functions of a woman's body, and slandering pretty much all of Mexico. In August 2015, a panel of three political data experts estimated that Trump's chances of getting the Republican nomination (again, just the nomination, not the presidency) stood at 2, 0, and −10 percent, respectively. And Larry Sabato, the head of the Center for Politics at the University of Virginia, said, "If Trump is nominated, then everything we think we know about presidential nominations is wrong."[3]

Most pundits everywhere were just as wrong.

Jump ahead to October 2016, with the presidential election a month away, and the surfacing of the infamous audio tape featuring Trump's smug crudity about grabbing women by their anatomy. "When you're a star, they let you do it. You can do anything."[4]

Yet another line crossed, which turned out not to be a line at all.

Then the election. Then the stupefaction, and the hand-wringing over getting the predictions so wrong, and the media's manifold mea culpa's about misunderstanding Trump's base.

And then the moment came, when the most powerful country in the history of humanity passed through the looking glass: the inauguration.

The White House press secretary du jour was Sean Spicer. In his first official press briefing, held on the first full day of Donald Trump's presidency, he chose to vilify the press for saying that the attendance of Trump's swearing-in was lower than it had been in 2009 for Barack Obama. He was outraged.

But then, there was that split screen picture circulated widely in the news and social media, showing an aerial picture of the Obama inauguration day crowd next to an aerial view of the Trump inauguration crowd, with the former field packed, and dwarfing, the sparse audience in the latter.

The photo comparison was all over the media: online, in print, on TV. It couldn't be more evident that the White House claims were both unsupported *and* insupportable. Spicer would soon fall victim to the ongoing game of musical chairs inside the White House—an administration that has surely shown us how to put the "fun" back into "dysfunction." But before his exit, he'd blather on for days about artificial turf and photo cropping. It was all piffle.

Yet the White House dug in, with the undead Kellyanne Conway defending Spicer, explaining that he'd been using "alternative facts." I have a confession to make: I love that term. It's a morbid kind of love, but love all the same. Chew it over for a second: alternative facts. As though they're choices on a menu that we can choose from and then place our order with our waiter at some imaginary restaurant—let's give it a name: maybe "Bistro Epistemo"?—and our dish comes back from the kitchen, with the alternative fact happily nestled on a fresh bed of nouveau reality.

Of course, it didn't end with alternative facts. Her neologism was a precursor to the one Trump himself uttered in the aftermath of white supremacist violence in Charlottesville, Virginia—violence, he said, which was caused in part by the "alt left," a group that has yet to materialize anywhere in the world. But the rub is this: if the photographic evidence featuring the crowds at the 2017 and 2009 inaugurations don't vaporize the White House claims, then there's no such thing as evidence.

It's true that institutions of power—political, social, military, ecclesiastical—have for centuries wanted things their own way, either claiming news they didn't like was fake news or manufacturing fake news for their own purposes. It's worth recalling that the term "propaganda" was coined in the early 1600s for a committee tasked with "propagating" the faith, or, if you like, a public relations firm that took holy orders.

But even the church couldn't always control fake news, even when it was produced in-house. Easter Sunday, 1475. Trent, Italy. A toddler goes missing. And a Franciscan preacher sermonizes that Jews had murdered the child, draining and then drinking its blood in a ghoulish parody of the Eucharist. The entire Jewish population of Trent was rounded up, and 15 of them were burnt at the stake. The papacy tried to halt the spread of the fake news, and the murders, but the rumors kept spreading; the Franciscan was eventually canonized, and one anti-Semitic website today still claims this story is true.[5] Some fake news sticks.

Then again, some doesn't. Jump now to 2003 and the Iraq War. Remember Comical Ali? His real name is Muhammad Saeed al-Sahhaf. And "Comical Ali" was a play on "Chemical Ali," the nickname applied to Ali al-Majid, the Iraqi defense minister who used chemical weapons, including mustard gas and sarin, in various attacks culminating with the 1988 attack on Halabja, in which over 5,000 people were killed. He was hanged in 2010. But Comical Ali, the spokesman for Saddam's regime during the Iraq War, became notorious—maybe even likeable—for his confident, almost avuncular, proclamations that Iraq would win the war, and was in fact winning it, even while American and coalition forces were moving on Baghdad. The invasion took 21 days. And every last claim that Comical Ali made during that time was not only wrong but seen as wrong at the time.

So if institutions of power have been trying to shove "because I say so" as a basis of ultimate authority down our collective throats throughout the ages, what's different about the "post-truth era" now? I think a few things.

The Origins of Specious

Truth claims appear widely and increasingly to be judged in popular media, and in institutions of power, on their perceived origins rather than on the validity and soundness of the arguments at hand. So if you happen not to like a given position, opinion, or news report, then go for the jugular—in this case, its origins—and dismiss it as "fake news," something Donald Trump has done with CNN, NBC, and other media organizations.[6]

And it's not just Trump. If you, dear reader, were to read, or hear about, an article in Breitbart News, it's likely that you'd dismiss it as fake news, given that people who read publications like this one do not tend to identify with the so-called alt-right. I would dismiss it, too, post-truth be told, because the origins of said article *are* suspect to me as well.

But as social divisions have deepened, as consumer markets have splintered, and as income disparities have grown, we seem to have returned to a kind of denominationalism, more social and political, rather than religious— one that reduces truth claims to nearly instant tribal affiliations: if the claim isn't from one of our own, then it can't be true.

But the question arises: why are we witnessing this reflexive focus on origins as truth-determining, and why now? I submit that it's because we're living in a moment of intense global anxiety, anxiety stemming from unprecedented levels of mass migration, which ratchet up existing social and political tensions to be as taut as piano wire. In her 2016 CBC Massey Lectures, Jennifer Welsh cited a jaw-dropping statistic, that the "total number of displaced people in the world today has reached a record 65 million [people]."[7]

And with this mass movement of people, the incendiary questions of who's in and who's out, who really belongs and who doesn't, increasingly drive political trends and movements around the world: the oft-cited rise of the anti-immigrant far right in Europe and its penetration into the mainstream. Remember the Hungarian camera woman who kicked a Syrian girl refugee? Look at the hostility in South Africa to migrant workers from neighboring Zimbabwe and elsewhere, or the repugnant conditions of off-shore detention centers in Australia, and, of course, Trump's fantasy wall along the Mexican border. These phenomena have a message: "If you're not from here, you don't belong here." This logic, of course, sputters into nullity in the face of historic grievances from First Nations. But logic has little to do with it. This focus on origins as the basis of truth or falsity is paradigmatic of the post-truth era.

I'd hasten to add, though, that the anxieties about incoming populations are not baseless. From June through July 2017, Italy received 15,000 refugees: that's 500 newcomers *a day*.[8] And it's clear that whenever "the other" arrives, especially in great numbers—whether those numbers are real or imagined—fear of "the other" escalates.[9] Many Brexit supporters felt the United Kingdom was changing too much, too quickly. Xenophobia and racism, of course, played their part in the referendum, as did a craven media and opportunistic politicians of the hollow men, stuffed men variety. But if cultures have load-bearing walls the way buildings do, then the added stresses will have to go somewhere, and they will go where they have always gone: along the social fault lines of race, class, gender, and so on.

The border town of Emerson, Manitoba, may well be the ongoing photo op of Canadian "niceness," being the ultimate destination for refugees streaming north from the United States. But a heart-wrenching portrait of the town in the *Walrus* portrays it as exasperated and exhausted from coping with the number of arrivals it's ill-equipped to deal with, and tensions are increasing.[10] And climate change will act as an accelerant on the already-volatile atmosphere produced by mass movements of people—let's not forget that the conflict in Syria was sparked by drought, which in turn was linked to a warming planet.[11] To adapt Oscar Wilde's barb at philosopher Herbert Spencer: Nature, grown weary of repeating herself for the benefit of *Homo sapiens,* will reassert herself on her own terms from here on.[12]

Perhaps it's this massive mix of stresses that produces the shrill tones coming from both the Right and Left. In this post-truth era, the political Right polices values the way the activist Left polices language, each with its fangs perpetually bared, and each, at least in my view, in need of vigorous flossing. The Left, having largely retreated into the academy, turns to language as its shibboleth of worthiness, and its preoccupation with nomenclature has compromised its ability—and maybe even its willingness—to build alliances when it most desperately needs them, settling instead for consuming its own.

As for the Right, it doesn't give a damn about allies. It already has them, as a glance at newspaper ownership and the proliferation of business sections, business news, and business reporting as well as business podcasts would all suggest, to say nothing of *business class* on airlines—as though "business" somehow constitutes a distinct class, and an elevated one at that. But where in all *this* business is labor reportage? It feels almost quaint to ask that question. And in the meantime, as the planet continues to bake, we see values on the one hand and language on the other continuing to act as filters, separating the clean thoughts from the unclean on their separate walkways into the same ark of ideological purity.

My sense is that we'll see even more reliance on origins as the principal determinant of truth. And I think it'll get uglier than it has already been, as I don't yet see any immunization against this cultural pathogen. No president has had his origins retrofitted, for example, the way its first black president has. To depressingly large parts of white America, Barack Obama *had* to be from elsewhere. He cannot belong, so his origins must be foreign, and those origins—falsely conceived—get lacquered over with yet another layer of falsity: that he's Muslim, twinning made-up geography with made-up biography to render him falser than false, and doubly inauthentic. All on the basis of "because I say so."

O Authority, Where Art Thou?

If "the truth" has become an ideological do-it-yourself project, we very soon start stumbling headlong into a quagmire of confusion over where to locate legitimizing authority.

Rachel Dolezal, the former head of the National Association for the Advancement of Colored People in Spokane, Washington, made headlines in 2015 when her public identity as an African American woman was revealed to have no basis, at least no biological basis. She was raked over the coals in major media and lampooned on TV comedy shows, and then she—predictably—wrote a book and did the interview circuit. Eventually she came clean, admitting that she didn't have black parents. But she continues to identify as black. Her reasoning is that race is socially constructed, a product of colonialism, and weaponized to maintain a white supremacist social order, an order she rejects. She claims to have learned this perspective on race, and to have embraced it, at Howard University—an historically black college, which she'd attended on scholarship, with the authorities apparently having assumed from her application and phone interview that she was African American. Her argument was not—it has to be said—uninformed. But it didn't win the day. And she's now apparently jobless and living on food stamps. "Because I say so," even in the post-truth era, appears to have its limits.

Limits we've witnessed in Canada with the story of Joseph Boyden. But the attention paid to his biology—or more precisely, his genealogy—was surpassed by the focus on his community—or rather his lack of one. While skeptics couldn't verify his claims to indigenous ancestry, they also couldn't find any First Nations community which claimed him as their own. In this instance, who you are is who others say you are. And as Hayden King pointed out, there's a long list of nonindigenous people who've been—as he aptly put it—caught playing Indian.[13]

In both cases, identifying oneself with the oppressed "other" was seen to have gone beyond compassion and basic humanity and into appropriation and deceit. And let's face it: there is a cult of the victim in popular media, and some people do find some kind of redemption in becoming a card-carrying member of that cult. Whatever their differences, both stories point toward the same conclusion: subjective identification with a given race or group does not in itself confer status as a member of that group. What is felt on the inside does not translate onto the outside as social reality.

But things get stickier when it comes to gender identity, where the opposite appears to be true. Much of the criticism of the now-defunct gender identity clinic at the Centre for Addiction and Mental Health (CAMH) in Toronto centered on clinicians, notably Dr. Ken Zucker who resigned from CAMH under pressure, for steering younger people away from being transgender adults—for, in effect, prescribing, or proscribing, his patients' sexual identities.

I know nothing about the science of sexual identity. But one statement Dr. Zucker made may help reveal the dilemma I'm driving at: "If a five-year-old black kid came into the clinic and said he wanted to be white, would we endorse that?"[14] That's the cultural crevice we seem to have stepped into: that subjectivity plays opposing roles when it comes to race on the one hand and gender or sexual identity on the other.

A couple of decades ago, you might see posters in urban centers outing various public figures as gay. In this instance, a figure's projected public identity—usually straight—was rejected as fraudulent by the activists. These public figures were, from the activists' point of view, denying, or underclaiming, their real identity. So the posters were gestures of reclamation, however coercive. But overclaiming a particular sexual or gender identity? No one seems to get outed for that. If someone says he or she is "it," then that person is seen to be whatever that "it" signifies.

Subjectivity is thus the locus of sexual/gender identity. But subjectivity is not. And we're left at this peculiar cross-roads where the signage is far from clear.

The Problem of Academic Problematizing

I see two other cultural strands twined into the post-truth fabric. If these two strands could somehow be personified, they'd be shocked—likely horrified—to find themselves so intimately entwined, not with each other exactly but with the same fetish object.

I see theoretical discourse within the academy, especially—but not limited to—literature departments, as the first strand. The second is communications strategies by heavyweight corporations, notably Big Tobacco, Big Oil, Big Pharma, and Big Sugar. And the fetish object they share is the habitual problematizing of the truth or, more accurately, the production of knowledge. But it may as well be called "the truth."

First is academic theorizing. I came of intellectual age in the 1980s, when literary theory was dominant—Marxism and all its variant forms, structuralism, post-structuralism, postcolonialism, psychoanalytic feminism, the New Historicism, the New Criticism, the New New Criticism.

Each had its own idiolect, featuring cool words like "praxis," "decentered," or "phallocentric."

French thinkers, above all Michel Foucault and Jacques Derrida, exerted wide influence and inspired near-reverence in literary studies—as well as revulsion among traditionalists. Foucault, with his archaeology of knowledge systems, and Derrida, with his interrogation of language and signification, represented a full-frontal assault on what we think we know and how we know it.

Many have traced this lineage of epistemic skepticism, identifying both the ancestry and the progeny of figures like Foucault and Derrida. Philosopher Kathleen Higgins is one of them, having appeared on an episode of *Ideas* we produced about post-truth.[15] She's not alone in rewinding to Friedrich Nietzsche and his famous image of the truth as a "mobile army of metaphors, metonyms, and anthropomorphisms."[16] She—like various others—see Nietzsche as the first of a series of what you might call radical gardeners who've overturned the philosophical sod we're now traipsing and tripping over, the uneven ground where the *terra* is no longer *firma*.

This lineage of epistemic skepticism sees truth as a function of power. And if truth is reducible to power, we're forever mired in the mucky territory of "because I say so," where claims to alternative facts made within its borders may not be so stupid after all, since rhetorical might equals right. And it's on this point that I think my former discipline of literary studies and literary theory has a lot to answer for. To be clear, problematizing knowledge is not itself the problem. It's, of course, legitimate, and necessary, to question received *doxa* and how knowledge is constructed. But the proportion of critical energy spent on problematizing knowledge, at the expense, and at times the denigration, of so many other modes of inquiry, has made its own unwelcome contribution to the relativized mess of public discourse right now.

And another thing. The greatest extinction event so far of the post-truth era is perhaps the contempt for experts and expertise. And I lay some of the blame for this decline in civil public discourse at the feet of recondite theoretical discourse. Climate change denial persists, not only in the general population but also in the uppermost reaches of governmental oversight—witness the appointment of climate change denier Scott Pruitt as head of the Environmental Protection Agency. Little wonder that depression rates among climate scientists are spiking. Climatologists are regularly trolled with vicious hate mail, and worse. We spoke to one on *Ideas,* Clive Hamilton in Australia, who told us that he's had his life threatened several times—and he's not unique in that.[17]

Therefore, if we're wondering why people now have "this attitude" toward experts, maybe it's partly because intellectual elites have long had this attitude toward people, and experts like climate scientists wind up on the wrong end of a time-delayed punch. The willful opacity of theoretical writing implies that it's acceptable to speak and write impenetrably, and to wear that same impenetrability as a signifier of intellectual depth. Only the cognoscenti know the codes, and if you don't know them, too bad—you're left out in the cold at the nightclub door not knowing the secret knock. Exponents of theory routinely justify their rhetoric as being as necessary as the technical terms of the sciences. I've read my fair share of theory. And this justification, in my considered view, is bullshit.

It's not about employing a language that embodies the technical precision of science—a notion bursting with naive assumptions about the way science works. It's about envying the status of science. The humanities have for decades suffered in silence as the sciences, especially theoretical physics, became the dominant discourse about ultimate reality. Whether it's outer space and the origins of the universe, or inner space and the workings of the brain, whether cosmology or biology, the sciences remain our shiniest decoder ring for understanding reality. And they tower over the humanities, attracting incomparably more funding, more media attention, and even more social validation. The sciences deliver certainty or, more accurately, are thought to deliver certainty. And what do the humanities deliver, exactly?

The lack of a ready-made answer to that question became unsustainable during the Thatcher–Reagan era of the 1970s–1980s, when neoconservative politics turned culture into markets, and citizens into consumers—and tilted the university onto a corporatist axis—on which it's still spinning. It was in this context that the ascendancy, and entrenchment, of jargonocentric theorizing occurred. Deregulation. The privatization of public services. The decline of unions and public commons. The rise of trickle-down "voodoo" economics. There is no such thing as society.[18] Publish or perish. It was all but inevitable that professionalized, scientific-sounding vocabularies would arise within Anglo-American universities, particularly within literature departments. They were vulnerable. They didn't need these recondite terminologies to explicate theories as much as they did to justify themselves, in short, to propagate. Theory was a signifier of the times.

Nothing else explains the astonishing rise of the academic fraud artist, Paul de Man, the made-in-America European intellectual and suave exponent of deconstruction, who lied about his academic credentials, lied about his criminal past—including writing an anti-Semitic piece for a collaborationist magazine during the Nazi occupation of his native Belgium—and never published a real book. Yet he got a free pass from fawning professors and administrators into epicenters of academic preeminence, like Harvard, Cornell, and Yale.

My contention is that the ascension of Paul de Man in particular incarnated the ascension of literary theory in general. Both flew largely unimpeded into the niche that institutional and social-political circumstances had created for them, where they took up residence and made theory-ese the official language, a language whose appeal was rooted in being abstruse, as in this line from de Man: "Narrative is the metaphor of the moment, as reading is the metaphor of writing."[19] What relationship does such rhetoric create with the person reading it? I think it's seigneurial, a shadow of Old World social relations, castle baron to serf. It's top-down, insouciant, and rather snotty. If it had subtitles, they would read: "I do not owe it to you to be comprehensible. You owe it to me to figure me out." And it creates an industry around itself.

In the late 1980s, I attended a conference in Glasgow where many of the heavy-hitters in theory would be speaking. The headliner was the patriarch of deconstruction, Jacques Derrida, who was to give a special evening lecture about his intellectual whipping boy, the metaphysics of presence. Derrida's own presence was impossible to miss, with his magnificent shock of white hair inspiring envy in those of us who are follicly challenged. What caught my eye were the tables of books on sale, primary texts by the theorists, secondary texts explicating their theories, and tertiary texts explaining the explanations. The more explicating, the higher the status of those being explicated—and the stronger this closed-loop economy becomes. Careers were made inside the loop of lit crit and grew to depend on its maintenance and expansion.

When the hour for Derrida's lecture arrived, the auditorium was packed, and the atmosphere was expectant and excited. When he entered, the hall fell silent, oddly similar to the moment when Bugs Bunny enters the concert hall as Leopold Stokowski.[20] As he began speaking to a rapt audience, the only audible sounds apart from his voice were the scribbles of assiduous note-taking. But his famously tortuous prose soon made the audience restless. Slowly, over the course of an hour, they started trickling out the side entrances. It was Glasgow after all, and the pubs were still open. I did notice, however, that the guy next to me was still taking notes, or so I thought. When I glanced over, I saw that he was actually drawing a cartoon giraffe, festooned with musical notes and even a dialogue balloon, indicating that the giraffe was singing "Chanson d'Amour."

My anecdote is, of course, not an argument against deconstruction or a grandiose assertion that that literary theory is somehow all wrong. It's clearly not even an argument. I saw too many traditionalists make the mistake of conflating their distaste for theory with disproof and counterargument. Their reflexive dismissals failed too often to engage directly with the theories they were rejecting and amounted to little more than the equivalent of wrinkling one's nose. Not good enough.

The point that I am trying to make is that the default reliance on complicated language is tantamount to the one percenting of communication. And it's both alienating and aggravating. The Oxford literary critic, John Carey, believes that there's a long vein of class-based aggression in literary theory's relationship with the public. In his book *The Intellectuals and the Masses,* Carey argues that contemporary literary theory inherited the same aesthetic of difficulty that defined literary modernism in the late 19th and early 20th centuries, when novels and poetry became increasingly sophisticated and harder to understand than they had been previously.[21] Carey sees the birth of this aesthetic as a reaction to the growth of mass literacy and mass culture in the mid- to late 1800s. Writers and intellectuals in class-ridden Britain felt threatened by the influx of the working- and middle-class "other" onto their cultural properties, so they built a wall—one made of words—to shield themselves from the "great unwashed," a phrase that incidentally originated in the Victorian era. They paradoxically saw themselves as the paragons of a culture which they themselves disdained, and it's by now well-trodden turf to point out how many of the great moderns had Fascist leanings and sympathies.

I don't believe it's anti-intellectual to call out this penchant of problematizing knowledge. I used to write in theory-ese while in graduate school, and it really isn't that hard. I find it far more intellectually rigorous and demanding to communicate with people outside your tribe and have your offerings subjected to public judgment. In my occupation, you learn the hard way that no matter how important what you have to say may be, it will get lost if the audience can't find it. And losing the message can provoke hostility when the messengers don't even seem to be trying.

The Truth: Brought to You by Corporate Sponsorship

Academic theorizing may make for a strange dancing partner with corporate communications, but it happened. What Big Tobacco, Big Pharma, Big Sugar, and Big Oil have been doing for much of the postwar period bears an uncanny resemblance to much critical discourse within the academy: namely, the problematizing of knowledge. The transgressions of these industries have been well documented. What's instrumental here is to understand the rhetorical strategy that these corporations used and still use.

Whenever the toxic effects of their products would come into question, variations on the following occur: they would publicly deny any causal links; they'd call for more studies to be commissioned, studies that they themselves would commission directly or indirectly; they'd announce conclusions that they'd already hardwired into the process; and they'd call for yet more studies to be done. Meaning is constantly deferred, what's knowable is repeatedly bracketed with uncertainty, and then it's back to business as usual. Vive la Derridean *différance*.

Big Tobacco knew as far back as 1964 that smoking caused cancer. One executive at R. J. Reynolds recognized the link between smoking tobacco and lung cancer. Reynolds destroyed his report. Then the presidents of six tobacco firms hired a public relations firm to beat back the truth. "This marked the beginning of what became, literally, an industrial-scale exercise in the promotion of an alternative scientific reality. It involved not just alternative facts, but an entire body of false scientific argument to deny that smoking caused cancer."[22] And they got away with it for decades, with the full extent of their homicidal sophistry coming to light only in 2001. In the West, smoking may have declined both as a consumer preference and in public acceptability. But Big Tobacco is still big: in 2015, according to the World Health Organization (WHO), over 1.1 billion people smoked tobacco, and cigarette consumption is increasing throughout the Mediterranean and in Africa.[23]

Big Pharma generates over $14 billion a year on antidepressants alone and is poised to make $2 billion more in the next few years.[24] And surprise, surprise, much of the research into antidepressants is tainted—even the potentially corrective research into the research itself. *Scientific American* found that "the vast majority of meta-analyses of antidepressants have some industry link, with a corresponding suppression of negative results. The latest study, published in the *Journal of Clinical Epidemiology,* which evaluated 185 meta-analyses, found that one-third of them were written by pharma industry employees."[25] Nothing like writing the review of your own book.

Big Sugar feeds itself on the global obesity epidemic. Again according to the WHO, the global rate of obesity has more than doubled since 1980. In 2014, 1.9 billion adults worldwide were overweight. No surprise that an industry lobby group, the so-called Sugar Research Foundation, had on its payroll not just one, but two prominent Harvard nutritionists, who "tore apart"[26] growing evidence that dietary sugar was behind a sharp increase in health problems and instead pointed their authoritative fingers at fat and cholesterol. This industry-led misdirect from 40 years ago is still being felt: there are now at least 600 million obese people around the world—not merely overweight—and that includes *42 million children under the age of 5.*[27]

Big Oil knew as far back as 1977 that its carbon-based fossil fuels were directly linked to climate change. And like Big Tobacco, it knew this *from its own research.*[28] So it spent millions on spreading misinformation to the public. As the historian of science and coauthor of *Merchants of Doubt,* Naomi Oreskes has shown that it also injected its perspective into the body politic, especially in the United States: overwhelmingly, those who deny that climate change is caused by humans vote Republican.[29] They've made denying climate science a marker of personal identity. As a strategy for marketing their "truth," it's undeniably brilliant.

The truth in each example was made to be whatever the corporations said it was. Evidence-based arguments were irrelevant, undermined, ignored, and suppressed. These multinationals paid good money for their truth; and in the post-truth era especially, the corporate customer is always right.

Maintaining the status of their truth in the digital age is tricky: the speed and accessibility of the Internet exceed anyone's direct control. But the hearsay nature of the web, especially that of social media—which is really neither social nor media—can be leveraged to aid and abet the post-truthers. Get your message out fast, have it infest as much virtual space as possible, and it may gain enough momentum to forestall any pushback. The near-instantaneous speed of the Internet has also spelled trouble for real journalism. Helen Boaden, the former director of BBC Radio, said on her retirement in 2016 that the speed of digital news can dilute authoritative, public service journalism. "It seems to me," she wrote, "that the media can sometimes rush very fast in order to stand still. . . . Do we, the media, do enough today, to explain and explore? Or are we too busy moving on to the next thing, in thrall to the pace of news?"[30] The faster that pace, the thinner real news becomes, and the greater the proliferation of fake news.

Hide the Sharp Objects

At this point, despair may seem to be a reasonable option. And that maybe "authenticity" as an operative trait of the media should skulk off to some unread corner of the dictionary and sit down quietly beside other defunct terms like "ectoplasm."

But we should beware of the comforts that despondency can offer. Feeling good about feeling bad is, at times, a kind of refuge for the chattering classes, to which I belong, a refuge we too often check ourselves into imagining ourselves looking on with melancholy wisdom as civilization implodes. We'd do well to remember that Samuel Beckett—never noted for his sunny disposition—wrote into *Waiting for Godot* the old saying about the two condemned prisoners crucified on either side of Christ: "Do not presume; one of the thieves was damned. Do not despair; one of the thieves was saved."[31]

The truth about the term "post-truth" is that it's used almost exclusively by people who care about the truth. Even the mythopoeic Donald Trump cares about the truth, at least in the sense of what others believe to be true. His obsessive diurnal and nocturnal watching of U.S. cable news cannot be explained by his wanting to learn about the world through authoritative news outlets. True, maybe TV is his natural habitat given that he was churned up like cud by reality television. But we shouldn't be shocked by his relentless bleating and tweeting about NFL players taking a knee, or his nyah-nyahing with North Korean leader Kim Jong Un. Trump's unhinged comments aren't merely acute symptoms of irritable bowel syndrome of the mind. They reveal that he's obsessed with the truth, albeit *his* truth, but truth nonetheless.

One happy effect of the post-truth moment is the renewed appetite for, and production of, that rarest and most endangered of journalistic species: investigative journalism. There's an archetypal image of the grizzled, cigar-chomping newsroom veteran, barking advice to a cub reporter: "The news, kid, is what they don't tell you." Given the grotesque overuse of embedded reporters during the Iraq War by far too many news agencies, the too-cozy relationship between public relations firms and journalists, and those unforgivable, God-awful press dinners in Ottawa or Washington,[32] I am convinced that the cigar-chomping veteran got it right.

And many journalists are getting it right, not only in the stories they're telling but in the caretaking of their relationship with the public. I think of Ira Glass, host and executive producer of *This American Life*. In 2010, I attended *the* public radio conference in the United States, called PRPD (Public Radio Program Directors). This conference is where deals are brokered and broken, where new programming is showcased, old friendships are rekindled, and ancient rivalries are reignited. If you're looking to get your program onto American public radio airwaves, you absolutely have to attend the PRPD.

In 2010, I was at Radio Netherlands Worldwide, heading a program called "The State We're In." And we'd caught wind that Ira was going to deliver a talk, which they've nicknamed "The Benediction." The Benediction occurs right at the end so people don't hightail it out of the conference earlier to catch their return flights home.

Ira was going to talk about programs that *he* was listening to, and apparently, ours was among those that he was going to highlight. Great news for marketing the show, so I made the trip to help capitalize on it. Ira said nice things about us and a slew of other programs. But what stuck with me were his prefatory remarks on findings by the Pew Research Center, which had been tracking belief in the following statement: "If it's in the media, it must be true."

The audience naturally laughed. The research confirmed what you've already guessed: that the belief had been in a steady arithmetical decline for decades—except in public radio, a finding that was met with genuinely warm applause.

But two years later, *This American Life* airs a story about horribly exploitative working conditions in a Chinese factory that makes iPads and iPhones. It was the most-downloaded episode in the program's long and illustrious history. But the story turns out to be false, a fake.

You have to appreciate the profile *This American Life* has to understand how disastrous this was.

It's arguably the most successful public radio program of all time, if you combine its audience numbers, its awards and recognitions, the intense devotion of its listeners, and its standing among radio producers around the world. It is a pillar. And it achieved its prominence not simply through journalistic rigor and dedication to audio craftsmanship but by privileging the relationship it has with listeners, or rather "the listener," because Ira typifies the public radio practice of speaking as though he's addressing one person—you. It's a peer-to-peer relationship. And that fake story undermined everything the show stood for.

Let's hit pause for a moment. If that same fake story were aired on many, if not most, other programs, whether TV or radio, in the United States or elsewhere, I can tell you what the show's or the network's response would likely be: it would circle the wagons. It would delay responding. It would deny, it would excuse, and it would explain it away—and maybe—I stress maybe—issue a perfunctory apology.

But not *This American Life*. In March 2012, it aired an *entire* episode that focused on the fake story that it had run the preceding January.[33] It called out its own program *and* its most popular episode. That's authenticity.

And the lesson to me was clear: treat your audience as though it's an adult, and it'll very likely respond as an adult. *This American Life* is still thriving. And rightly so. However, journalistic authenticity entails more than striving for an honest relationship with the audience. It also has to have the possibility of meaningful impact; otherwise, there's no reason to pay attention to it.

In my experience, no caste of journalist has the greatest potential for creating either massive impact or pornographic futility, the way photographers do, especially war photographers. The reason for this, I think, is that photojournalists cannot do hotel journalism, as it's disparagingly called in the trade. They have to be right where the story is happening if they're going to tell that story through pictures, either still or moving. So they see all the horror, the humanity, the hubris, and the humility in situations that are unimaginable to most of us.

Maggie Steber is one such photojournalist. Maggie won World Press Photo for her work in Haiti, a country she's been covering for decades. But as she told my old colleague, Eric Foss, and me when we interviewed her for a CBC TV documentary, reality can grind you down: "I have photographed death in Haiti so much, and I have seen so much death, that ultimately I think you come to a point where you just say: that's all I can do. And you just think: I just can't go back and witness it anymore, and photograph it anymore, because I don't see what the fuck it's going to matter anymore."[34] Meaningful impact: those two words haunt my profession.

But Maggie went on: "Does that mean I think we shouldn't do it? Oh no, by no means. You have to keep thrusting this stuff in front of people." Maggie's right.

Powerful, predatory men are being called to account in ways that were unthinkable even a few years ago, all because of persistent and courageous reporting—much of it done by women it should be stressed—in getting these stories imprinted onto public consciousness. Harvey Weinstein comes immediately to mind. It took the *New York Times* and the *New Yorker* to tell us what the proverbial "they" didn't want told.

Before him, Bill Cosby. Still further back, Dominique Strauss-Kahn.

And, of course, Fox News, which has now officially reached quorum and can be formally referred to as a pig pen: former CEO Roger Ailes, who unfortunately passed away midway through 2017. Bill O'Reilly, who—unfortunately—has not yet passed away. Still on the roll call of Fox News predators past and present: Francisco Cortes, Jamie Horowitz, Eric Bolling, Charles Payne, and, my namesake, Greg Kelly.

Notice what these the more famous names here all have in common, apart from position, influence, and piggery? They're all old and astonishingly ugly. I'm serious in speculating that there's a whole orchard of unsavory psychological fruit to be picked here, when it comes to the pathology of the powerful predatory male who's still on the prowl well past his best-buy date.[35]

Of course, we don't have to venture south of the border to find man-pigs brought down by reporting that tells the truth to power, as the case of former CBC radio host Jian Ghomeshi would attest. Justice has been uncertain, overdue, compromised, diluted, and delayed when you look down this very cursory list. But these stories would not have been heard at all had it not been for the trinity of interrelated beliefs: that the truth exists, that the truth matters, *and* that it can be made to matter widely.

Sustaining that belief is tough. I will admit that I have often wondered whether anything we in the media have done, or ever can do, makes a whit of difference. The gap between the 1 percent and the remaining 99 percent continues to expand like an obscene universe. Corporations rival, or even surpass, the powers of elected governments. And elected governments everywhere are less credible and appear to be growing weary of democracy itself. Add to this unholy mix environmental degradation and climate change, the latter of which to my mind is *the* story of our time, which will drive all other stories in the decades to come. You can begin to understand the allure of despair.

But—I remind myself—one of the thieves was saved. I take it as axiomatic that doing one's utmost to tell the truth to power—even risking or losing one's life—may not result in anything. But doing nothing will guarantee nothing. This isn't the stark proposition it may seem to be. It's always been this way and always will be, just as epistemological labyrinths have always been with us and always will be. But the truth is that the truth *is*. I can assert this without embarrassment or endless qualifying clauses for one reason: because of the single most powerful interview I have ever seen.

This interview did not occur within the context of broadcast journalism. It took place in an OPP interrogation room in February 2010. And it has confirmed forever, at least for me, the credo that the right questions asked the right way at the right time can save lives.

There'd been a spate of break-ins and sexual assaults in Tweed, Trenton, and the Ottawa area. Two women went missing. Tire tracks were found near the home of one of the missing women, so the police set up a dragnet and eventually found a vehicle whose tread appeared to match. That vehicle belonged to Colonel Russell Williams, commander of CFB Trenton, Canada's largest military air base. Colonel Williams was brought in for questioning. The interrogator was Detective Staff Sergeant Jim Smyth.

I have watched this interrogation on YouTube dozens of times. And every time, I'm struck by how note-perfect it is. The right questions, asked the right way, at the right time. Detective Smyth in his quiet, methodical, business-like way approaches Williams with what I now see as a double-helix of inquiry. One of those filaments is a patient, step-by-step presentation of evidence, which will eventually push Williams up against a wall of absolute incontrovertibility. The other filament is the creation of a psychological debt with Williams, time and again indicating his desire to help Williams as far as he can at every stage of the interrogation. Even when the evidence mounts against Russell, Smyth doesn't offer a scintilla of judgment against the monster sitting across from him. One arm of the helix was progressively constrictive and informational, the other constantly open and relational. It was a masterpiece.

Right at the outset, Detective Smyth sets Colonel Williams at ease as they enter the interrogation room. Williams even smiles up arrogantly at one of the video cameras Detective Smyth points out to him. Smyth asks the colonel: "What would you be willing to give me to help me move past you in this investigation?" And his relationship with the suspect is instantly established, as if to say: *I think you're probably innocent. I'm just doing my job. I need your help.* The detective asks for fingerprints and a blood sample—and then adds, seemingly casually, maybe also footwear impressions? Colonel Williams agrees to it all. Four hours later, Williams would be offering a full confession.

From the moment they enter the room, Smyth constructs an inviting hall of mirrors for Williams to enter, and once entered, he can exit only by telling the truth. Smyth's body language would mirror that of Williams, crossing and uncrossing his arms or leaning forward or back. He would verbally mirror words and phrases that Williams says. And he would mirror Williams emotionally as well, whenever the latter expressed concerns, to which Smyth would say "me, too" or "so do I." Then there were the silences, some of them lasting for more than four minutes at a time. Smyth used these silences to mirror and magnify the tension mounting inside Williams whenever he'd fall silent as a new piece of damning evidence was presented to him.

At one point, Detective Smyth shows Williams an impression of tire prints taken at the home of one of the missing women and of the tires on the vehicle Williams drove to the station.

Of course, they match. He then shows Williams, or "Russell" as he keeps calling him (avoiding the deferential "Colonel Williams"), the footwear impressions taken just outside one of the victim's homes, impressions that match the boots which Williams—incredibly—wore to the interrogation. But he avoids direct implication and says instead: "Your boots walked to the back of Jessica Lloyd's house."[36] Your boots. He lets it sink in, and then a few minutes later tightens up the line of questioning: "You and I both know you were at Jessica Lloyd's house and I need to know why."

As the informational strand constricts, Smyth continues to build up the psychological debt with Williams by keeping the relationship open: "I don't think you want the cold-blooded psychopath option," he tells Williams. He strikes a confidential tone and informs Williams that some people enjoy the notoriety of being known as a psychopath—he mentions serial rapist and killer Paul Bernardo. And then—cunningly—he tells Williams: "I don't see that in you. If I saw that in you, I wouldn't even be back in here talking to you, quite frankly." But, of course, Detective Smyth is in that interrogation room because he suspects Colonel Williams of being exactly like Paul Bernardo: a murderous psychopath.

Psychopaths thrive on control, a fact Smyth leverages when he warns Williams that with the footwear and tire impressions, things are getting out of control "really, really fast." And that it's all "getting beyond my control." He announces that Williams's residences and computers are being searched, and his wife now knows what's going on. So Smyth tightens the question line another notch: if a body is found, he tells Williams, you will have no cards left to play. "What are we going to do?" he asks Williams. Note the "we"—*I'm still not a threat to you.* He repeats the question: "Russell, what are we going to do?" Silence.

And it's at this point that the entire interrogation pivots. Williams doesn't answer the question. Instead, he responds plaintively: "Call me 'Russ,' please." Smyth had pierced the barrier. Williams is reaching out to him. Williams needs an ally, just as Smyth needed Williams's help earlier. The mirroring is now complete. This is the moment when Detective Smyth calls in the psychological debt he'd been building up all along. Williams asks Smyth how to minimize the impact of anything he might say on his wife. Then it breaks wide open.

Detective Sergeant Smyth utters a simple, six-word sentence that brings the whole interrogation—and the horror that women and entire communities were living through—to an end. He tells Williams: "We start by telling the truth." Williams falls silent once more, for nearly 30 seconds, taking long breaths and exhaling hard. His jaw tightens. His temple flexes with tension. He finally breaks the silence and in a near-whisper says: "ok." Smyth mirrors Williams one last time and says "ok" equally softly.

With his characteristic even tone, Smyth asks: "Where is she?" referring to the body of Jessica Lloyd. He doesn't mention her name or refer to her body. He backs off implying culpability as he's already established that. What he needs at this critical juncture is one bit of information from Williams and has to give him unpressured latitude to get it. It worked. Colonel Williams, or "Russ," asks for a map.

Nothing in this tour de force of an interrogation resembles anything we see in a Hollywood movie or in television dramas. There's no in-your-face screaming, no histrionic accusations, and absolutely nothing physical: no torture, no hitting, no touching—not even an insult. Just the right questions asked the right way at the right time.

It's impossible to know how many women's lives this interrogation saved. But given the trajectory of Williams's crimes, which began with dozens of fetish burglaries and escalated to two home-invasion sexual assaults before ending with two murders, it is a certainty that lives were saved.

This interrogation has also become a personal and professional touchstone for me. Whenever I hear the siren call of the post-truth moment luring me into its seductive waters of cynicism or despair, I direct myself back to that uncanny direction of Detective Sergeant Smyth: *we start by telling the truth*. Because it's more important than ever to do so in public discourse, especially in the media we produce. It's not just the economy and pop culture which have become globalized. The problems we face as a species are also globalized, many of which have reached extreme proportions. And as we know with extreme cases, asking the right questions the right way at the right time can literally be a matter of life and death.

Therefore, we in the media must choose life[37] and commit and recommit to this first principle: that we start not with obsessing over ratings, counting clicks, or attracting "likes," or preoccupying ourselves with awards, or promotions, or even job security.

We start by telling the truth.

But not "because I say so."

Notes

1. Peter Schickele, *The Wurst of P.D.Q. Bach* (1971).

2. Michael Kruse and Taylor Gee, "The 37 Fatal Gaffes That Didn't Kill Donald Trump," *Politico Magazine,* September 25, 2016.

3. Larry J. Sabato, Kyle Kondik, and Geoffrey Skelley, "Republicans 2016: What to Do with the Donald?" *Sabato's Crystal Ball,* August 13, 2015.

4. David A. Fahrenthold, "Trump Recorded Having Extremely Lewd Conversation about Women in 2005," *Washington Post,* October 8, 2016.

5. Jacob Soll, "The Long and Brutal History of Fake News," *Politico Magazine,* December 18, 2016.

6. Brian Stelter, "President Trump Focuses Anti-Media Ire on NBC after Tillerson 'Moron' Report," *CNN Media,* October 4, 2017.

7. Jennifer Welsh, *The Return of History* (Toronto: House of Anansi Press, 2016), p. 113.

8. Sylvia Marchetti, "Italy Is Pleading with Europe to Help Deal with a Record Influx of Refugees," *Time,* July 11, 2017.

9. Cf. Aladin al-Mafaalani, "Fighting at the Table: Conflict as Successful Integration," part 4 of "Us and Them: Diversity, Division and a World of Difference," *CBC Radio Ideas,* June 29, 2017.

10. Michael Lista, "Is Canada Really a Safe Haven?" *Walrus,* September 6, 2017.

11. Henry Fountain, "Researchers Link Syrian Conflict to a Drought Made Worse by Climate Change," *New York Times,* March 2, 2015.

12. Cf. Oscar Wilde, "The Decay of Lying," *Nineteenth Century,* January 1889.

13. Hayden King, "Joseph Boyden, Where Are You From?" *Globe and Mail,* December 28, 2016.

14. Hanna Rosin, "A Boy's Life," *Atlantic Monthly,* November 2008.

15. Naheed Mustafa (producer), "The Truth about Post-Truth," *CBC Radio Ideas,* January 19, 2017.

16. Kathleen Higgins, "Post-Truth Pluralism: The Unlikely Political Wisdom of Nietzsche," *Breakthrough,* Summer 2013.

17. Clive Hamilton, in "Are We F—ked? Decoding the Resistance to Climate Change," Mary O'Connell (producer), *CBC Radio Ideas,* September 7, 2017.

18. Margaret Thatcher, from interview *Women's Own,* September 23, 1987.

19. Quoted in Robert Alter, "Paul de Man Was a Total Fraud," *New Republic,* April 5, 2014.

20. Chuck Jones (director) and Michael Maltese (writer), "Long Haired Hare," *Looney Tunes,* Warner Bros., 1949.

21. John Carey, *The Intellectuals and the Masses: Pride and Prejudice among the Literary Intelligentsia 1880–1939* (London: Faber, 1992).

22. Clive Irving, "Inside Big Tobacco's Academy of Lies, the Inventor of 'Alternative Facts,'" *Daily Beast,* March 3, 2017.

23. Cited in "WHO Global Report on Trends in Tobacco Smoking 2000–2025," *WHO,* 2017.

24. "Global Depression Drug Market Poised to Surge from USD 14.51 Billion in 2014 to USD 16.80 Billion by 2020," *Nasdaq Global Newswire,* May 10, 2016.

25. Roni Jacobson, "Many Antidepressant Studies Found Tainted by Pharma Company Influence," *Scientific American,* October 21, 2015.

26. "How the Sugar Industry Artificially Sweetened Harvard Research," *PBS NewsHour,* September 13, 2016.

27. Susan Blumenthal and Samara Levin, "Global Obesity: A Growing Epidemic," *Huffpost,* February 2, 2016 (updated February 2, 2017).

28. Shannon Hall, "Exxon Knew about Climate Change Almost 40 Years Ago," *Scientific American,* October 26, 2015.

29. Naomi Oreskes in "Decoding the Resistance to Climate Change," *CBC Radio Ideas,* September 17, 2017.

30. Helen Boaden, "BBC Radio Director Helen Boaden Resigns, Criticising State of Journalism," *Guardian,* September 29, 2016.

31. Samuel Beckett, Act 1: *Waiting for Godot.*

32. Some observers think it was the roasting of Donald Trump by President Obama at one such press dinner that inspired Trump's ambitions to undo Obama's core legislation. See Roxanne Roberts, "I Sat Next to Donald Trump at the Infamous 2011 White House Correspondents' Dinner," *Washington Post,* April 28, 2016.

33. Ira Glass, "Retraction," *This American Life,* March 16, 2012.

34. Maggie Steber in *Beyond Words: Photographers of War,* produced by Greg Kelly and Eric Foss for *CBC News Sunday,* 2005.

35. According to the model Zoe Brock, Harvey Weinstein chased her around his hotel room in nothing more than his bathrobe, demanding a massage from her. After she locked herself in the bathroom, he apparently started crying and

said: "You don't like me because I'm fat." Nardine Saad, "The Full List of Harvey Weinstein Accusers Includes Fledgling Actresses and Hollywood Royalty," *Los Angeles Times,* October 17, 2017.

36. Jessica Lloyd and Cpl. Marie-France Comeau were both murdered by Colonel Russell Williams.

37. Deuteronomy 30:19: "I [God] have set before you life and death, blessing and curse. Therefore, choose life."

CHAPTER FOUR

Post-Truth: Marcuse and New Forms of Social Control

Lisa Portmess

Post-truth political speech—the lies, disinformation, alternative facts, and propaganda that undermine rational discourse and political decision-making—operates to influence, obfuscate, and distract, executing messages and image content that allow for deniability, amplification, and distortion. Troll farms, targeted Facebook and Google ads, web brigades, Twitter bots, and other fake news production have proved able to disrupt elections, deliver votes on national referendums, accentuate social divisions, fuel racial animosity, and communicate fake news in coded speech that skillfully communicates with targeted groups. As Malware does with its hostile software, fake news has its own executable code in viral contagion, video/audio manipulation, and active content that conceals intentionality and political will. In benign forms, fake news, coded memes, and image manipulation entertain—sharks swimming on flooded highways and Onion-like satire of political events—and blur the boundary of news and non-news.

Yet post-truth political discourse in its serious vein has contributed to the rise of emotional, inflammatory, and aggressive communication that reflects the power of new technologies to shape political opinion and democratic elections. For all of its media and comedic appeal, post-truth discourse serves serious political and communicative purposes that strengthen individual and institutional authoritarian ideologies and invite disruptive intrusion by foreign actors. Influential new technologies operate as powerful shadow enablers in political arenas, even as intelligence experts examine political interests that fund the data mining and data analytics of such firms as Cambridge Analytica, believed instrumental in both the U.S. election and the EU referendum, and sites like Blactivist on Twitter and Facebook, linked to Russian accounts, that infiltrate in order to heighten racial discord. In these ways, post-truth discourse, in its power to deflect, obfuscate, and conceal intent, gives rise to urgent political questions about knowledge production, new technologies, and concealed power. This chapter explores tacit assumptions about knowledge in the contemporary debate over post-truth and argues for a conception of post-truth that acknowledges new forms of social control that are more dispersed, unstable, and contested than the philosopher Herbert Marcuse envisioned in his writings on technology and society. A matrix of human intentionality and techne conceals the social relations and positionality of post-truth discourse in ways unforeseeable by Marcuse in his concern with the technological rationality of an earlier era.

Post-truth politics raises familiar epistemological questions in new contexts—about reason and human irrationality, the fallibility of perception, the social context of knowing, the impact of technology on the knowing subject, the politics of knowledge, and the role of emotion and identity in establishing belief. But it also raises trenchant questions about power, social control, wealth, race, and inequality associated with historical critiques of capitalism and its technological instrumentalities. Herbert Marcuse was a prescient analyst of technology, disinformation, and the realm of consciousness as a site of domination and repression. Themes of his critique thread through contemporary analysis of capitalism and disinformation even if he could not foresee the destabilized order out of which new forms of social control would emerge.

In 1964 Marcuse published *One Dimensional Man: Studies in the Ideology of Advanced Industrial Society* as a critique of advanced industrial society created unfreedom in the uncritical consumption it promoted and thwarted revolutionary resistance. Dulled by consumption through mass media and advertisement and the withering away of critical capacities, the one-dimensional self struggles for meaning in a social world in which Marcuse believes the great refusal by outcasts of society holds promise for social transformation and for the resurgence of epistemic virtues. For Marcuse it is ultimately the individual who must seek liberation from the post-truth world of advanced capitalism, its means of production, and its ideology. Disinformation, whether a permanent feature of advanced democracies and advanced capitalist societies or an episodic aberration at times of heightened political partisanship, threatens human well-being and intellectual freedom whether as an instrument of state domination or as the cascade of information and fake news we now experience.

Post-Truth Disinformation

Post-truth disinformation differs in striking ways from earlier less technologized (yet highly effective) forms of disinformation, such as Soviet *Dezinformatsiya* in the Stalin era, German disinformation campaigns during World War II, and disinformation used by the United States, the French, the British, and others as an instrument of war. Disinformation today is democratized (anyone can create and effect large-scale distribution), socialized (available by peer-to-peer sharing on social media), atomized (divorced from brand or source), anonymized in creation and distribution, personalized through micro-targeted messaging, and conveyed by largely self-regulated social media platforms.[1] Such disinformation floods social media platforms, television and Google and Facebook ads, stoking division in the United States on immigration, white supremacist marches, and NFL players' protests of police violence. Ubiquitous and frequently indistinguishable from conventional news and advertisement formats, fake news cascades through the body politic, streamlined to reach readers whose preferences are known by sophisticated predictive analytics.

In the first use of the term "post-truth" in the *Nation* in 1992, Serbian American playwright Steve Tesich lamented "a government of lies" that perpetrated the Iran/Contra scandal and a complacent public that preferred lies to truth.[2] The war in the Persian Gulf later deepened the patriotic desire to see the war as the government chose to frame it. For Tesich, when all turned out to be lies, it was plain that the public had chosen "a glorious victory" over uncomfortable truths and had become complicit in yielding to totalitarian forces. "In a very fundamental way," Tesich wrote, "we as a free people, have freely decided that we want to live in some post-truth world" (Tesich, Kreitner).

Tesich's observation reminds us that disinformation has a history, and each country a biography of the fraught relationship of its people to official information. In times of war or fractious partisan discord, disinformation flourishes and people are hungry for the confirmation of the beliefs of their group. Tesich's reflection on the complicity of citizens is reenacted in the post-truth era by every act of scrolling through social media platforms in which users submit to being sold to the advertiser as they *like*, or a British population that accepts Tony Blair's statement that the Iraq War was the foundation on which the war against terrorism was being won and that the war was essentially benign in its effects. By this statement "Blair was creating a form of hyper-reality—an imaginary world that, he could not help himself believing, was coming into being as a result of the war."[3] As Blair put it in his speech to the Labour Party conference in September 2004: "I only know what I believe," a statement, John Gray observes, "was a manifesto for post-truth politics."[4]

In post-truth analysis, much attention is given to the usurping of new technologies by corporate and political interests, both foreign and domestic. As a commodity, fake news generates wealth for international media conglomerates that have little incentive for self-regulation. Noam Chomsky, in a July 2017 interview with Google staff, criticized the failure of media to ask serious questions of media dependence on corporate interests beyond the narrow issue of how to respond to fake news. "Why, for the last generation, have we constructed socio-economic policies and political policies which are developing a perfect storm which could destroy us?"[5] Such "distortion of the world" that is created by deepening inequality and capital concentration is the condition in which fake news flourishes, and this condition, for Chomsky, is more fundamental than the fake news it enables. Chomsky argues that only resistance by citizens against media conglomerates trafficking in fake news and the hold of corporate advertising on mainstream media will address "the distortion of the world"—the narrow focus of contemporary media journalism.

Chomsky envisions the possibility of a less-distorted world of information in which investigative journalism has the freedom to speak what it discovers and resist consensus journalism described in his earlier work with Edward Herman, *The Manufacturing of Consent: The Political Economy of the Mass Media* (1988).[6] But Chomsky's dream of a free investigative journalism comes up against the powerful, conjoined interests of mainstream journalism and powerful political actors, and addresses neither the vulnerability of readers to post-truth discourse, the rise of individual authoritarianism, nor the sophisticated media production of misinformation packaged as fact. In his essay "Some Social Implications of Modern Technology," Marcuse wrote:

> Technology, as a mode of production, as the totality of instruments, devices and contrivances which characterize the machine age is thus at the same time a mode of organization and perpetuating (or changing) social relationships, a manifestation of prevalent thought and behavior patterns, an instrument for control and domination.[7]

There is no doubt that new forms of disseminating information perpetuate changing social relationships. Nor even that information provides instruments for control and domination. But what is less clear is that social media technologies have the kind of totality that Marcuse believes typical of technology as a mode of production, or that technology manifests prevalent thought and behavior. In partisan information environments, information is particularized, atomized, and customized to users, making the very conformity of the social world Marcuse envisioned a much more fragmented social and information environment rather than the compliant efficiency of technological rationality. Nor have social technologies developed the transparency required by laws governing transparency in television and radio political campaign messages or been forthcoming about the proportion of bots among its account holders and advertisers.

The wildness and the concealed intentionality of post-truth politics create decentralized forms of social control, micro-targeted and customized messaging to individuals according to their psychographic profiles. This engenders a very different kind of knowledge production, intended to destabilize, disrupt, accentuate division, and exert control in variable and covert ways. Such is the new *unfreedom* of the contemporary disinformation environment—atomized, subversive, and concealed in how it exerts political intentionality and influence.

Philosophical Questions of Truth and Fact in a Post-Truth Era

Philosophical questions of truth are among the most thought-provoking commentaries on post-truth politics. Such philosophical analyses examine the notion of *truth,* which the expression "post-truth" references, and the nature of fact suggested by "fake news." Is it truth itself that has been damaged, obscured, and drowned in the disinformation environment? Or is the information environment one in which there's either no truth to be obscured or a reaffirmed sense of truth reinscribed in every condemnation of fake news? And what should be said about facts? Are facts what we need to assert in challenging post-truth discourse? Or are facts themselves a fiction of ideology?

Kathleen Higgins, in her article "Post-Truth Pluralism: The Unlikely Political Wisdom of Nietzsche," argues that the post-truth era is a permanent feature of our developed democracy rather than an aberration.[8] "The Internet multiplies the perspectives and truths available for public consumption. The diversity of viewpoints opened up by new media is not going away and is likely to intensify. This diversity of interpretations of reality is part of a long-standing trend. Democracy and modernization have brought a proliferation of worldviews and declining authority of traditional institutions to fix meanings."[9] Thus, rather than pine for a return to an earlier era, we should see "today's divided expert class, and fractious publics, not as temporary problems to be solved by more reason, science, and truth, but rather as a permanent feature of our developed democracy."[10] On this view, the proliferation of belief systems and different worldviews does not prevent pragmatic action in the world even though it renders more complex the democratic process of addressing contemporary problems. Such multiple perspectives can be seen as an opportunity for human development and "creative formulations of alternative possibilities for concerted responses to our problems."

Our post-truth condition, for Higgins, is the condition of our present and our future, one we must navigate in order to advance liberal values (Higgins).

In appeals for pragmatic cooperation among competing tribes in highly charged political cultures, Higgins argues for a post-truth pluralism that seeks pragmatic solutions and common ground in which we discover "sites of possible intervention" that make pragmatic action in the world possible. To do this, progressives, she argues, would need to have a different understanding of the truth than that which reduces political disagreement or black and white categories of fact and fiction. The very notion of fake news plays on this, obscuring the reality that "human beings make meaning and apprehend truth from radically different standpoints and worldviews, and that our great wealth and freedom will likely lead to more, not fewer disagreements about the world."[11] Thus, for Higgins, it is a philosophical shift that is needed, to a conception of truth that recognizes post-truth pluralism as a permanent feature of developed democracies. Yet here too concerted action is needed against disinformation that degrades the very democratic mechanisms that protect political pluralism. A shift to post-truth pluralism is consistent with action against troll farms and social bots that produce disinformation at critical moments in political life—at the eve of referendum or the eve of the election of a president. Fake news as a concept is neutral as to philosophical questions of truth. One can adopt Higgins's philosophical position on truth yet still urge greater action by social media tech giants to regulate fake news on their sites and endorse current efforts to ensure that their platforms are not tools of foreign governments.

In "Let's Get Metaphysical about Trump and the 'Post-Truth Era,'" Crispin Sartwell considers it a "bizarre misinterpretation" to believe that truth is disintegrating or in crisis.[12]

> Fabrications do not undermine truth—they presuppose it. Lies can harm people, but they can't harm truth itself. They conceptually depend on it. The right conclusion from all this isn't that truth is disintegrating, but that truth is hard and intrusive, that it does not readily bend to human will or agreement or narrative. The power of the Russian intelligence services or a Sean Spicer press briefing is considerable, but it does not include the ability to bend the fabric of reality.[13]

Higgins's position—which acknowledges the philosophical difficulty in grasping the nature of truth as well as the inescapable intrusiveness of truth—suggests an alternative approach to post-truth quandaries. Even if different political communities are described as living in "different realities"— each consuming different streams of information and each deciding how to think by seeking the consensus of people like themselves—each community still has confidence that it possesses the truer version of reality. "Both sides need the truth, and they need it not to be relative to any group's particular set of beliefs. . . . There's nothing unusual about a situation in which people disagree about what the truth is."[14] On Sartwell's view, navigating the post-truth environment requires de-escalation of the harrowing language of fake news as the death of truth. It is far better to seek depolarization and engagement that resist escalationist claims that post-truth threatens the very basis of reasoning, evidence, and logic.

Yet Sartwell's argument, though it assuages the worry that truth itself is eclipsed by fake news (whatever the disagreements are that philosophers have about the nature of truth itself), does not assuage the Orwellian fear that fascist propaganda emerges in rich disinformation environments and turns lies into truth. Sartwell assures his readers of the security of the notion of truth but not the security of the environment in which we search for it. In that environment, imposter web pages that amplify divisive social and political messages surface, with manipulated images generating fear of streaming immigrant border crossings, Muslim terrorists, and militant Black Lives Matters activists. Even if Sartwell is right that the *philosophical* problem of truth isn't any harder in this post-truth era, there is no doubt that the landscape for truth discovery is more treacherous in a post-truth era of disinformation.

As Sartwell resists the notion of the disintegration of truth and denies that the notion of truth is in crisis, other post-truth commentators scrutinize the notion of "fact" and "truthifiability" and express doubt about asserting too sharply a fact-based strategy against post-truth. In "What's the Opposite of Post-Truth? It's Not as Simple as 'the Facts,'" Steven Poole challenges approaches to post-truth that assert the primacy of fact in combating fake news.[15] Poole cites the Nobel laureate in physics, Frank Wilczek, who believes that we should think less of whether an idea is true, and more of whether it is "truthifiable"—"whether it can inspire further creative research that would otherwise be shut down by overly aggressive and hasty fact-checking."[16] To insist adamantly on facts, Poole argues, is likely to intensify tribal warfare and harden divisions. "There was never a golden age of truth."[17]

Yet Poole recognizes that deliberate misinformation and lies are serious and require resistance by readers armed with critical skills. He argues that whatever means readers use to discern what they read, it is finally up to them to decide what they are going to believe.

The underlying difficulty of today's polemics about post-truth is that many well-meaning residents of the reality-based community are talking as though it is always obvious and uncontroversial what is a "fact" and what isn't. And yet the very idea of a fact is a social construct with an origin. (As the philosopher Alasdair MacIntyre has written: "Facts, like telescopes and wigs for gentlemen, were a 17th century invention.") Facts are fuzzy and changeable: in scientific practice, matters of truth and evidence are always at issue. The best scientific theories are social constructs. Whether they should be taken as accurately describing reality is still an unresolved

debate in quantum physics; and, as the biologist Stuart Firestein has written: "All scientists know that it is facts that are unreliable. No datum is safe
from the next generation of scientist with the next generation of tools."[18]

But Poole does not fully take account of the greater difficulty for readers in a
post-truth information environment in deciding what to believe, even if we
agree that facts are fuzzy and changeable and matters of truth are always at
issue. The *caveat lector* approach of Poole's requires sophisticated skill in discerning authoritative information, awareness of the ubiquity of social bots
and troll-sourced information, and forensic skills only experts have in detect-
ing sophisticated manipulated video and audio.[19] In a highly developed disinformation environment, such skills are in large part beyond the capacity of
most readers, with searching engines and autocompletes producing Holocaust denial sites as the first results for the question "Did the Holocaust happen?"[20] Poole's position holds out hope for the development of such advanced
skills in readers and their communities, against powerful interests and the
invisible analytics that stream individuated content, with a weakened notion
of fact that renders fact-checking, techniques of source discernment, and
political action against intrusive disinformation. Complicating efforts to create greater skill in readers is the gradual transformation to greater use of
images and video in post-truth politics. With their visceral effects and the
greater susceptibility of viewers to trust what they see, post-truth images are
less likely to be recognized by viewers as fake than fake news is.

Daniel Levitin, in his book *Weaponized Lies: How to Think Critically in the
Post-Truth Era,* argues for the importance of teaching the kinds of critical
skills that Poole advocates.[21] Truth matters, he asserts at the start, and our
best defense against misinformation is in developing "infoliteracy" that
teaches readers how to evaluate source quality, recognize faulty arguments,
and distinguish pseudo-facts that masquerade as facts and biases that distort
information. In three broad sections he addresses issues in evaluating numbers; issues in evaluating words and identifying expertise, recognizing coun-
terknowledge (misinformation packages to look like fact); and issues in
evaluating the world, knowing what you don't know, becoming wary of logical fallacies, and recognizing that information and misinformation cohabit
side by side. But essential as such critical thinking skills are, fake news
requires political action that strengthens democratic institutions in monitor-
ing election intrusion, investigative journalism that reveals the fake news of
Trojan horses,[22] pressure on social media conglomerates to identify fake
news and better inform users of suspect content, and consideration of legal
and regulatory mechanisms that require greater responsibility for eliminat-
ing the kind of fake news that surfaced by 4chan trolls on Facebook and
Google after the Las Vegas shooting in October 2017, identifying the wrong
gunman as a Trump-hating liberal. Weaponized lies as these cannot be

countered by critical thinking alone, especially as counterknowledges are packaged with even greater sophistication.[23]

Julian Baggini takes on the question of truth from an entirely different perspective in his book *A Short History of Truth: Consolations for a Post-Truth World,* asserting that talk of a "post-truth" society is premature and misguided.[24] Our preoccupation with post-truth indicates that truth matters; lies still land politicians in hot water. Yet he acknowledges that there is a loss of interest in political truth, defeatism in distinguishing truth from falsehood and a preference for choosing political leaders based on emotion. Voters seek simple narratives and respond to simple policy aims in times of information complexity. But the antidote, Baggini argues, is not a return to simple truths.

> To rebuild belief in the power and value of truth, we can't dodge its complexity. Truths can be and often are difficult to understand, discover, explain, verify. They are also disturbingly easy to hide, distort, abuse or twist. Often we cannot claim with any certainty to know the truth. We need to take stock of the various kinds of real and supposed truth out there and understand how to test their authenticity.[25]

In each of the 10 types of truth Baggini explores—eternal truths, authoritative truths, reasoned truths, empirical truths, moral truths, and holistic truths, among others—he illustrates how the means of establishing truth are imperfect and carry within them the possibility of distortion. Knowing this, he believes, helps to guard against this misuse and realize "that the claim we live in a post-truth world is the most pernicious untruth of them all."[26] After a short exposition of each of the 10 types of truth, Baggini observes that the post-truth society is in part the failure of cultivating epistemic virtues such as skepticism, openness to other perspectives, a spirit of collective enquiry, a readiness to confront power, a desire to create better truths, and a willingness to let our morals be guided by the facts.[27] Baggini concludes that we all recognize that truth is not a philosophical abstraction but instead central to how we live and understand ourselves, each other, and the world.[28]

Baggini's meditation on truth echoes the position Sartwell voiced. Truth is complex, philosophical theories of truth differ, and simple assertions of fact fall short. Rather than indicate societies that have moved beyond truth, post-truth politics points instead, Baggini argues, to social fragmentation and diminished epistemic virtues. Knowledge is inescapably social, and different theories of truth are hard to reconcile. Even in a post-post-truth world, individuals must ultimately make of experience what they will.

Yet Baggini says little about the systemic causes of the degradation of political discourse and its intersection with human fallibility—themes that preoccupy Matthew d'Ancona in his book *Post Truth: The New War on Truth and How to Fight Back,* which traces the rise of the misinformation industry and the "digital bazaar,"[29] and Evan Davis's *Why We Have Reached Peak Bullshit and What We Can Do about It,* who seeks to explain the irrational appeal of bullshit and the possibility that it has other purposes than truth (and that deception as well as discretion in telling the truth has its role in social life). For Davis, coded message and other forms of indirect speech, on the surface clearly false or evasive, can be subtly informative and convey what direct speech hesitates to say, in ways that exaggeration, myth, and embellishment also do. We wouldn't want to relinquish these creative and expressive forms of language. Yet for Davis, who gives wider berth to untruth, there is something that won't change: "For all the rubbish we speak, ultimately the fate of human beings is driven by reality not words."[30] And this—in a time of the powerful brought low by lies and the undeniable force of natural disasters—portends the ebbing away of this post-truth era, as once the virulent McCarthy era ebbed.

Conclusion

In his writing on technology Herbert Marcuse sounded dire warning about the role of disinformation in advanced capitalist societies and hoped for the spirit of refusal to rise in rare individuals who create a new and radical subjectivity. In this transformation he believed oppressive technological rationality could be overcome and a new reality principle born. As this chapter has argued, the new technologies of the contemporary post-truth environment, with "mass customization of messaging, narrative, and persuasion,"[31] have engendered concealed authoritarian exploitation, "cognitive hacking,"[32] and the creation of what Chomsky terms "distorted worlds." Few individuals subject to tailored disinformation can alone take on the sophisticated analytics and teeming counterknowledges that flood the information streams and ground knowledge acquisition and political judgment. Only collective action, increased research, and international cooperation can strengthen institutions tasked with investigating breaches of information systems, protect the electoral process in democratic states, punish criminal intrusion and data theft, hold tech giants to account, and educate individuals and organizations in the critical appraisal of information. For these tasks, nations and the international community need to thwart the new forms of social control that thrive on vast armies of social bots, post-truth lies, and weaponized information—and work to reclaim public spaces for democratic deliberation.

Notes

1. Kelly Born, "Six Features of the Disinformation Age," *Project Syndicate,* October 2, 2017, https://www.project-syndicate.org/commentary/fake-news-government-inadequate-responses-by-kelly-born-2017-10.

2. Steve Tesich, "The Watergate Syndrome: A Government of Lies," *Nation,* January 6/13, 1992, 12–14. See also Richard Kreitner, "Post-Truth and Its Consequences: What a 25-Year-Old Essay Tells Us about the Current Moment," *Nation,* November 30, 2016, https://www.thenation.com/article/post-truth-and-its-con sequences-what-a-25-year-old-essay-tells-us-about-the-current-moment/.

3. John Gray, "Post Truth by Matthew d'Ancona and Post-Truth by Evan Davis Review: Is This Really a New Era of Politics?" *Guardian,* May 19, 2017, https://www.theguardian.com/books/2017/may/19/post-truth-matthew-dancona-evan-davis-reiews.

4. Ibid.

5. Ed Sykes, "Noam Chomsky Flips the Debate about Fake News on Its Head, in a Room Full of Google Staff," *The Canary,* July 4, 2017, https://www.thecanary .co/uk/2017/07/04/noam-chomsky-flips-the-debate-about-fake-news-on-its-head-in-a-room-full-of-google-staff-video/.

6. Edward S. Herman and Noam Chomsky, *Manufacturing Consent: The Political Economy of the Mass Media* (New York: Pantheon Books, 1988).

7. Herbert Marcuse, "Some Social Implications of Modern Technology," *Technology, War and Fascism: Collected Papers of Herbert Marcuse* (New York: Routledge, 1998), p. 41.

8. Kathleen Higgins, "Post-Truth Pluralism: The Unlikely Political Wisdom of Nietzsche," The Breakthrough Institute, Summer 2013, https://thebreakthrough .org/index.php/journal/past-issues/issue-3/post-truth-pluralism.

9. Ibid.

10. Ibid.

11. Ibid.

12. Crispin Sartwell, "Let's Get Metaphysical about Trump and the 'Post-Truth Era.'" *Wall Street Journal,* May 5, 2017, https://www.wsj.com/articles/lets-get-metaphysical-about-trump-and-the-post-truth-era-1494022098.

13. Ibid.

14. Ibid.

15. Steven Poole, "What's the Opposite of Post-Truth? It's Not as Simple as 'the Facts,'" *New Statesman,* May 18, 2017, https://www.newstatesman.com/culture/books/2017/05/what-s-opposite-post-truth-it-s-not-simple-facts.

16. Ibid.

17. Ibid.

18. Ibid.

19. Olivia Solon, "The Future of Fake News: Don't Believe Everything You Read, See or Hear," *Guardian,* July 26, 2017, https://www.theguardian.com/tech nology/2017/jul/26/fake-news-obama-video-trump-face2face-doctored-content.

20. Frank Pasquale, "From Holocaust Denial to Hitler Admiration, Google's Algorithm Is Dangerous," *Huffington Post,* February 6, 2017.

21. Daniel J. Levitin, *Weaponized Lies: How to Think Critically in the Post-Truth Era* (New York: Dutton Press, 2017).

22. Julian Borger, Lauren Gambino, and Sabrina Siddiqui, "Tech Giants Face Congress as Showdown over Russia Election Meddling Looms," *Guardian,* October 22, 2017.

23. Levitin, *Weaponized Lies.*

24. Julian Baggini, *A Short History of Truth: Consolations for a Post-Truth World* (London: Quercus, 2017).

25. Ibid., 8.

26. Ibid., 10.

27. Ibid., 106.

28. Ibid., 108.

29. Matthew d'Ancona, *Post Truth: The New War on Truth and How to Fight Back* (London: Ebury Press, 2017).

30. Evan Davis, *Why We Have Reached Peak Bullshit and What We Can Do about It* (London: Little, Brown, 2017), p. 298.

31. Rand Waltzman's "The Weaponization of Information: The Need for Cognitive Security." Testimony presented before the Senate Armed Services Committee on Cybersecurity on April 27, 2017.

32. Ibid.

References

Baggini, Julian. *A Short History of Truth: Consolations for a Post-Truth World.* London: Quercus, 2017.

Born, Kelly. "Six Features of the Disinformation Age." *Project Syndicate.* October 2, 2017. https://www.project-syndicate.org/commentary/fake-news-government-inadequate-responses-by-kelly-born-2017-10.

d'Ancona, Matthew. *Post Truth: The New War on Truth and How to Fight Back.* London: Ebury Press, 2017.

Davis, Evan. *Why We Have Reached Peak Bullshit and What We Can Do about It.* London: Little, Brown, 2017.

Gray, John. "Post Truth by Matthew d'Ancona and Post-Truth by Evan Davis Review: Is This Really a New Era of Politics?" *Guardian.* May 19, 2017. https://www.theguardian.com/books/2017/may/19/post-truth-matthew-dancona-evan-davis-reiews.

Herman, Edward S. and Noam Chomsky. *Manufacturing Consent: The Political Economy of the Mass Media.* New York: Pantheon Books, 1988.

Higgins, Kathleen. "Post-Truth Pluralism: The Unlikely Political Wisdom of Nietzsche." The Breakthrough Institute. Summer 2013. https://thebreakthrough.org/index.php/journal/past-issues/issue-3/post-truth-pluralism.

Kreitner, Richard. "Post-Truth and Its Consequences: What a 25-Year-Old Essay Tells Us about the Current Moment." *Nation.* November 30, 2016. https://www.thenation.com/article/post-truth-and-its-consequences-what-a-25-year-old-essay-tells-us-about-the-current-moment/.

Levitin, Daniel J. *Weaponized Lies: How to Think Critically in the Post-Truth Era.* New York: Dutton Press, 2017.

Poole, Steven. "What's the Opposite of Post-Truth? It's Not as Simple as 'the Facts.'" *New Statesman.* May 18, 2017. https://www.newstatesman.com/culture/books/2017/05/what-s-opposite-post-truth-it-s-not-simple-facts.

Sartwell, Crispin. "Let's Get Metaphysical about Trump and the 'Post-Truth' Era." *Wall Street Journal.* May 5, 2017. https://www.wsj.com/articles/lets-get-metaphysical-about-trump-and-the-post-truth-era-1494022098.

Solon, Olivia. "The Future of Fake News: Don't Believe Everything You Read, See or Hear." *Guardian.* July 26, 2017. https://www.theguardian.com/technol ogy/2017/jul/26/fake-news-obama-video-trump-face2face-doctored-content.

Sykes, Ed. "Noam Chomsky Flips the Debate about Fake News on Its Head, in a Room Full of Google Staff." *The Canary.* July 4, 2017. https://www.theca nary.co/uk/2017/07/04/noam-chomsky-flips-the-debate-about-fake-news-on-its-head-in-a-room-full-of-google-staff-video/.

Tesich, Steve. "The Watergate Syndrome: A Government of Lies." *Nation.* January 6/13, 1992.

CHAPTER FIVE

Extraordinary Popular Delusions and the Manipulation of Crowds

Sergio Sismondo[1]

Some Post-Truths in the Post-Truth Era

Have we entered a post-truth era? Did we turn a corner with the U.S. election and its aftermath, with steady streams of fake news, easily debunked but widely circulating conspiracy theories, and outright lies placed front and center? Even if not, the enormous attention to "fake news," with much effort to distinguish the real and the fake, shows genuine fears that a post-truth era is on us.

Some might accuse electoral politics of having been a post-truth arena for a long time. However, by the rules of the game in democratic contests, politicians generally only bend the truth. When caught lying outright, for example, in attempts to escape responsibility for their actions, they provide complex justifications and near-apologies. The Trump campaign and administration abandoned that game, working mainly in the bombastic modes that Trump had successfully used in reality TV, not a genre noted for its concern with traditional realism. The currency of reality TV is emotional connection, not factual accuracy.[2] Thus, in an article in the *Atlantic,* Salena Zito writes that Trump supporters were "taking him seriously, not literally" (while the press was taking him literally, not seriously).[3]

The coalition that Donald Trump assembled included people generally fearful about legal and illegal immigration, voters concerned about free trade and the erosion of good jobs, people upset at all parts of the political establishment and its connections with Big Finance, a broad range of white supremacists and vocal misogynists, and—of course—those deeply concerned about Hillary Clinton's e-mails. That coalition was fueled by deep feelings of anger directed scattershot at inconsistent targets; anger was something on which the voters were taking Trump very seriously. There is, however, nothing unusual about campaigns being driven by fears, concerns, and angers. Feelings and emotions are the basic stuff of mass democracy, so it's unclear that any of the fears, concerns, or anger represent anything particularly "post-truth."

Examining the 60 most prominent distinct items on Google that characterized "post-truth" or the "post-truth era," in the summer of 2017 a research assistant assembled a database of how commentators were defining these terms, mostly in the course of essays on politics or public culture.[4] I grouped commentators' portrayals of post-truth under five themes:

1   The emotional resonance and feelings generated by statements are coming to matter more than their factual basis.

2   Opinions, especially if they match what people already want to believe, are coming to matter more than facts.

3   Public figures can make statements disconnected from facts, without fear that rebuttals will have any consequences. Significant segments of the public display an inability to distinguish fact and fiction.

4   Bullshit, casual dishonesty, and demagoguery are increasingly accepted parts of political and public life; this should not, however, be confused with ordinary lying, which is nothing new.

5   There has been a loss of power and trust in traditional media, leading to more fake news, news bubbles, and do-it-yourself investigations. This theme is associated with attention to communication structures, including social media.

To these I added a further one that we can assume sits behind and supports or leads to most of the others:

6   There has been a loss in respect for or trust in experts.

I add this last theme because of the many denunciations of elites, especially elites who happen to be marked by their expertise. During the Brexit campaign, Michael Gove sidestepped issues about the economic cost of Brexit, saying that "people in this country have had enough of experts."[5] A part of the U.S. vote was a loud vote against expertise. Hillary Clinton became, among other things, a symbol for technocracy, and this was articulated as a struggle to connect with voters. The wholesale rejection of expertise by voters and the more selective rejection of expertise being continued in some of the Trump administration's appointments suggest that optimism about the coexistence of democracy and expertise may be misplaced, or perhaps that expertise, in general, is increasingly seen as "sectarian."[6]

All of the six prominent claims I just listed represent the post-truth era as a broad cultural phenomenon. As a result, these different post-truths are compatible with each other; indeed, one can read two or more of them in most commentaries. For example, Stephen Colbert succinctly summed up several of them a decade ago, striking a chord with his term "truthiness": the *feeling* of truth, not necessarily connected to truth.[7] Ultimately, many people seem to care more about truthiness than about truth. But how did this happen?

Post-Truth Accusations: Blame the Philosophers

Some of the most prominent explanations of the post-truth phenomenon blame philosophers. Without much explanation, journalist Peter McKnight blames the post-truth era on philosophical postmodernism,[8] a position he characterizes in terms that suggest that he has been reading the feminist science and technology studies scholar Donna Haraway: there is no "view from nowhere" or "God's eye" view, but only a kind of "perspectivism" about truth.

> It was . . . the modern university, that bastion of left-wing thought, that set the stage for Mr. Trump's inauguration. During the Reagan years, the university found a new champion called postmodernism, that much ballyhooed . . . philosophy that provides justification for the Trump administration's tortuous relationship with the truth.

There are any number of similar accusations, building on a family of consistent themes. Let me provide a few more examples.

S. D. Kelly argues that philosopher Jacques Derrida's trenchant insistence on the mutual dependence of words and texts for their respective meanings, and the consequent lack of meaning of both, has taken root in U.S. culture at large. This is because fully 40 percent of working Americans hold college degrees, and they are putting Derrida's analyses into practice:

> The world is no longer logocentric, words no longer mean anything, and this is not Trump's fault. Trump is not to be held solely responsible for the fact that, when he is front of a crowd, or in a debate, or in an interview, telling it like it is, there is no longer an is. Our politicians make a practice

of speaking words into the void and seeing what happens next. If the madness that follows the political rhetoric at a rally demonstrates the dismantling of society itself, don't blame the practitioners. Blame the theoreticians for a change. Blame Derrida.[9]

One last example. As reported by science writer John Horgan, filmmaker Errol Morris claims that historian of science Thomas Kuhn helped usher in the current regime.[10] Horgan disagrees, because he doesn't think that Kuhn's work—and he gratuitously throws philosopher Bruno Latour into the mix—has been read by climate change deniers, vaccine skeptics, Fox News commentators, and other vanguard post-truthers. For Horgan, Kuhn and Latour are "radical postmodernists," who hold views that *could* support the post-truth era, but he treats it as absurd to think that they've been particularly influential on public affairs.

For all their anti-Enlightenment inclinations, none of Haraway, Derrida, Kuhn, or Latour offers much support to the post-truth era. Their various positions and arguments are more subtle than these commentators suppose, recognizing that established truth is a powerful force in the world and understanding genuine truths as complex constructions: established truth shapes not only what people believe and say but also what they do and make, and who they become; and even the best pieces of knowledge are shaped materially, politically, socially, and culturally. I am hard-pressed to see much in common between any of the six claims about the post-truth era I listed and prominent relativist philosophical thought.

However, on the key issue, Horgan is surely right, because any attempt to blame relativist or postmodern scholars grossly overestimates their reach. What was the concrete route from philosophy to politics? Kelly, unlike many others, sees the problem; in her hand-waving suggestion that given that 40 percent of the U.S. workforce has attended college, she identifies the postmodern infection as coming from professors indoctrinating their students with the teachings of Derrida and other anti-Enlightenment philosophers. But she assumes that most college students take at least one humanities course in which they come into contact with Derrida and kin, that they understand and accept the larger anti-Enlightenment arguments, and that they carry those arguments out into their political engagements. All of those assumptions are obviously false. Moreover, in my experience as a professor, undergraduate students are quite likely to espouse simplistic relativisms before taking any university classes.

Accusations against relativist scholarship betray a certain insulation from the real world of public truths. Those who write commentaries for a living might be misled into thinking that mere words, even if widely circulated in academic spheres, can constitute truths that play roles in structuring public life and actions. The construction of public truths typically requires infrastructure, tools, resources, effort, ingenuity, and validation structures. Even an important Twitter account does not by itself make what is generally taken to be knowledge.

Paranoia about Pizza

Let's look at an iconic example of an extreme post-truth episode, the spread of the pizzagate conspiracy theory. The theory began its life immediately before the 2016 election on a white nationalist Twitter account, as a claim that there was a pedophile ring linked to important members of the U.S. Democratic Party.[11] The story spread quickly on such sites as 4chan and Reddit, and—with very creative reading of supposed code words in leaked Democratic Party e-mails—stabilized as the claim that Hillary Clinton was the head of a sex trafficking operation centered on a Washington pizzeria named Comet Ping Pong. The theory was heavily promoted by social media hacker David Seaman, author of the book *Dirty Little Secrets of Buzz*.[12] It gained a larger audience when it was promoted by the radio host and writer Alex Jones, "America's leading conspiracy theorist,"[13] on InfoWars.com and then circulated on other white nationalist websites. The theory made it into the White House: although Donald Trump did not publicly endorse it, his advisor and (very briefly) National Security Advisor General Michael Flynn did, and Trump has praised Jones and Infowars on several occasions. Jones retracted his endorsement of the pizzagate theory when one Edgar Welch traveled with a high-powered rifle from North Carolina to Comet Ping Pong to investigate; he fired several shots but failed to find any evidence of the sex ring. Even after the pizzagate story had mostly died, a YouTube video by a relatively obscure host, David Zublick announcing the imminent arrests of politicians and others involved in the pedophile ring, received 300,000 views.

The whole episode is horribly disturbing, but it may be only yet another among many recent instantiations of what Richard Hofstadter calls a "paranoid style" in politics.[14] Though Hofstadter's focus is on American politics, the style can take root in politics anywhere: such "extraordinary popular delusions" underlie crusades, witch hunts, and riots everywhere.[15] Writing in 1964—though it could as easily have been 2016—Hofstadter noted:

> American politics has often been an arena for angry minds. In recent years we have seen angry minds at work mainly among extreme right-wingers, who have now demonstrated . . . how much political leverage can be got out of the animosities and passions of a small minority.

He recounts a number of episodes from the late 18th through the mid-20th centuries—anti-Mason, anti-Catholic, and anti-Communist movements—that exhibit the paranoid style and fervor it can create. The style finds an opponent whose apparently secretive or unfamiliar rituals and practices are thought to nurture conspiracies, often involving illicit sex and other acts dangerous to the nation's moral fiber.

> The enemy is clearly delineated: he is a perfect model of malice, a kind of amoral superman—sinister, ubiquitous, powerful, cruel, sensual, luxury-loving. . . . Very often the enemy is held to possess some especially effective source of power: he controls the press; he has unlimited funds; he has a new secret for influencing the mind (brainwashing); he has a special technique for seduction (the Catholic confessional).

In 2016, we had pizzagate.

In pizzagate and other instances of paranoia, we are so far from the kinds of narratives normally seen in the works of such scholars as Haraway, Derrida, Kuhn, and Latour that I don't think that we can reasonably draw any connections. Certainly, the fact that even the best pieces of knowledge are shaped politically, socially, and culturally appears irrelevant to any evaluation of the pizzagate theory, its conniving creators, and credulous supporters. While it might not have been easy to get the pizzagate narrative to be taken seriously by many people, it involved a far narrower and very different range of resources than we see in, for example, the establishment of any scientific theories and involved a striking disregard for evidence.

If we can see post-truth-like episodes and politics in many times and places, what, if anything, makes the present moment particularly post-truth? Perhaps the distinctiveness of the moment stems from a shift in the balance, in which emotional resonance, heartfelt opinion, clever bullshit, and alternative media have gained just enough ground over mainstream evidence, facts, and expertise to have rattled many people—and to have affected an election of importance around the world.

Post-Truth Chemical Imbalances

Allow me a detour through some of my own research on the pharmaceutical industry, to illustrate some focused approaches to communication.

To increase their sales, pharmaceutical companies try to expand awareness of diseases for which their drugs can be prescribed, increasing the likelihood that physicians will diagnose those diseases and that other people will see themselves as having those diseases. This is what critics call "selling sickness" or "disease-mongering."

For example, without doubt the incidence of depression has been affected by the extensive promotion of the disease and of drugs with which to treat it.[16] Given the availability of a drug that inhibits the uptake of serotonin, and then drugs affecting other molecules, pharmaceutical companies picked up and promoted first a "serotonin-deficiency" theory of depression and later a more general "chemical imbalance" theory. Drug companies are so effective at public relations that they convinced both doctors and the public at large that there are widespread imbalances. There has never been good evidence for either theory![17] This has become clear enough that a number of psychiatrists are now insisting that the field as a whole never held any "chemical imbalance theory."[18]

To physicians, the most visible conduits of pharmaceutical information are sales representatives. They beat paths from office to office, trying to earn a minute or so of a physician's time to make a targeted sales pitch, tailoring what they have to say to the physician's attitudes and personality.[19] In addition to bringing food for the staff and drug samples to be given away to patients, sales reps bear reprints of the articles their companies have created to give scientific backing to their pitches. An article is a gift of knowledge, an apparent step away from the normal commercialism of the representatives. Not only does the knowledge buttress sales jobs, but its status as a gift provokes a return, in the form of prescriptions.

Sales representatives have limited status and influence, so the pharmaceutical industry often develops and turns to "key opinion leaders" ("KOLs") to disseminate scientific information.[20] As the term itself suggests, pharmaceutical companies hire KOLs to influence others, to lead opinions in the directions that the companies prefer. For this reason, relations between the companies and KOLs are ideally, from the point of view of the companies, part of general "KOL management" plans.

One way in which researcher KOLs can help establish a pharmaceutical company's preferred knowledge base is by serving as (unpaid) authors on "ghost-managed" manuscripts—these are manuscripts that pharmaceutical companies control or shape, in ways opaque to readers, through multiple steps in the research, analysis, writing, and publication process.[21] When potentially major drugs come out, their manufacturers flood medical journals with articles about the disease and the drug.

This is a carefully orchestrated process. Companies propose and design multiple manuscripts around studies by lumping and splitting data. Hired medical writers produce first drafts and edit many papers, and medical education and communication companies expertly shepherd manuscripts through the publication pipeline—not only writing medical manuscripts but also communicating with the formal authors of those manuscripts, submitting them to medical journals where they should have impact, and tracking their progress and effects.

In the promotion of the chemical imbalance theory of depression, pharmaceutical companies established close connections with psychiatrists and other physicians who wrote textbooks, articles, and clinical practice guidelines. They also hired thousands upon thousands of physicians to give presentations to other physicians, using slides and scripts generated by the companies.

Through these means and others, the companies appear to have success-fully established depression both medically and culturally. They helped phy-sicians see it often and helped patients interpret their feelings and experiences in terms of it—perhaps even shaping their identities around it and their chemical imbalance.

Depression may seem like a special case, because it is a mental illness and because the boundaries between the disorder and sadness are malleable. However, any number of bodily illnesses have been shown to have been strongly affected by marketing efforts, including such common chronic dis-eases as hypertension, diabetes, high cholesterol, and osteoporosis, as well as less common conditions such as restless legs syndrome and irritable bowel syndrome.[22]

The pharmaceutical industry doesn't assume that congenial perspectives will develop on their own, and nor does it rely on information to spread itself. Instead, companies shape information to support core narratives around their products, place that information strategically for important markets, and employ thousands of intermediaries to present that informa-tion to targeted individuals.

Following Money and Power

Information, ideas, attitudes, and epistemic practices do not move by themselves. To understand the landscape of pharmaceutical knowledge and opinion, we need to pay attention to interventions by actors working for and with the pharmaceutical industry. To understand the landscape of climate change knowledge and opinion, we need to pay attention to interventions by actors working for and with the fossil fuel industry.[23] Similarly, I think that to understand the landscape of the post-truth epistemic shift, we need to pay attention to interventions by specific interested actors. To understand how the paranoid style has become more mainstream, how undercurrents of pub-lic discourse have risen to the surface, we need to follow the money and the power.

Clearly, the past two decades have seen enormous changes in political economies of information and attention. But one of the most successful new players over the past two decades has been a mainstream media company, Fox News. Launched by Rupert Murdoch in 1996, Fox News emphasized colorful graphics, explosive language, and a systematic blurring of the line between news and opinion—all in the service of a fiercely partisan support of right-wing politics and causes. Fox has helped to fuse political partisan-ship with positions in a culture war, helping to firm up an ideological sup-port within the politics by demonizing opponents in the war. In the process,

it nurtured all of the elements of post-truth, from a focus on emotional resonance to disdain for (other) mainstream media to a respect for conspiracy
theories. Fox's overall model has been highly profitable.

Over the same period, the rise of new social media, and especially of Facebook, Twitter, and YouTube, has fractured communication. The one-to-many
model of communication dominant through most of the 20th century has
ceded ground to a many-to-many model of communication. Putting the
change in terms of models of communication, though, detaches it from the
actions of new social media companies.

In its efforts to gain advertising revenue, Facebook is directly competing
with traditional media. Facebook's News Feed is a brilliant personalizing
tool for showing users what they're likely to want to see and read, tracking
what users share, comment on, like, read, and even linger over. The tool frac-
tures mass media, and then Facebook can use a parallel tool to fracture its
advertising content, personalizing the array of ads a user is likely to see. The
result is that Facebook users increasingly see items that they find congenial,
and that tends to reinforce attitudes and views they already have—all of
which goes some way toward lessening the influence of traditional sources of
authority. Educated liberals will tend to see news stories of social progress
and its failures. Within the "paranoid style" demographic of Facebook users,
news will tend to confirm paranoias.

Twitter may represent a different part of the dissolution of the modern
fact, in that this and other social media platforms can be easily used as tools
of very ugly kinds of politics. *Guardian* commentator Lindy West, announcing that she is abandoning Twitter, writes with exasperation: "After half a
decade of troubleshooting, . . . it may simply be impossible to make this
platform usable for anyone but trolls, robots and dictators."[24] Well-organized
prompting encourages digital brownshirts to pile abuse (including offline
abuse, after "doxxing") on vocal opponents of white supremacist and similar
groups and the politicians with which they ally. Given that Twitter (the company) has made no significant efforts to deter abusers, the platform has stabilized as a site for actions that would be illegal in many places.

Social media scholar danah boyd has described how, in the early 2000s, it
became popular among young "hackers"—people with computer skills and
interests and a certain oppositional attitude—to play pranks in which they
focused the attention of many others on some particular story, image or
song.[25] The activity grew, as did the skills and tools, and the initial pranking
gave rise to manipulation motivated by ideology or money. "They also learned
how to game social media, manipulate its algorithms, and mess with the
incentive structure of both old and new media enterprises." People had
learned how to "hack the attention economy." Social media platforms and
advertisers had been building a new attention economy—becoming "attention merchants"—[26]but noncorporate actors were creatively running their
own schemes at the margins of that economy.[27]

Combining old and new media approaches is a site like Breitbart. It has strong ideological convictions like Fox, though more explicitly centered on white nationalism and eschewing some free-market ideals. Yet it has gained status largely by relying heavily on dissemination via social media—coordinating on social media with neo-Nazis and the like.[28] The alt-right includes many attention hackers, now adults keen to put their skills to use promoting white nationalism and attacking black and women leaders. Breitbart chair and former White House advisor Steve Bannon exhorted his young protégé Milo Yiannopoulos:

[You are] Social Media and they have made it a powerful weapon of war. . . . There is no war correspondent in the west yet dude and u can own it and be remember[ed] for 3 generations—or sit around wasting your God-given talents jerking off to your fan base.

Many political parties have drawn on the possibilities offered by Facebook's and Twitter's ability to spread "memes" across affinity networks and the former's ability to individualize experiences. One of the best-known hackers for hire is Cambridge Analytica, used by the "Leave" campaign in the Brexit vote and by the Trump campaign in the U.S. election, in both cases to target voters in key districts, feeding them information, stories, and images intended to focus attention and emotions. However, while Cambridge Analytica has attracted notice, because of its presumed role in two surprising winning campaigns, its questionable tactics, and its association with alt-right causes,[29] the U.S. Democrats also ran a sophisticated social media campaign, relying on broadly similar tools to target ads at key voters.

The opportunities for targeted propaganda were enormous. Thus, Russia jumped into the fray, weaponizing social media. Its most successful campaign has been in the United States, especially during the 2016 election. Through fake intermediaries, Russia purchased ads on Facebook during the election. More important, though, it created fake Facebook and Twitter accounts in swing states, hacked into little-used accounts, and with the help of "bots" that reposted and retweeted preferred content started spreading propaganda. Much of it was targeted: negative stories, insinuations, and vicious comments about Hillary Clinton. Russian hackers also made use of the United States' most durable divides, especially around race relations and gun rights: Russia "harvested American rage."[30] Posing as U.S. citizens, Russian impostors created new online activist organizations on the right and the left, even funding actual protests to give those organizations legitimacy and force.[31] Six of the fake sites—Being Patriotic, Blacktivists, Heart of Texas, LGBT United, Secured Borders, and United Muslims of America—were shared 340 million times.[32] Facebook has found more than 450 other fake sites.

President Vladimir Putin, of course, denied any official Russian involvement in any of the various social media propaganda campaigns. In an interview he did allow, though, that "free-spirited" hackers might have awakened in a good mood one day and spontaneously decided to contribute to "the fight against those who say bad things about Russia."[33]

This is not only a U.S. story. There are questions about Russia's involvement in the UK Brexit vote. In the midst of public scrutiny around fake accounts, Facebook deleted more than 30,000, and perhaps as many as 70,000, Russian-linked fake Facebook accounts that were spreading propaganda during the 2017 French presidential election.[34] It also deleted tens of thousands of fake accounts during the 2017 German federal elections.

Russia may or may not have been involved in pizzagate.[35] However, at least one actor was deploying it systematically: tweets with the hashtag #pizzagate were disproportionately high in swing districts, not in districts likely to vote Trump.[36] The paranoia was being used deliberately.

Establishing Public Truths

As political economies of information and attention have been radically disrupted, old epistemic resources have lost value. In particular, many authoritative gatekeepers have lost much of their authority and are no longer keeping the important gates. The action has moved elsewhere.

The old media's most visible response to eruptions of lies and bullshit has been to emphasize fact-checking. Fact-checking, though, is a nonstarter. Most people hold closely to their beliefs, especially if those beliefs are woven into constellations of attitudes, feelings, interests, and more. Rebuttals in the form of naked facts are useless: few common aphorisms are as wrong as Justinian's "the truth shines with its own light."

The spread of lies, nonsense, and emotions should not be the only issue. Whether in the echo chambers of social or older media, we might be just as concerned with the power to direct attention as we are with fake news. Both play into instrumental and behaviorist approaches to politics (and other arenas), treating publics as people to be manipulated rather than convinced. Epistemic competition is as much about which truths are considered salient and important as about which claims can be considered true and false, and these choices have important consequences.

The fracturing done by social media is not necessarily a democratizing change. The many-to-many model of communication, or the fact that almost everybody has the ability to vie for other people's attention, does not necessarily distribute communicative agency. Powerful actors can put in place mediators and amplifiers to manipulate the new social media crowds. If the new era merely blows up old knowledge structures, then it isn't very likely to be democratization and, in fact, most likely leads to authoritarianism.

Although we have only taken some steps in that direction so far, the emergence of a genuinely post-truth era might be more possible than most people would imagine. The *fact* as we know it is often a *modern* fact, arising out of particular configurations of practices, discourses, epistemic politics, and institutions.[37] As solid as those configurations have been, it is not far-fetched to imagine them disrupted—indeed, parts of them have been disrupted. And thus we need to reconfigure practices, discourses, epistemic politics, and institutions.

We can start with a return to some old-fashioned critical tools. Sheila Jasanoff and Hilton Simmet, in a hopeful article encouraging dialogue, write that the following questions need to be asked of assertions expected to become public knowledge:

Who made the claim?

In answer to whose questions or purposes?

On what authority?

With what evidence?

Subject to what oversight or opportunity for criticism?

With what opening for countervailing views to express themselves?

And with what mechanisms of closure in cases of disagreement?[38]

To give these questions real force, we need to develop institutions that better support practices within which these questions are raised persistently. We need to develop more or less stable sociotechnical orders that bring together these institutions and associated achievements, arguments, discourses, norms, techniques, technologies, and various forms of capital. I do not know what such institutions and orders look like, but in the emerging political economies of information and attention, our old ones may not, by themselves, be fully up to the task.

Notes

1. Elements of this chapter appeared in two editorials: Sergio Sismondo, "Post-Truth?" *Social Studies of Science* 47, no. 1 (2017): 3–6, and Sergio Sismondo, "Casting a Wider Net: A Reply to Collins, Evans and Weinel," *Social Studies of Science* 47, no. 4 (2017): 587–92. The chapter also owes a debt to conversations with Khadija Coxon.

2. On some related issues and a rich discussion of this point, see Chapter 7 by Khadija Coxon in this volume.

3. Salena Zito, "Taking Trump Seriously, Not Literally," *Atlantic*, September 16, 2016.

4. Thanks go to Heather Poechman for her research assistance.

5. Henry Mance, "Britain Has Had Enough of Experts, Says Gove," *Financial Times*, June 3, 2016.

6. Stephen Turner, "What Is the Problem with Experts?" *Social Studies of Science* 31, no. 1 (2001): 123–49.

7. Linking the first two themes earlier, Colbert notes the individualism of truthiness: "It's not just that I *feel* it to be true, but that I feel it to be true. There's not only an emotional quality, but there's a selfish quality." See Nathan Rabin, "Stephen Colbert (interview)," *A.V. Club,* January 25, 2016, http://www.avclub.com/article/stephen-colbert-13970.

8. Peter McKnight, "Trump as Postmodernist: Truth No Longer Bound by Facts," *Toronto Globe and Mail,* January 28, 2017.

9. S. D. Kelly, "Blame Jacques Derrida for Donald Trump," *Mere Orthodoxy,* March 31, 2016, https://mereorthodoxy.com/tag/jacques-derrida/.

10. John Horgan, "Did Thomas Kuhn Help Elect Donald Trump?" *Scientific American* (blog), May 25, 2017, https://blogs.scientificamerican.com/cross-check/did-thomas-kuhn-help-elect-donald-trump/.

11. For a partial account, see Andrew Breiner, "Pizzagate, Explained: Everything You Want to Know about the Comet Ping Pong Pizzeria Conspiracy Theory but Are too Afraid to Search on Reddit," *Salon,* December 10, 2016. https://www.salon.com/2016/12/10/pizzagate-explained-everything-you-want-to-know-about-the-comet-ping-pong-pizzeria-conspiracy-theory-but-are-too-afraid-to-search-for-on-reddit/.

12. Jeff Stein, "FBI's Russia Probe Expands to Include 'Pizzagate' Threats," *Newsweek,* March 22, 2017.

13. Joe Coscarelli, "An Interview with Alex Jones, America's Leading (and Proudest) Conspiracy Theorist," *New York,* November 17, 2013.

14. Richard Hofstadter, "The Paranoid Style in American Politics," *Harper's Magazine,* November 1964, 77–82, 85–86.

15. Charles Mackay, *Extraordinary Popular Delusions and the Madness of Crowds* (New York: Harmony Books, 1980; 1st ed. published 1841).

16. For example, David Healy, "Shaping the Intimate: Influences on the Experience of Everyday Nerves," *Social Studies of Science* 34, no. 2 (2004): 219–45.

17. On serotonin, see Jeffrey R. Lacasse and Jonathan Leo, "Serotonin and Depression: A Disconnect between the Advertisements and the Scientific Literature," *PLoS Medicine* 2, no. 12: e392, and Robert Whittaker, *Anatomy of an Epidemic: Magic Bullets, Psychiatric Drugs, and the Astonishing Rise of Mental Illness in America* (New York: Broadway Paperbacks, 2010). On the chemical imbalance theory more generally, see, for example, Irving Kirsch, "The Emperor's New Drugs: Medication and Placebo in the Treatment of Depression," in F. Benedetti, P. Enck, E. Frisaldi, and M. Schedlowski, eds., *Placebo. Handbook of Experimental Pharmacology,* vol. 225 (Berlin, Heidelberg: Springer, 2014).

18. For example, Ronald W. Pies, "Nuances, Narratives and the 'Chemical Imbalance' Debate," *Psychiatric Times,* April 11, 2014, http://www.psychiatrictimes.com/blogs/nuances-narratives-chemical-imbalance-debate.

19. Shahram Ahari and Adrienne Fugh-Berman, "Following the Script: How Drug Reps Make Friends and Influence Doctors," *PLoS Medicine* 4, no. 4 (2007): e150.

20. Sergio Sismondo, "Key Opinion Leaders: Valuing Independence and Conflict of Interest in the Medical Sciences," in Isabelle Dussauge, C.-F. Helgesson and Francis Lee, eds., *Value Practices in the Life Sciences* (Oxford: Oxford University Press, 2015), pp. 31–48.

21. Sergio Sismondo, "Ghosts in the Machine: Publication Planning in the Medical Sciences," *Social Studies of Science* 39, no. 2 (2009): 171–98.

22. For example, Jeremy Greene, *Prescribing by Numbers: Drugs and the Definition of Disease* (Baltimore: Johns Hopkins University Press, 2007); Ray Moynihan and Alan Cassels, *Selling Sickness: How the World's Biggest Pharmaceutical Companies Are Turning Us All into Patients* (Vancouver: Greystone Books, 2005); Steven Woloshin and Lisa M. Schwarz, "Giving Legs to Restless Legs: A Case Study of How the Media Helps Make People Sick," *PLoS Medicine* 3, no. 4 (2006): e170.

23. Naomi Oreskes and Erik M. Conway, *Merchants of Doubt: How a Handful of Scientists Obscured the Truth on Issues from Tobacco Smoke to Global Warming* (New York: Bloomsbury, 2011).

24. Lindy West, "I've Left Twitter. It Is Unusable for Anyone but Trolls, Robots and Dictators," *Guardian,* January 3, 2017.

25. danah boyd, "Hacking the Attention Economy," *Points,* January 5, 2017, https://points.datasociety.net/hacking-the-attention-economy-9fa1daca7a37.

26. Tim Wu, *The Attention Merchants: The Epic Scramble to Get Inside Our Heads* (New York: Alfred A. Knopf, 2016).

27. For other versions of these schemes, see Khadija Coxon, "Attention, Emotion, and Desire in the Age of Social Media," in C. G. Prado, ed., *Social Media and Your Brain: Web-Based Communication Is Changing How We Think and Express Ourselves* (Santa Barbara, CA: Praeger, 2017), pp. 37–56.

28. Tara Golshan, "2 Big Takeways from a Scandalous Report on Internal Breitbart Documents," *Vox,* October 5, 2017, https://www.vox.com/2017/10/5/16433172/buzzfeed-report-breitbart-documents-milo.

29. Cambridge Analytica was an illegal participant in the UK Brexit vote, its services having been donated to the "Leave" campaign at a heavily discounted rate. The company also attempted to play a brokering role with WikiLeaks to find or generate a scandal concerning Clinton's e-mails. One of the investors in Cambridge Analytica is Robert Mercer, who is also an investor in Breitbart, and one of the executives is Bannon. See Kara Scannell, Dana Bash, and Marshall Cohen, "Trump Campaign Analytics Company Contacted WikiLeaks about Clinton Emails," *CNN,* October 25, 2017, http://www.cnn.com/2017/10/25/politics/cambridge-analytica-julian-assange-wikileaks-clinton-emails/index.html.

30. Nicholas Confessore and Daisuke Wakabayashi, "How Russia Harvested American Rage to Reshape U.S. Politics," *New York Times,* October 9, 2017.

31. Shaun Walker, "Russian Troll Factory Paid US Activists to Help Fund Protests during Election," *Guardian,* October 17, 2017.

32. Bob Dreyfuss, "Russian Trolling of US Social Media May Have Been Much Greater Than We Thought," *Nation,* October 23, 2017.

33. Scott Shane, "The Fake Americans Russia Created to Influence the Election," *New York Times,* September 7, 2017.

34. Joseph Menn, "Russia Used Facebook to Try to Spy on Macron Campaign," *Reuters,* July 27, 2017, https://www.reuters.com/article/us-cyber-france-facebook-spies-exclusive/exclusive-russia-used-facebook-to-try-to-spy-on-macron-campaign-sources-idUSKBN1AC0EI.

35. The unusual popularity of the David Zublick YouTube video announcing imminent arrests of the pedophile ring bears the hallmarks of Russian influence. See Confessore and Wakabayashi, "How Russia Harvested American Rage to Reshape U.S. Politics."

36. Massimo Calabresi, "Inside Russia's Social Media War on America," *Time,* May 18, 2017.

37. Variously understood and analyzed by, for example, Peter Dear, "Totius in Verba: Rhetoric and Authority in the Early Royal Society," *Isis* 76, no. 2 (1985): 144–61; Mary Poovey, *A History of the Modern Fact: Problems of Knowledge in the Sciences of Wealth and Society* (Chicago: University of Chicago Press, 1998); Steven Shapin, *A Social History of Truth: Civility and Science in Seventeenth-Century England* (Chicago: University of Chicago Press, 1994).

38. Sheila Jasanoff and Hilton Simmet, "No Funeral Bells: Public Reason in a 'Post-Truth' Age," *Social Studies of Science* 47, no. 5 (2017): 764.

CHAPTER SIX

The Post-Truth Temperament: What Makes Belief Stray from Evidence? And What Can Bring Them Back Together?

Juan Pablo Bermúdez

In a coastal British town in the late 19th century, a man is about to send his ship, filled with passengers, on a trip across the sea. He knows the rusty ship has recently needed repairs, and experienced people in the docks warn him it may not be seaworthy, pointing to some of its flaws. For a while, the shipowner worries about these things, and even considers sending the ship to maintenance, which would cost him a lot of money. But on further reflection he overcomes these concerns. After all, the ship has gone through so many trips, braving so many storms, always coming back safely to shore. Why would this time be any different? Besides, Divine Providence would not leave these poor families unprotected on their way to seeking a better life. He thus reaches the sincere belief that his ship is "thoroughly safe and seaworthy." After the ship sinks in the middle of the sea, he collects the insurance money without saying a word.

In his classic essay "The Ethics of Belief" (1877/1999), William K. Clifford argues that the shipowner is "verily guilty" of the death of the ship's passengers. That much seems clear. But what is it exactly that makes him guilty?

Not that he had a false belief (we can all be blamelessly mistaken about the way the world is) or that his belief was insincere (his conviction *was* sincere). What makes him guilty, Clifford argues, is *the way in which* he reached his belief. With all the evidence right in front of him (his awareness of the ship's repeated need for repairs; the testimony of others warning him), "he had no right to believe" that the ship was safe for travel. Moreover, *even if* the ship had successfully arrived at the other shore, the man would *still* be guilty, for precisely the same reason: "He had acquired and nourished a belief, when he had no right to believe on such evidence as was before him."

Clifford's view is quite radical: we are always wrong to believe anything without sufficient evidence and to ignore relevant evidence. Many have argued this is going too far: sometimes available evidence cannot fully determine belief, and sometimes it makes sense to believe against the evidence: a cancer patient knows recovery is very unlikely, but she also knows that believing she will get better increases the odds of improvement.[1]

That said, we can probably agree that something has gone wrong when a person's beliefs go against the solid and easily accessible evidence pointing in the contrary direction. And yet this seems to happen frequently, both in private conversation and in public discourse. Many believe *against the evidence* that man-made climate change is not real; many believe that organic food is better for your health; and so on.[2] Fake news go viral on social networks every day, and even after they are debunked people hold on to the opinions they have formed on fake grounds.[3] In this our beliefs seem to be as faulty as that of Clifford's shipowner.[4]

But this chapter is not about the ethics of belief: I will not discuss the moral issues surrounding belief formation and revision. It is rather about the *psychology of belief,* and the problems that concern us are: why are some people more prone to believing against the evidence and to resisting belief revision? It seems that we are living in a *post-truth* era (Keyes 2004), in which belief no longer has to follow fact; and if so it is crucial to ask: what can account for the cases in which belief separates from evidence? And what can get them back together?

I start by searching for the key feature of the post-truth phenomenon: while often associated with emotion overpowering reason, and with discourse practices that blur the distinction between honesty and dishonesty, the first section argues that, at its core, post-truthfulness is about a specific mode of argumentation. The rest of the chapter then explores personality dispositions that have been said to generate this post-truth kind of argumentation. The *partisan account* holds that conservatives, given their idiosyncratic psychological characteristics, tend to engage in more post-truth thinking than liberals. The *cognitive account,* on the other hand, claims that it is impulsive thinkers—relying on fast intuition rather than on thorough reflection—who tend toward post-truthfulness the most. While both are popular candidates for an explanation of the post-truth temperament, the available evidence turns out to go against both of them. Instead, there are reasons to think that people tend to engage in post-truth thinking if they receive surprising evidence not with curiosity and wonder but as a *threat* to their identity. It is this tendency to greet surprising evidence with self-defensive attitude that triggers the mode of thinking proper to post-truthfulness. Thus, the post-truth temperament is self-defensive; and if we want people to not fall back on it too much, they just have to feel less threatened by scientific evidence and more curious about it.

Before we jump in, a brief warning: there are many cases in which evidence is inconclusive, and there it makes sense for people to disagree, even if this disagreement is tainted with underappreciation for the facts. The most worrisome cases are, however, those in which there is solid and widely available evidence in favor of one side of the issue, agreed upon by the experts, and people still fail to converge toward the evidence. This chapter focuses on post-truthfulness as it is revealed in the latter.

Post-Truthfulness and Motivated Reasoning

Consider the mental steps that the shipowner goes through to reach the sincere belief that his ship is safe:

1. *Bringing prior motivations to the table*: The man starts the process having his desire to use his ship for a transoceanic trip.
2. *Facing counter-motivational evidence*: He realizes the ship may need repairs, and other people's testimony corroborates this.
3. *Sensing the costs implied by accepting the evidence*: Accepting the evidence implies repairs that will cost a lot of money.
4. *Rationalizing the problem away*: His deliberation downplays the negative evidence and amplifies positive features of the situation, thereby succeeding in canceling out the discordant evidence's epistemic influence.
5. *Believing against the evidence*: The outcome is a sincere motivation-concordant, evidence-discordant belief.

Steps 1–3 set the stage for the problem: there is desire-discordant evidence, and attending to it is uncomfortable. Step 4 solves the uneasiness: reasoning leads the shipowner to discredit the evidence, which produces an evidence-discordant belief, and reaffirms the preexisting motivation.

Replace the shipowner's economic motivation with a *political* motivation—for example, a desire for my (or my group's) views about a politically loaded topic to be true—and you will have an instance of post-truth reasoning. Think about Sarah, the climate change denier, a conservative well aware that her group believes climate change is not caused by human action. As a member of her group, Sarah desires this shared belief to be true (step 1). Unexpectedly, however, she finds information online that shows more than 96 percent of climate scientists agree that climate change is largely driven by human action (step 2). What to do?

In this case, the costs for Sarah of accepting the evidence at face value (step 3) are not economic—as in the shipowner's case—but of a more existential nature: yielding to the evidence would imply contradicting her group with respect to a widely shared belief. This might endanger the group's acceptance of Sarah as an upstanding member. Insofar as my Sarah's group membership would be very costly to lose (after all, she relies on her group for much affective and practical support), accepting the present evidence would have a steep cost for her. Thus, it is understandable if Sarah reasons her way out of the issue (step 4) by arguing that many climate scientists still disagree and that the evidence must certainly be way less clear-cut than the neat charts in this website suggest. This reasoning leads to Sarah retaining her climate-denial belief (step 5).

Often "post-truth politics" is presented as a public debate scenario that tends to favor emotion and personal expression while sacrificing precise argument. This suggests that post-truthfulness bypasses reasoning. But that is oftentimes not the case: rather than the absence of reasoning, post-truthfulness is a certain kind of argumentative reasoning. You can see this by discussing with someone like Sarah who defends a post-truth view: instead of merely reacting emotionally, they rationalize their views by discrediting contrary evidence, pointing to apparent gaps in it, or highlighting their own supportive evidence. Of course, the post-truth argument's sophistication varies greatly between people, but the mere fact that these arguments exist shows that, rather than an absence of reasoning, post-truthfulness should be conceived as reasoning in the service of a preexisting motivation or goal.

Donald Trump is, of course, an endless treasure trove of post-truth material. Here is a gem: in a recent interview, while disparaging the news media as "fake," he paused for an instant, deep in thought, and said: "I think one of the greatest of all terms I've come up with is 'fake.' I guess other people have used it, perhaps, over the years, but I've never noticed it."[5]

The structure of Trump's thought process is eerily similar to the shipowner's:

1. *Prior motivations*: Trump has a preexistent desire to show he has created great things; which leads him to consider that perhaps the term "fake" is one of them.
2. *Facing the evidence*: He realizes that there is contrary evidence—some other people have probably used it too.
3. *Sensing the costs*: Accepting the evidence at face value would imply admitting he was wrong about something.

4. *Rationalizing it away*: His deliberation downplays the negative evidence (he had never noticed anyone using the term) and amplifies positive features of the situation (so even if others had used it before, at least he came up with it independently).

5. *Believing against the evidence*: This reasoning process produces a new, sincere belief: he created the word "fake."

If it wasn't so frightening, the naïveté of the whole process might even seem endearing: here is a person willing to argue that he coined a common English word.[6] You can see Trump going through this kind of mental process in many of his declarations: boasting, then briefly noticing contrary evidence, then arguing to reaffirm his boastful belief.

Crucially, Sarah and Trump's cases are not instances of deception. Deceiving someone generally implies that you mislead him or her into believing a proposition *p*, while you yourself believe that *p* is false.[7] But the transparency of Trump's thought process reveals there is no deception strategy at play. What we have instead is a man using his reasoning to disregard discordant evidence and convince himself of something that suits his preexisting desire. Since no intention to deceive others is required, and the outcome often is a sincere, evidence-discordant belief, post-truth reasoning is closer to *self-deception* than to deception. It is not about someone trying to hide the truth from us. It is about someone hiding the truth from himself while believing himself to be truthful.

But how is self-deception even possible? Standard cases of self-deception are those of "people who falsely believe—in the face of strong evidence to the contrary—things that they would like to be true" (Mele 2001, p. 25). This can occur when this desire for *p* to be true biases the processes of evidence acquisition and manipulation, for example, by misinterpreting *p*-discordant evidence as not really discordant (e.g., other people may have used the word "fake" before, but I hadn't realized that they had) or leading one's attention to focus on information that confirms *p* and away from information that disconfirms *p* (e.g., after my preferred candidate wins the presidential elections, I tend to reflect on her successes and dismiss her blunders, thus ending up sincerely convinced that she is doing a great job).

This process (in my preexisting desire biases my acquisition and evaluation of evidence) is what psychologists call *motivated reasoning*: a pattern of thinking where my assessment of the evidence's worth is unintentionally subordinated to my preexisting motivations and preferences. In these cases, people's reasoning leads them not to adjust their commitments in accordance with the evidence but to assess the evidence in accordance with their commitments. Crucially, this happens unintentionally—some even say "unconsciously"—which is how the person can go on to endorse her resulting belief with complete sincerity, often more strongly than before.[8]

Thus, post-truthfulness is neither a matter of blindly following emotion while shutting down reason nor a matter of insincere deception. At its core, we should understand "post-truthfulness" as the cases of motivated reasoning in which the biasing desire is a political one (expressing a political value or an association with a certain group). This kind of reasoning is key to post-truthfulness because it can explain many of its other associated traits.

First, motivated reasoning explains how an emotional argument supporting your preexistent political commitments can be more convincing than a technical, evidence-based argument against them—hence the prevalence of appeals to emotions in political discourse. Moreover, motivated reasoning is a great tool to make honesty and dishonesty coexist: "In the post-truth era, we don't just have truth and lies," writes Ralph Keyes (2004), "but a third category of ambiguous statements that are not exactly the truth but fall short of a lie." Keyes describes the "post-truth era" as the time in which everyone (from politicians to academics, from accountants to nonfiction writers) engages in practices that blur the distinction between honesty and dishonesty: "massaging the truth," "enhancing the truth," "contextualizing," "creative retelling," and so on. Arguably, these communication practices largely derive from psychological exercises of motivated reasoning, which allow dismissal of countervailing evidence to coexist with sincerity. Indeed, through motivated reasoning people can unintentionally reshape a fact's description to make it fit more neatly into their own agenda. Third, motivated reasoning can also be seen as a crucial contributor to the apparent trend toward political polarization in contemporary democracies. Motivated reasoners tend to double down on their beliefs and discredit the evidence and the figures who speak against it.

Thus, motivated reasoning is arguably at the core of many faces of the post-truth phenomenon: the prevalence of emotion expression over detailed argument, the blurring lines between honesty and dishonesty, and political polarization. If so, it is then crucial to understand what makes people tend toward motivated reasoning? If there are people who have a *post-truth temperament* (a set of more or less stable personal cognitive and motivational dispositions that lead people to engage exceptionally often in post-truth thinking), then what personal traits make people more susceptible to motivated reasoning?[9] In other words, what character traits lead someone to evaluating evidence in accordance with prior commitments, rather than prior commitments in accordance with evidence? Two answers to these questions are common and appealing.

The trend toward post-truthfulness has recently coincided with a revitalization of right-wing political movements. This has led some to claim that post-truth thinking has an intimate connection with conservative political outlooks. There may be something in the conservative mindset (e.g., the tendency to protect my group's traditional lifestyle in the face of external threats) that particularly triggers motivated reasoning toward the rejection of cultural change and foreign ideas. This is the *partisan account* of the post-truth temperament.[10]

However, if it turns out that the post-truth temperament is not particularly linked to a political outlook, it may have its roots in a particular thinking style. The current trend toward digital, online, participatory communication (the so-called Web 2.0) has tremendously accelerated the pace and amount of information processing. This has arguably had the effect of making us rely on faster, more intuitive modes of thinking and of making deep and careful reflection a rare occurrence. What if fast, intuitive thinking was at the core of post-truthfulness? An increase in reliance on this shallow mode of thinking could likely explain the increase of motivated reasoning. Thus, people who have a fast-intuitive thinking style would tend to engage in post-truth thinking; and the decline of slow, reflective, critical reasoning would explain why our beliefs seem increasingly distant from evidence and fact. This is the *cognitive account* of the post-truth temperament.[11]

Is one of these a correct interpretation of the post-truth temperament? In what follows I assess whether the relevant empirical evidence supports the partisan or the cognitive accounts. The outcome, as will become clear, is that it does *not*. Despite appearances, post-truthfulness is neither about the politics you support nor about how slowly and carefully you think. Or so I will argue. Let us begin with the partisan account.

Two Political Temperaments

There is a long tradition of social science studying liberal and conservative personality traits. Accumulated empirical evidence makes it clear that there are several psychological differences between them.[12] Differences are so striking indeed that you can practically tell whether someone is a liberal or a conservative by just looking at his or her bedroom. Dana Carney and colleagues (2008) listed the visible objects of people's living spaces in a U.S. city and found that conservatives' bedrooms were cleaner, had more organization supplies (e.g., calendars and postage stamps), and were more conventionally decorated (e.g., with sports paraphernalia and bottles of alcohol). Contrastingly, liberal bedrooms were messier and less well lit, and their spaces contained more and more diverse items of cultural expression, like books, music records, travel memorabilia, and art supplies.

What can account for these differences? To summarize the findings, we can group the differences between conservatives and liberals into *epistemic* and *motivational asymmetries*.[13]

Epistemic asymmetries: Conservatives are markedly intolerant of ambiguity. They prefer categories that are well defined and thus tend to resist ambivalent characters (who combine good traits and bad traits), preferring black-and-white situations. Since they dislike ambiguity, they tend to close problems off quickly, solving them in ways intuitive and familiar to them, and rigidly maintaining these solutions in the face of challenges. They are thus less likely to consider alternative viewpoints and more likely to think others would reach their own conclusions if they thought things through.

By contrast, liberals are much more tolerant of—or even pleased by—ambiguity and uncertainty. They like spending more time and effort understanding a situation's multiple aspects, a story's different sides. Hence, they tend to consider alternative viewpoints and seek diverse solutions to problems. This makes them more likely to seek compromise in disagreements.[14]

Motivational asymmetries: Conservatives appear to be more sensitive to risks: they perceive mortality, and potential threats posed by social groups and figures, as more salient. They place greater value on loyalty, tradition, and group cohesion, whereas liberals value individual uniqueness and expression more than their counterparts. Just as people's taste buds are not equally sensitive to tangy or sweet flavors, similarly liberals and conservatives tend to respond differently to moral features of a situation. Liberals have a strong moral sensitivity to issues of fairness and harm but are not very sensitive to issues of respect for authority, group loyalty, and moral purity or disgust. Conservatives seem to be highly sensitive to *all five* of these moral intuitions: fairness, harm, respect for authority, group loyalty, and moral purity/disgust.[15] Thus, conservatives tend to consider group loyalty and respect for authority as much more morally relevant than liberals.

Do these epistemic and motivational asymmetries generate a tendency to motivated reasoning, therefore linking a certain partisan personality to the post-truth temperament?

Post-Truthfulness across the Political Divide

On a first look, a connection between conservatism and post-truthfulness seems quite plausible: conservatives are more ambiguity intolerant, seek quicker resolutions, are more stubborn on their views, and value loyalty and respect for authority. How could this temperament not lead to motivated reasoning? But let us see whether this view holds up after a closer look.

Defenses of the partisan account rest on two different strategies: (1) conservatives simply tend to believe more falsehoods than liberals, and (2) there are psychological differences that make conservatives more prone to prejudice and bias. The first strategy will simply not work: Mooney (2012) convincingly documents that conservatives tend to have more false beliefs and to reject and deny scientific views. But, to go back to Clifford's shipowner, one thing is *what* people believe, and something else is *how they acquire* their beliefs. Simply having many false beliefs does not entail that you are unintentionally disregarding motivation-discordant evidence: the evidence may just not have been available to you in the first place. Conservatives may tend to have more false beliefs (about science, international politics, the economy, etc.) because their evidence base is smaller, because their trusted sources of information are particularly biased or misleading, or because they have fewer intellectual resources to assess the evidence. I do not claim any of these is the case, but *if* one of them were, then conservative false beliefs would simply be caused by a lack of relevant evidence, not by a tendency to motivated reasoning. If you want to show that conservatism is somehow at the basis of the post-truth temperament, then you have to show that being conservative leads you not to having more false beliefs than liberals but to acquiring more beliefs *via motivated reasoning* than liberals. And a tally of false beliefs cannot achieve this.

The second strategy seems more promising, because it looks for an association between conservative psychological traits and the disposition to motivated reasoning. But there are actually two distinct arguments here: you could claim that the disposition to motivated reasoning is linked to conservative *motivational dispositions* or to conservative *epistemic dispositions*. Let us look at each one independently.

Post-Truth Thinking and Conservative Motivations

Conservatives place a higher value on the defense of tradition, respect for authority figures, and group cohesion. They also perceive other groups and their ideas as more threatening. Therefore, they may be more likely to disregard evidence that goes against their shared worldview. Conversely, because they do not care as much for group loyalty or respect for authority, and because they value diversity, liberals may be less likely to disregard belief-discordant evidence. But they still do.

In August 2017, James Damore, then a Google engineer, sent an internal memo to other company employees. The memo criticized Google's diversity policies, arguing that they reflected liberal biases and that a less-biased look at the scientific evidence on the differences between men and women would suggest a redesign of such policies. Damore's memo caused huge controversy, and profuse media coverage led to massive bullying, violent threats against him, and ultimately to his swift firing by Sundar Pichai, Google's CEO.

Seemingly to justify the firing, Pichai claimed that "to suggest a group of our colleagues have traits that make them less biologically suited to that work is offensive and not OK."[16] But that misrepresents the memo: Damore's argument was about how various traits, like skills and interests, are distributed across the entire population, not between Google employees—a quite distinct group that most likely does not mirror the entire population's distribution.

Scientific evidence does not support many of Damore's population-distribution claims,[17] and his population-level approach dramatically misses the mark when assessing the issue of diversity in tech firms (Lee 2017). What is crucial for our present concerns is that this is a case in which, when they feel one of their core moral intuitions is under attack (in this case, equality of treatment), liberals react like any other outraged majority would do: by disregarding the purported evidence, discrediting the speaker, and even excluding the speaker from the community. The logic of outrage is the same; only the value that caused the outrage differs.

Against the motivational asymmetry argument, this suggests that liberals also engage in motivated reasoning, discrediting value-discordant evidence, even when the value in question (in this case, equality and fairness) is a liberal one.

But those in the left are susceptible to motivated reasoning even when the value in question is a traditionally right-wing one. A team of researchers in Colombia recently gathered a group of supporters of a right-wing political figure (Álvaro Uribe) and a group of supporters of a left-wing leader (Gustavo Petro). They showed each group independently some statements by their respective political champion and asked them whether they agreed with the claims. Unsurprisingly, Uribe's supporters expressed high levels of agreement with Uribe's claims, as did Petro's supporters for his. People in both groups offered a range of arguments in defense of their leader's statements. After this, the researchers revealed that Uribe's purported statements were actually made by Petro, and Petro's apparent claims were in reality Uribe's. In hindsight, it was clear that the quotes did not match the figures (Uribe was portrayed as arguing for Latin American solidarity and Petro as claiming foreign investment was the solution to labor issues). But not even one participant realized something was off until the researchers revealed the truth.[18]

In defense of their respective authority figure, both right- and left-wing groups followed the same motivated-reasoning steps:

1. *Prior motivations*: Desire for preferred political leader's claims to be right.
2. *Facing the evidence*: Statements are presented by this leader.
3. *Sensing the costs*: Criticizing the statements would be costly (particularly when surrounded by other supporters of the movement).
4. *Rationalizing it away*: Individuals thus find ways to make sense of the statements, defending them despite possible dissonance with the rest of their political outlook.
5. *Believing against the evidence*: The reasoning process generates a belief in the claims purportedly made by their political leader.

A similar analysis can be done for the Google memo situation. Both cases are consistent with the evidence of motivated reasoning in political groups: conservatives and liberals are equally likely to engage in motivated reasoning (Kahan 2016). Regardless of their specific political orientation, people tend to defend orientation-concordant evidence and to dismiss orientation-discordant evidence. And all this suggests that the motivational argument for the partisan account does not work: people with a certain political position are not significantly more motivated to engage in post-truth reasoning than others.

Post-Truth Thinking and Conservative Thinking Styles

Recall that conservatives have turned out to be more averse to ambiguity, more likely to accept intuitive and familiar solutions, and less likely to consider alternative views. Does this entail that conservatives are more *cognitively* biased toward motivated reasoning than liberals?

In a recent study, Washburn and Skitka (2017) asked both liberal and conservative participants to interpret pieces of (apparently authentic, but actually manipulated) scientific evidence about politically divisive topics, like climate change and immigration. In all cases, the evidence admitted of two interpretations: a simple, intuitive interpretation that always turned out to be wrong (based on simply comparing the numbers explicitly presented) and a complex interpretation that was always right (based on making intermediate calculations to reach a more accurate comparison). Experimenters manipulated the evidence so that participants' political stance was in some cases compatible with the simple-incorrect interpretation and in some cases compatible with the complex-correct interpretation.

These were the key predictions: if the epistemic asymmetry argument is correct, then conservatives will be more likely than liberals to misinterpret the evidence (choosing the intuitive-incorrect interpretation over the complex-correct one) in the cases in which the correct interpretation goes against their political preferences. Also, if the epistemic asymmetry argument is correct, liberals will be more likely than conservatives to interpret the evidence correctly *even when* the complex-correct interpretation goes against their political preferences. In short, since conservatives tend to value group loyalty, they will tend to interpret the evidence in accordance with their group's way of thinking, even when that interpretation is wrong; and liberals would tend to interpret the evidence correctly, even when the correct interpretation goes against their own group's views and is harder to reach.

The results? Liberals and conservatives are *just as likely* to misinterpret the evidence when the correct interpretation goes against their political preference. Both groups tended to follow biased cognitive processes (picking the simple-incorrect interpretation) when that is what favors their political preference. In other words, regardless of their political outlook, people are more likely to seek an interpretation consistent with their own group's values and beliefs.

We humans, in general, have a tendency to deceive ourselves about evidence that threatens our dearly held values, beliefs, and commitments. We already tend to see the world as confirming our beliefs, focusing on confirming details much more than on disconfirming details.[19] This tendency works independently of our political outlook: it is a bipartisan issue.

That said, even if current evidence does not support the partisan account of the post-truth temperament, the possibility still remains that what is at the core of the post-truth temperament is a matter of cognitive dispositions: maybe people who are more susceptible to cognitive biases, who think less carefully, tend to engage more in motivated reasoning precisely because of this. This is the *cognitive account* of the post-truth temperament, and it is what we will go on to examine now.

Is Reflection an Antidote for Post-Truthfulness? Assessing the Cognitive Account

Try to answer the following question:

David is looking at Carol, while Carol is looking at Hector. You know that David is married and that Hector is unmarried. Is a married person looking at an unmarried person?

(A) Yes

(B) No

(C) Cannot be determined.[20]

If you are like most people, you would pick (C): it cannot be determined. And you would be wrong. Intuitively, the answer *feels* right; it has an immediate appeal. But let's use some hypothetical thinking. Carol can be either married or unmarried. What happens if she is married? Then a married person (Carol) would be looking at an unmarried person (Hector). And if she is unmarried? Then a married person (David) would be looking at an unmarried person (Carol). Either way, the right answer is (A): Yes.

This is not a very complex problem: all it takes to find the right answer is two steps of hypothetical thinking. And yet most of us get it wrong. It is not because we are dumb (if our lives depended on it, we would surely get it right!) but rather because we are *lazy*: if it is not necessary, we'd rather go with our intuition and avoid doing the more effortful hypothetical process.

Recent cognitive science has proved that, because we tend to avoid cognitive effort, we tend to fall into biases while solving all kinds of cognitive problems, from reasoning to decision-making, from moral evaluation to social stereotypes.[21]

That said, some people have a more *intuitive* temperament, and others have a more *reflective* temperament. The Cognitive Reflection Test (CRT) was designed to assess how intuitive or reflective a person tends to be. It simply asks people three questions that elicit a deceptively intuitive but wrong answer.[22] People with high CRT scores are less likely to blindly follow the intuitive heuristics that lead to the cognitive biases that haunt us while solving many everyday problems.[23]

Now, the crucial question: is an intuitive disposition (and its associated higher likelihood of falling into cognitive biases) at the basis of post-truthfulness? If this were so, then reflective people—as measured by the CRT—would tend to engage *less* in motivated reasoning when they face contrary evidence. This would have the positive upshot that, if we want to reduce motivated reasoning, we would just have to find ways for people to think more deeply about the issues. In this increasingly fast-paced world, asking people to slow down and think the important things through would lead to them assessing their views on the basis of evidence, instead of evidence on the basis of their views.

This is, indeed, precisely *the opposite* of what the available evidence has found so far: not only does reflectivity not decrease motivated reasoning, but actually when reflective people face discordant evidence, they tend to radicalize their own position rather than revise it. In a landmark study, Dan Kahan (2013) investigated the relations among political outlook, CRT scores, and the tendency to engage in motivated reasoning. He found that, regardless of their political orientation, more reflective people have a greater tendency to engage in motivated reasoning than intuitive people.[24]

In conclusion, the evidence speaks against the cognitive account of the post-truth temperament. Post-truthfulness is not a matter of irrational biases: slow, reflective, and careful thinkers are even more prone to—and, of course, better at—motivated reasoning than faster, more-intuitive thinkers. Being more reflective does not make you more likely to change your mind in the face of evidence; it just makes you better at dismissing the evidence or accommodating it within your own position. "So convenient a thing it is to be a reasonable creature, since it enables one to find or make a reason for everything one has a mind to do," says Benjamin Franklin (1886/1917, p. 49).

Post-Truthfulness as Epistemic Self-Defense

So post-truth thinking is not a trait particularly associated with conservatism. It is not a matter of fast, biased thinking either. What is it about, then?

To move forward, let us go back again to the structure of motivated reasoning:

1. Prior motivations
2. Facing the evidence
3. Sensing the costs
4. Rationalizing it away
5. Believing against the evidence

The accounts we have considered identify the post-truth temperament's crucial elements with different steps of this process. The cognitive account focuses on step 4: people tend toward motivated reasoning because their rationalization processes are largely based on biased, intuitive modes of thinking. This is, however, not the case: careful, reflective thinkers engage in motivated reasoning too. The partisan account, in its epistemic-asymmetries version, also focused on the differences between conservatives and liberals in step 4.

The motivational-asymmetries version of the partisan account had a different approach, focusing on step 1 instead: prior motivations proper to conservatives (e.g., loyalty and authority) would make them tend more strongly toward motivated reasoning than liberals. But we have found that not to be true: prior motivations lead liberals to motivated reasoning just as much as conservatives.[25]

I would like to propose that the crucial step that leads to motivated reasoning is step 2: facing the evidence. To see why, consider that the aforementioned cases of post-truth thinking all have one thing in common: when faced with contrary evidence, our post-truth thinkers assume a defensive stance toward it. This is not a necessary reaction: belief-discordant evidence can also be seen, for instance, as an intriguing invitation to gain new knowledge about the world. But the post-truth temperament construes it as potentially harmful and thus reacts to it with a sort of epistemic fight-or-flight mechanism: either dismiss it and do not even pay attention to it or attack it and refute it.

Motivated reasoning thus turns out to be the cognitive strategy we employ to face a situation that we see as a threat. And since what is under threat is a certain political motivation (either a personal political value or a belief that we share with those in our political group), the discordant evidence is a threat to our identity. Sarah the climate skeptic, Google's liberal employees, and partisans defending their leader's fake claims—all these characters have in common that they react to surprising evidence by adopting an epistemic self-defense mode, reasserting their identities via rationalized affirmations of their values and commitments.

In a sense, this reaction makes perfect sense: in a world where we are constantly bombarded by negative feedback (frustrated personal and professional plans, unexpected political outcomes, belief-dissonant information from countless news sources, etc.), motivated reasoning is an often-useful way to defend our personal integrity and to reassert our vital connections with the groups we belong to. When in self-defense mode, reasoning serves not as a tool to assess validity and seek truth but as a means of clarifying who we are in the midst of all the dissonance.

From this perspective, it is *expressively* rational for individuals to engage in motivated reasoning, using argumentation to express identity and allegiance.

This is particularly so in collective environments, where our social identity (our relationships of belonging to groups we identify and interact with every day) is at stake. Understandably, then, the outcomes of facing dissonant evidence often are either its rejection or a radicalization of prior beliefs. Then it is to be expected that a more careful assessment of the evidence will lead to greater political polarization based on belonging, instead of a fact-based convergence on the truth.[26]

Thus, the post-truth temperament is not about political outlook; it is not about whether you are intuitive or reflective. It rather seems to be about perceiving evidence contrary to your beliefs as a threat to your own identity. If this is true, the two crucial nodes of the post-truth temperament would be the disposition to feel new, dissonant information as threatening and the tendency to defend yourself from that threat through motivated reasoning.

Stay Curious

But how can we know that the self-defense account is a more accurate description of the post-truth temperament? If this account is correct, we could predict that people who tend to construe surprising information not as threatening but rather as intriguing would engage less in motivated reasoning. In other words, people who are not repelled by, but rather attracted to, surprising and dissonant information should engage less in motivated reasoning.

Evidence in favor of this prediction recently appeared almost by accident. Dan Kahan and colleagues (2017) were researching how to make science documentaries more engaging, and for this reason they had to come up with a way to measure *scientific curiosity*: people's disposition to seek out scientific information simply for the pleasure of learning. After they came up with a reliable way to measure it,[27] they were surprised to find that, contrary to all other available cognitive proficiency measures, science curiosity *countered* motivated reasoning. More scientifically curious people tended to converge toward a fact-based interpretation of politicized evidence, regardless of political orientation. Thus, for example, when asked about how much risk global warming poses for human health and prosperity, liberals and conservatives tend to be increasingly polarized as their reasoning proficiency (numeracy, cognitive reflection, science comprehension, etc.) increases. But scientifically curious liberals and conservatives tended to *converge* rather than polarize on their assessments of how much risk global warming posed for human health and prosperity.

Therefore, curiosity seems to do what reflection and cognitive ability cannot: cancel out the effects of motivated reasoning. How can it possibly do this?

Looking for an answer, Kahan and colleagues exposed each participant to two journalistic reports of (legitimate) scientific findings: one supporting that global warming is a serious threat and the other supporting that it is not serious. What was new to this study was that each participant found one report with a *surprising* headline (either "Scientists Report Surprising Evidence: Arctic Ice Melting Even Faster Than Expected" or "Scientists Report Surprising Evidence: Ice Increasing in Antarctic") and another report with an *unsurprising* headline (either "Scientists Find Still More Evidence That Global Warming Actually Slowed in Last Decade" or "Scientists Find Still More Evidence Linking Global Warming to Extreme Weather"). Thus, each participant saw one article confirming his or her view and another disconfirming it. But each one of these articles was sometimes presented as surprising and other times as unsurprising. Participants were asked to "pick the story most interesting to you."

Given the common need to defend our self-identities by reaffirming our beliefs, we would expect that people simply gravitate toward the stories that confirm their preexistent positions, regardless of whether they were presented as surprising or unsurprising. This was indeed the case but only for people who were not scientifically curious. More scientifically curious people gravitated toward the surprising story, both when it was belief-concordant and when it was belief-discordant.

Thus, evidence suggests that science curiosity mitigates the tendency to motivated reasoning. It makes people seek new and surprising evidence, even when it speaks against the worldview they are invested in. In other words, curiosity cancels out the tendency to construe new information as threatening—the very reaction that triggers the post-truth mechanisms of self-defense.[28]

Strangely, then, the only thing that seems to work as an antidote to motivated reasoning is the taste for learning new things about the world. If you are the kind of person who enjoys learning, novel evidence may appear to you as something attractively intriguing, despite it not being consistent with the prior commitments you bring with you to the epistemic situation. In other words, you can feel more free to explore the evidence, without feeling that your personal identity is at risk.

As far as we currently know, then, curiosity may be the only thing that consistently makes people keep their guard down, refrain from reacting self-defensively, and simply take a good look at the evidence. In other words, curiosity may lead to a more harmonious relationship between evidence and belief.

If this is true, curiosity and wonder would turn out to have incredible political significance. The feeling of epistemic threat, and the subsequent reaction of self-defense, is a key engine of the post-truth temperament and its related societal symptoms: the intensification of political polarization, the dominance of emotion and self-expression over fact-based argument and dialogue, and the acceptance of speech practices that blur the line between honesty and dishonesty. This presents us with a crucial task: finding and creating effective tools to increase and amplify people's sense of curiosity and wonder about the world.

Clifford is surely right to claim that beliefs should adjust to the evidence when evidence is strong and easily available. And we as a political collective should find ways to make our beliefs responsive to such evidence. But this is often a task that clashes with our sense of who we are, and thus, our beliefs often stray away from evidence. This will surely continue to exist as long as dissonant evidence appears to be a threat to our social identity. Unless we find ways to make the epistemic task of evidence assessment a more pleasurable and less existentially threatening activity, post-truth will win the day.

Acknowledgments

Many thanks to Santiago Amaya, Alejandro Rosas, Sergio Barbosa, and Mark Kingwell for their detailed and tremendously helpful comments and suggestions. Undoubtedly, the chapter still has many limitations, for which I am solely responsible.

Notes

1. Since Clifford's essay, the ethics of belief has been a topic of intense philosophical debate. Chignell (2016) offers a good recent overview.

2. On evidence for anthropogenic climate change, see Cook et al. (2016); on evidence that organic food is no better than regular food for health, see Smith-Spangler et al. (2012).

3. For analysis, see Sunstein (2017) and Bermúdez (2017).

4. "Doxastic involuntarists" (i.e., people who think we have no voluntary control over our beliefs) disagree with Clifford's view that we have epistemic responsibilities over our beliefs, but a certain version of his view can be more palatable to them: even if we have no direct voluntary control over our beliefs, we still have *indirect* voluntary control over them: we are in control of setting ourselves in a position in which our beliefs can be more or less receptive to evidence (by, e.g., paying more attention to the evidence). It is in this sense that we can attribute epistemic responsibility to the shipowner: not directly for his belief but indirectly for his carelessness about belief-formation habits.

5. The statement was made in an interview with Arkansas governor M. Huckabee on October 8, 2017. It was highlighted by Dale (2017).

6. In case you are wondering, instances of the word are attested as far back as the 18th century. Therefore, no, Trump could not have possibly made it up.

7. See Keyes (2004) for an interpretation of post-truth as a generalized environment of deception. Mele (2001) argues convincingly that sometimes

deceiving someone into believing *p* does not involve the deceiver's believing that
~*p*, but he himself accepts these are not the norm.

8. For more on motivated reasoning, see Kunda (1990) and Flynn et al. (2017).

9. For now I am merely assuming that post-truth thinking has internal
causes (e.g., personality traits) and is not entirely caused externally (i.e., by situations and contexts). There certainly are situational aspects that facilitate or
diminish motivated reasoning, but if we can find some personality traits that
make someone more or less susceptible to motivated reasoning, then it makes
sense to talk about a post-truth temperament. In the immediately following sections I will revise views that place conservatism and lack of reflectiveness at the
core of the post-truth temperament. I will argue that these are not satisfactory
accounts, but in the last two sections I will argue that post-truthfulness can be
seen as to some extent caused by the temperamental trait of self-defensiveness
and countered by the temperamental trait of science curiosity.

10. See Mooney (2012) for an extended defense.

11. Arguments like these can be inferred from Carr's (2010) condemnation of
"shallow thinking" and Heath's (2014) case for a "slow politics" in the age of the
Internet. Mele (2001) also defends a version of the cognitive account, by charac-
terizing cognitive biases—particularly confirmation bias—as key mechanisms
leading to self-deception.

12. The strategy can be traced back at least to Adorno and colleagues' (1950)
studies of the "authoritarian personality." An influential meta-analysis by Jost
and colleagues (2003) brought the available evidence together and generated
floods of new interest (for an update, see Jost 2017). Lengthy discussion can be
found in Mooney's tellingly titled *The Republican Brain: The Science of Why They
Deny Science—And Reality* (2012). However, two key caveats are in order. First,
"conservatism" and "liberalism" are very ambiguous and context-dependent
terms. Particularly, one can distinguish liberalism and conservatism about *economic* issues (e.g., the size and role of the state, redistribution, and risk sharing) from liberalism and conservatism about *social* issues (e.g., abortion, gay
marriage, and the role of religion in public life) (Gerber et al. 2010). That said,
liberalism and conservatism in both dimensions tend to cluster together in
many U.S. populations (Keyes 2004), leading to a rather dualistic political
landscape in that country. This brings us to the second caveat: the great majority of empirical findings employ U.S. populations; this makes the findings susceptible to not being applicable to other countries, or even to minorities within
the United States itself. There are reasons to suspect that some other communities (e.g., Western European countries) share some of the same patterns, but
many others should not. This must be verified empirically before attempting
any generalizations.

13. Based on Jost's (2017) taxonomy. He distinguishes between asymmetries
in *existential motivations* (mostly related to perceptions of safety and threat) and
in *relational motivations* (mostly related to identity and belongingness). I merge
the two since much of the greater threat perceptions of conservatives have a relational component (concerns about negative influences of other groups).

14. This is a very rough sketch of the complex empirical landscape. A review (Jost 2017) shows conservatism significantly correlates with higher scores in measures of dogmatism, cognitive rigidity, need for structure and cognitive closure, and intolerance for ambiguity; and liberalism significantly correlates with higher scores in measures of tolerance for uncertainty, need for cognition, and cognitive reflection.

15. See Haidt and Graham (2007) and Haidt (2012). While the theoretical validity of Haidt's "moral foundations" framework is still very much up for debate, it is interesting as a heuristic tool, and its main empirical results seem well substantiated for the U.S. population in general (although see Davis et al. 2016, who found it does not replicate well in African Americans).

16. For the memo, see Conger (2017). For the CEO's declarations, see Pichai (2017).

17. Though it does support others: see Stevens and Haidt (2017) for a meta-analytic review.

18. The investigation was led by Henry Murraín (Semana 2017). It is worth stating that this is preliminary study, still in need of corroboration (but see Cohen 2003).

19. For confirmation bias, see Hart et al. (2009). For the phenomenon in political contexts, see Taber and Lodge (2006).

20. The problem, originally from Levesque (1986, p. 85), was studied by Stanovich (2011, pp. 106–7).

21. For recent summaries, see Kahneman (2011) and Evans (2010).

22. For example, imagine that there is a patch of lilies on a lake, and the lilies double in size once a day. The lilies cover the whole lake in 48 days. How long will it take for them to cover half of the lake? (Intuitive—wrong answer: 24. Reflective—correct answer: 47.) Originally developed by Frederick (2005), the test has been widely used and discussed. There is much current debate about its appropriateness (e.g., Szaszi et al. 2017), but it retains its place as the go-to tool for measuring thinking styles, because it does not rely on self-report, and it reliably correlates with other cognitive measures. The CRT is usually related to so-called dual-system theories, but independently of them it remains a useful method for assessing people's cognitive dispositions.

23. Frederick (2005), Hoppe and Kusterer (2011), and Liberali et al. (2012). Keep in mind that reflectivity is not a measure of cognitive *ability* but of cognitive *disposition*. Reflective people are not necessarily more capable of solving cognitive problems: they are more likely to spend the time and the effort to solve it.

24. These results also hold for other measures of reflectivity, or even cognitive ability, like numeracy and science literacy (Kahan et al. 2012; Kahan and Corbin 2016; Drummond and Fischhoff 2017).

25. In another interpretation, the motivational argument could be seen as focusing on step 3: conservatives' higher sensitivity to risk and threat that leads them to post-truth tendencies. But, again, this is not something the evidence has supported, since liberals also perceive evidence against their core values as threatening.

26. For self-affirmation theory, see Sherman and Cohen (2006). In connection with motivated reasoning, see Kahan (2013, 2017). For a different argument

for the inefficacy of further reflection, see Mark Kingwell's contribution to this volume.

27. Researchers measured scientific curiosity with a mix of self-report measures (answers to questions like "How often do you read science books?") and behavioral measures (choosing to watch scientific documentaries vs. gossip TV programs, and the amount of time spent watching each).

28. As the researchers themselves insist, it is worth stressing that this is merely a preliminary finding that needs further corroboration. One may worry, for example, that science curiosity is merely tracking a "sensationalism" preference: when asked to pick the most interesting story, more curious people simply pick one framed as most surprising. This could lead them to align themselves with the most sensational (rather than evidence-based) stories.

References

Adorno, T. W., Frenkel-Brunswik, E., Levinson, D. J., & Sanford, R. N. (1950). *The authoritarian personality*. New York: Norton.

Bermúdez, J. P. (2017). Social media and self-control: The vices and virtues of attention. In C. G. Prado (Ed.), *Social media and your brain* (pp. 57–74). Santa Barbara, CA: Praeger.

Carney, D. R., Jost, J. T., Gosling, S. D., & Potter, J. (2008). The secret lives of liberals and conservatives: Personality profiles, interaction styles, and the things they leave behind. *Political Psychology, 29*(6), 807–840.

Carr, N. (2010). *The shallows: What the internet is doing to our brains*. New York: Norton.

Chignell, A. (2016). The ethics of belief. In E. N. Zalta (Ed.), *The Stanford Encyclopedia of Philosophy* (Fall 2016). Retrieved from https://plato.stanford.edu/entries/ethics-belief/.

Clifford, W. K. (1877/1999). The ethics of belief. In T. Madigan (Ed.), *The ethics of belief and other essays* (pp. 70–96). Amherst, NY: Prometheus.

Cohen, G. L. (2003). Party over policy: The dominating impact of group influence on political beliefs. *Journal of Personality and Social Psychology, 85*(5), 808–822.

Conger, K. (2017). Exclusive: Here's the full 10-page anti-diversity screed circulating internally at Google (updated). *Gizmodo*. Retrieved from https://gizmodo.com/exclusive-heres-the-full-10-page-anti-diversity-screed-1797564320.

Cook, J., Oreskes, N., Doran, P. T., Anderegg, W. R., Verheggen, B., Maibach, E. W., . . . & Rice, K. (2016). Consensus on consensus: A synthesis of consensus estimates on human-caused global warming. *Environmental Research Letters, 11*(4). doi: 10.1088/1748-9326/11/4/048002.

Dale, D. (2017). Trump defends tossing paper towels to Puerto Rico hurricane victims: Analysis. *Toronto Star*. Retrieved from https://www.thestar.com/news/world/2017/10/08/donald-trump-defends-paper-towels-in-puerto-rico-says-stephen-paddock-was-probably-smart-in-bizarre-tv-interview-analysis.html.

Davis, D. E., Rice, K., Van Tongeren, D. R., Hook, J. N., DeBlaere, C., Worthington, E. L., & Choe, E. (2016). The moral foundations hypothesis does not replicate well in black samples. *Journal of Personality and Social Psychology, 110*(4), e23–e30. https://doi.org/10.1037/pspp0000056.

Drummond, C., & Fischhoff, B. (2017). Individuals with greater science literacy and education have more polarized beliefs on controversial science topics. *Proceedings of the National Academy of Sciences, 114*(36), 9587–9592.

Evans, J.St.B.T. (2010). *Thinking twice: Two minds in one brain.* New York: Oxford University Press.

Flynn, D. J., Nyhan, B., & Reifler, J. (2017). The nature and origins of misperceptions: Understanding false and unsupported beliefs about politics. *Political Psychology, 38*(682758), 127–150.

Franklin, B. (1886/1917). *The autobiography of Benjamin Franklin.* New York: Houghton Mifflin.

Frederick, S. (2005). Cognitive reflection and decision making. *Journal of Economic Perspectives, 19*(4), 25–42.

Gerber, A. S., Huber, G. A., Doherty, D., Dowling, C. M., & Ha, S. E. (2010). Personality and political attitudes: Relationships across issue domains and political contexts. *American Political Science Review, 104*(1), 111–133.

Haidt, J. (2012). *The righteous mind: Why good people are divided by politics and religion.* New York: Vintage.

Haidt, J., & Graham, J. (2007). When morality opposes justice: Conservatives have moral intuitions that liberals may not recognize. *Social Justice Research, 20*(1), 98–116.

Hart, W., Albarracín, D., Eagly, A. H., Brechan, I., Lindberg, M. J., & Merrill, L. (2009). Feeling validated versus being correct: A meta-analysis of selective exposure to information. *Psychological Bulletin, 135*(4), 555–588.

Heath, J. (2014). *Enlightenment 2.0: Restoring sanity to our politics, our economy, and our lives.* New York: Harper.

Hoppe, E. I., & Kusterer, D. J. (2011). Behavioral biases and cognitive reflection. *Economics Letters, 110*(2), 97–100.

Jost, J. T. (2017). Ideological asymmetries and the essence of political psychology. *Political Psychology, 38*(2), 167–208.

Jost, J. T., Glaser, J., Kruglanski, A. W., & Sulloway, F. J. (2003). Political conservatism as motivated social cognition. *Psychological Bulletin, 129*(3), 339–375.

Kahan, D. M. (2013). Ideology, motivated reasoning, and cognitive reflection. *Judgment and Decision Making, 8*(4), 407–424.

Kahan, D. M. (2016). The politically motivated reasoning paradigm, part 2: Unanswered questions. In R. Scott & S. Kosslyn (Eds.), *Emerging trends in the social and behavioral sciences: An interdisciplinary, searchable, and linkable resource* (pp. 1–15). Hoboken, NJ: Wiley.

Kahan, D. M. (2017). The expressive rationality of inaccurate perceptions. *Behavioral and Brain Sciences, 40,* 26–28.

Kahan, D. M., & Corbin, J. C. (2016). A note on the perverse effects of actively open-minded thinking on climate-change polarization. *Research & Politics, 3*(4), 1–4.

Kahan, D. M., Landrum, A., Carpenter, K., Helft, L., & Hall Jamieson, K. (2017). Science curiosity and political information processing. *Political Psychology, 38,* 179–199.

Kahan, D. M., Peters, E., Wittlin, M., Slovic, P., Ouellette, L. L., Braman, D., & Mandel, G. (2012). The polarizing impact of science literacy and numeracy on perceived climate change risks. *Nature Climate Change, 2*(10), 732–735.

Kahneman, D. (2011). *Thinking, fast and slow.* New York: Farrar, Straus and Giroux.

Keyes, R. (2004). *The post-truth era: Dishonesty and deception in contemporary life.* New York: St. Martin's Press.

Kunda, Z. (1990). The case for motivated reasoning. *Psychological Bulletin, 108*(3), 480–498.

Lee, C. (2017). I'm a woman in computer science. Let me ladysplain the Google memo to you. *Vox.* Retrieved from https://www.vox.com/the-big-idea/ 2017/8/11/16130452/google-memo-women-tech-biology-sexism.

Levesque, H. J. (1986). Making believers out of computers. *Artificial Intelligence, 30*(1), 81–108.

Liberali, J. M., Reyna, V. F., Furlan, S., Stein, L. M., & Pardo, S. T. (2012). Individual differences in numeracy and cognitive reflection, with implications for biases and fallacies in probability judgment. *Journal of Behavioral Decision Making, 25*(4), 361–381.

Mele, A. R. (2001). *Self-deception unmasked.* Princeton, NJ: Princeton University Press.

Mooney, C. (2012). *The republican brain: The science of why they deny science—and reality.* Hoboken, NJ: Wiley.

Pichai, S. (2017). Note to employees from CEO Sundar Pichai. *Google Blog.* Retrieved from https://www.blog.google/topics/diversity/note-employees-ceo-sundar-pichai/.

Semana. (2017). Lo que digan Uribe o Petro [Whatever Uribe or Petro Say]. *Semana.* Retrieved from http://www.semana.com/nacion/articulo/el-experimento-sobre-la-irracionalidad-de-los-seguidores-de-uribe-y-petro/ 536884.

Sherman, D. K., & Cohen, G. L. (2006). The psychology of self-defense: Self-affirmation theory. *Advances in Experimental Social Psychology, 38*(6), 183–242.

Smith-Spangler, C., Brandeau, M. L., Hunter, G. E., Bavinger, J. C., Pearson, M., Eschbach, P. J., . . . Bravata, D. M. (2011). Are organic foods safer or healthier than conventional alternatives? A systematic review. *Annals of Internal Medicine, 157*(5), 348–366.

Stanovich, K. (2011). *Rationality and the reflective mind.* New York: Oxford University Press.

Stevens, S., & Haidt, J. (2017). The Google memo: What does the research say about gender differences? *Heterodox Academy.* Retrieved from https://heterodoxacademy.org/2017/08/10/the-google-memo-what-does-the-research-say-about-gender-differences/.

Sunstein, C. R. (2017). *#Republic: Divided democracy in the age of social media.* Princeton, NJ: Princeton University Press.

Szaszi, B., Szollosi, A., Palfi, B., & Aczel, B. (2017). The cognitive reflection test revisited: Exploring the ways individuals solve the test. *Thinking and Reasoning, 23*(3), 207–234.

Taber, C. S., & Lodge, M. (2006). Motivated skepticism in the evaluation of political beliefs. *American Journal of Political Science, 50*(3), 755–769.

Washburn, A. N., & Skitka, L. J. (2017). Science denial across the political divide. *Social Psychological and Personality Science.* Retrieved from http://journals.sagepub.com/doi/abs/10.1177/1948550617731500.

CHAPTER SEVEN

Reality for the People

Khadija Coxon

Those of us in the knowledge industry—professional spaces like academia, traditional forms of journalism, and print publishing—tend to interpret controversies as intellectual battles, and post-truth hits particularly close to home for the philosophically inclined. As a popular philosophers' version of the story goes, post-truth descends from the postmodernism associated with figures like Lyotard, Derrida, and Foucault, with its aims to destabilize core Western intellectual categories and values. I'm wary of this narrative, on multiple levels. Not least is a doubt that the forces of post-truth care about Lyotard et al., mixed with suspicion of philosopher's myopia—the instinct to parse every difference via some well-worn conceptual dichotomy, like realism versus antirealism. But I won't go down those roads here. Instead, I'll pose a question meant to take us in a different direction: what precisely is post about post-truth?

Traditionally, "post" means "after," functioning as what linguists call an indexical, a bit of language that points, ostensibly, to temporal order. In this sense, the prefix directs our attention to a before to signal relation with an after. But the meaning of "post" differs in the case of post-truth, and here is where its narrow affinity with postmodernism may actually be instructive. As the *Oxford English Dictionary* pointed out in 2016 when it named "post-truth" word of the year, in the mid-20th century terms like "post-national" and "post-racial" were signals of what would become widespread semantic change. The meaning of "post" exceeded chronological logic by encompassing ideas of conceptual irrelevance. Postmodernism, post-structuralism, post-feminism, post-indexical, post-truth—these are all ways of pointing not to time or order but to real or aspired-to redundancy. The terms dismiss a once-venerated idea or ideology, still pointing not to direct attention in any pattern or linear progression but to jolt recognition of an attitude.

Notice that post-truth is constructive: it builds legitimacy and energy around appeals to emotion, so that what matters to determining not only our knowledge but also our orientation to the world increasingly comes down to the perceived authenticity and honesty of raw expressions of feeling. The destructive part of this process is the diminishment of truth and facts, of course appalling to those of us who value knowledge in some familiar sense. But a diminishing process isn't a philosophical claim of the order that truth or facts are relative, nor a rejection of something like an Enlightenment ideology status quo. When we interpret post-truth as an argument or a set of concrete claims about truth, we are missing how the phenomenon functions as a kind of indirection. Framing sacred truth as a cow produces indignation, and, deep in it, we miss how the power dynamics of expertise and knowledge production are shifting. There is pointing, at our expense.

This chapter calls for a shift of attention from the destructive to the constructive space of post-truth, from truth to feeling, asking how and why affect, feeling, and emotion have gained economic value in the system that produces, distributes, and circulates knowledge, understanding, and perception of our shared world. Borrowing a philosopher's turn of phrase, I'll call this kind of value "epistemic currency." To get moving, I'll explore how affect functions as epistemic currency through a case in easy sight: the networked space of reality TV and social media. Here, appeals to emotion bear family resemblances to truth, in that they function as particularly powerful strategies of authentication. We can then trace the roots of these strategies—which are far less esoteric than postmodernism—to the rise of psychotherapeutic discourses in the 20th century.

Seeing how affect becomes epistemic currency, I suggest, reveals post-truth as an understudied symptom of what some have called a "turn to the demotic," a turn to the people's systems of meaning. Affect is highly marketable as epistemic currency, because, unlike expertise—the bedrock of appeals to truth and facts—capacity for affective expression is an equal-access resource. Post-truth is part of a complex of technologies that offer the demos a certain kind of freedom, freedom of affective expression. This affords a reality for and of the people. It's a pernicious state of affairs, and not wholly nor perhaps even primarily, because the value of truth has been undermined or deflated. The political significance of elevating the people's systems of meaning has been cut loose from the goal of giving the *demos* power (*kratos*). Reality for the people is demotic but not democratic.

Networked Reality

Don't you ever go after my fucking husband!
—Lisa Rinna, Season Five, *Real Housewives of Beverly Hills*

Social media and reality TV are among the most indicted sites of the kinds of appeals to emotion associated with post-truth. U.S. president Donald Trump's persona has to a large extent been produced and distributed via reality TV and social media, and the Trump team's expert navigation of these spaces is implicated in the post-truth phenomenon in complicated ways. Particularly confounding for commentators on the 2016 U.S. election has been the contrast between Trump's seemingly constitutional propensity to lie, boldfaced and baldly, and populist perception of his opponent Hillary Clinton as untrustworthy and dishonest. There are many facets of this contrast, not least of them misogyny and straightforward lies, but I want to focus on how personas like Trump's exemplify success in laying claim to a kind of authenticity that depends on appeals to emotion.

Since the early 2000s, radical economic restructuring of television and other media has led to a new kind of celebrity, produced rather than presupposed by media exposure, whose primary asset is ordinariness rather than stardom.[1] In this new celebrity economy, entrepreneurial nonactors can be made into commodities by marketing a kind of authenticity that is neither natural nor internal, but rather constructed deliberately through complex processes that are historically new and not well understood. As Laura Grindstaff and Susan Murray have persuasively argued, the most significant marker of a nonactor's authenticity is coherent performance of intense, raw emotion, which must both encapsulate a distinct persona and rapidly circulate across multimedia in the interests of consumer products.[2]

One of the goals of constructing authenticity through appeals to emotion is to produce what Grindstaff and Murray call "branded affect."[3] Different subgenres of reality TV—the game-doc, the makeover show, the docusoap—rely on different strategies to produce branded affect, to different degrees of success. Following Grindstaff and Murray, I am interested in the docusoap as an example of what may be the most powerful site for branding affect and producing ordinary celebrity.[4] Kim Kardashian, arguably the most well-recognized reality TV celebrity in the world, is famous for the over-the-top emotionality that defines her particular brand of affect, which got off the ground and continues to circulate via the docusoap *Keeping Up with the Kardashians.* Focusing on specific cast members, plotlines, and stylistic devices of the docusoap franchise *Real Housewives,* I want to consider closely how appeals to emotion function as authentication strategies and to show how the circulation of these strategies across multimedia confers value on emotion as epistemic currency.

Precarity and disposability are integral features of the work of ordinary celebrity, and docusoap actors are under tremendous competitive and entrepreneurial pressure to be interesting yet relatable enough to leave audiences always wanting more of their personae. The *Real Housewives* series all revolve around casts that include recurring and new members. There are well-recognized status hierarchies among cast members, and status goes along with being marketable enough as a branded commodity to be recast season after season. The undeniable queen bee of the *Real Housewives of Beverly Hills* (*RHBH*), and maybe of all of the *Real Housewives* franchises, is Lisa Vanderpump, a British expat restaurateur whom the show's executive producer Andy Cohen has described as irresistible for her striking resemblance to a character from a Jackie Collins novel. Vanderpump is an original character on the *RHBH* series, having been cast and recast for all eight seasons. She lives in a fabulous Beverly Hills mansion, carries a tiny Pomeranian as a fashion accessory, and, in general, resembles a soap opera character, except in one important respect: she claims not to be independently wealthy, repeatedly distinguishing herself from a caricatured Beverly Hills socialite by insisting that she works every day to pay her bills.

Zealously foregrounding the necessity of work is a ubiquitous authentication strategy of *Real Housewives* cast members. A useful example concerns the introduction of two new cast members during Season 5 of *RHBH*. Both have worked in Hollywood for over 20 years and are mostly known as daytime soap opera actresses. The first is Eileen Davidson, who still has a recurring role on a daytime soap. Davidson's demeanor is relatively reserved, and she describes herself as more focused on her craft as an actor than on public relations or Hollywood celebrity. The second is Lisa Rinna, who knows Davidson from their early days in the soap opera biz but who is now the more recognized celebrity, in part because she works loosely in multiple domains, from hosting television shows to having owned a Hollywood fashion boutique to selling a successful line of products on the Home Shopping Network. Rinna is loud, outspoken, and vivacious, a personality that seems to match her huge eyes, distinctly oversized lips, and 1990s shag haircut. She repeatedly and frequently refers to herself as a "hustler" who will "do anything for a buck."

In the course of the season, Davidson and Rinna each become embroiled in their own separate feuds with other cast members, propelled by structurally analogous yet importantly different scenes. On the one hand, Davidson's feud with Brandi Glanville is unremarkable. It begins when the two are at a group dinner, and Glanville, a great fan of Davidson's soap opera celebrity, begs Davidson to reenact a scene from that day's taping of the broadcast soap. When Davidson refuses, Glanville threatens to get things started by throwing her (white) wine at Davidson and then, drunk and full of giggles, lightly tosses the contents of her glass forward, into Davidson's face.

Davidson attempts to be gracious but holds a lukewarm grudge. The feud, the scene, and Davidson's role in them are not memorable. In fact, in animated GIFs (graphics interchange format) associated with the scene, the focus is on neither of the protagonists but on Rinna's wide-eyed, open-mouthed look of astonishment, emphasized by her trademark lips.

On the other hand, Rinna's feud with Kim Richards, and the most climactic scene of it, helps to crystallize Rinna's brand of over-the-top melodramatic affect. Tension builds gradually between Rinna and Richards throughout the season and comes to a head at another group dinner when Richards implies incriminating information about Rinna's husband. Screaming, "Don't you ever go after my fucking husband!" Rinna throws not just the contents of her wine glass but the glass itself, which crashes loudly and shatters, wine and glass flying everywhere. The moment provokes high levels of distress within the group, with cast members running in different directions, some crying, some shouting, many fleeing the scene. This was the "money shot" of the season, almost instantly proving that Rinna is what some viewers call a real real housewife—someone so utterly watchable that she's bound to be recast. Through an ironic twist on anti-mimesis, Rinna demonstrated her expertise as a method actor of her own persona—an outrageous, reactive, unpredictable soap opera-esque former soap opera star. Unlike Davidson, a mere working actor, Rinna made herself into a new kind of celebrity by presenting larger-than-life, brandable emotions that authenticate her for the audience.

Rinna's success at self-branding is not merely a matter of individual effort or acting skill, though I have no doubt that she is both talented and a hustler. A point that cannot go without mention is that, as Grindstaff and others have shown,[5] the work of casting directors and producers is indispensable to the production of affect in reality TV. Docusoaps are particularly difficult to cast, because they are the most loosely structured of all the subgenres of reality TV, and they thus depend on the cast members to generate emotion-laden relational conflict and to present highly watchable personas. Producers must extract legible expressions of emotion that will be read as authentic, a task that in some ways overlaps with the work of theater and film directors but differs in important respects. Reality TV shows typically involve multiple producers in competition with each other, and they are arguably more motivated to use manipulative and otherwise ethically questionable tactics. And more to the point, the authenticity of emotion in the space of reality TV transcends the value of subtlety. Reality TV emotions must be highly intense and condensed, in particular because they need to translate very rapidly across multimedia, particularly in the form of GIFs. Indeed, "Don't you go after my fucking husband!" instantly became a widely circulated GIF, and the life of Rinna's personal brand of affect has been further extended through multiple memes that highlight her highly reactive facial expressions and her striking physical features, while repeating her always emotionally evocative commentaries and catchphrases.

Docusoaps exploit the networked infrastructure of reality TV, social media, and other types of media to produce and circulate branded affect not only through specific characters but also through categories of affect more generally associated with the franchise. An interesting example emerges when we consider that the real housewives regularly observe with exasperation, incredulousness, and humor that the show is "like high school" or claim that the women from the show are "worse than teenagers." While these comments imply that the group personality emerges naturally from a particular constellation of women, it is the scaffolding of both the genre and its integral relationship with multimedia that generates the *Real Housewives* brand of feminized immaturity—itself a form of branded affect.

Let us consider what cast members call "stirring the pot." I am inspired here by Alice Marwick and danah boyd's incisive ethnographic study of how teenage girls mobilize the concept of drama in their uses of social media.[6] Marwick and boyd present drama as an emic term, which is to say that it comes from the research subjects' vernacular and is described on its own terms, without translation into external categories or concepts. As Marwick and boyd illustrate, drama includes but is not reducible to a number of more conventional categories more commonly used to translate the communicative and relational strategies of teenage girls, such as gossip, rumor, bullying, and relational aggression. Important for our purposes is Marwick and boyd's observation that the networked infrastructure of social media is integral to drama.

Season 6 of the *RHBH* provides a useful example of stirring the pot. In the relevant story line, Yolanda Hadid has been diagnosed with Lyme disease and now often doesn't participate in group events. When she does show up, she is a shadow of her former physically stunning supermodel self, refusing to wear makeup and having had her breast implants removed. In her absence, some of her castmates discuss Hadid's Instagram account, saying it is peculiar that she frequently posts pictures of herself in hospitals in the role of an invalid. They see a tension between these and other posted images, such as one where she looks exuberant and healthy on a yacht vacation in Alaska. Rinna provides the scene with its most emotionally intense moment by breaking down in tears and claiming guilt about having participated in a conversation in which someone repeated a rumor that Hadid was not suffering from Lyme but from Munchausen. Rinna denies believing the rumor and speaks only of her moral emotions about having given the rumor life. She claims she must confess to Hadid.

Erika Girardi warns Hadid that the other women are gossiping and spreading a rumor about her. Hadid expresses shock, confusion, and resignation, indicating that by continuing to mention the rumor, Rinna is guilty of stirring the pot. When the other women find out, some suspect Girardi herself of pot-stirring. At some point, Rinna claims to realize just how much Vanderpump, the British expat restaurateur, dislikes Hadid. She then indicates that she had been unknowingly manipulated by Vanderpump, who originally planted the idea of mentioning the rumor on camera. Rinna calls out the other women for pretending not to know that all along the rumor had already been widely circulating on social media and throughout the group. Vanderpump reacts with bewilderment, breaking her characteristic British lack of vulnerability, getting teary, and claiming that Rinna misconstrued her original words. She suggests she is being bullied and that Rinna is a loose cannon. Rinna suggests she is being bullied. The rest of the season concerns feuds over who really stirred the pot, a question that comes down to the true emotional motivations of Rinna and Vanderpump. Hadid becomes one of many detectives, disgusted by all the claims of bullying when she is the one under attack. Hadid does not return for the next season, although both Vanderpump and Rinna are recast. They are now head-to-head for the title of queen-bee.

Like teenage girls' drama, stirring the pot includes but also supersedes rumor, gossip, and bullying. Gossip involves two or more people who discuss an absent party,[7] and it is clear that the women initially engage in gossip about Hadid. However, as Hadid is drawn into the discussion, which involves and is also simultaneously taking place online, it is less clear that gossip is at issue. One of the teens in Marwick and boyd's study indicates that, once one begins to gossip about themselves, they have entered the realm of drama. Similarly, the more involved Hadid gets in the discussion of herself, the more she seems like a participant in the pot-stirring. And although the pot-stirring involves a rumor, the point of interest is not so much the rumor itself. The question of whether Hadid has Lyme disease becomes irrelevant, as the story line comes to revolve around the question of who is the chief pot-stirrer.

There is interesting tension around the concept of bullying. Marwick and boyd make clear that the teenage girls in their study do not apply the concept to themselves, being reluctant to ascribe lack of agency to parties in relations of drama. They suggest instead that bullying is a concept imposed from the outside by adults. Interestingly, while it is common for cast members under fire for stirring the pot or other reasons to claim to be victims of bullying, it is equally common for other cast members to dismiss these claims as a way of exploiting a buzzword to manipulate the audience. The audience's perception is formed not only or even primarily through watching the show itself but through tabloids and discussions on social media and the blogosphere, spaces where cast members are also typically active participants. Many cast members of *Real Housewives*, like the teenage girls in Marwick and boyd's study, view bullying as an externally imposed concept that does not describe their social relations authentically.

Pot-stirring mimics something like what Marwick and boyd have presented as teenage drama, but it involves a distinctive authentication strategy: it always pushes for an emotional truth of a matter, whether that truth precedes the pot-stirring or not. Although the idea is presented by the women pejoratively, and they are rarely willing to claim responsibility for participating in it, pot-stirring defines the group in important ways. It determines status hierarchies and chances of being recast or fired. Effectively stirring the pot is not easy, and it is not simply a matter of being outspoken. Some cast members, such as Glanville of the Beverly Hills franchise or Jill Zarin of the New York City franchise, were at some point valued on the show for their over-the-top pot-stirring ways, but both eventually came to alienate the audience and were fired. Who is the realest housewife of them all? The one who can most effectively stir the pot without turning off the audience in the process.

Perhaps the most historically distinctive aspect of reality TV's production and circulation of affect as an authentication strategy is that it places form and content in such a tightly woven relationship. The kinds of appeals to emotion I've discussed in the context of *Real Housewives*—from Vanderpump and Rinna's presentation of themselves as dependent on labor for survival to the broader group's strategic use of stirring the pot—could not have existed before the advent of highly networked multimedia platforms. They depend on GIFs, memes, emojis, and the complex and networked infrastructures of reality television, both traditional and newer digital forms of tabloid journalism, the blogosphere, and social media.

Psychotherapeutic Reality

> There's a lot of talk in this country about the federal deficit. But I think we should talk more about our empathy deficit—the ability to put ourselves in someone else's shoes; to see the world through those who are different from us—the child who's hungry, the laid-off steelworker, the immigrant woman cleaning your dorm room. (Barack Obama, Northwestern Convocation, 2006)[8]

> What is required now is nothing less than a leap to global empathic consciousness and in less than a generation if we are to resurrect the global economy and revitalize the biosphere. (Jeremy Rifkin, *Empathic Civilization*, 2010)[9]

In 2014, there was a huge backlash against a *New Yorker* article by psychologist Paul Bloom that argued for limitations on empathy's moral significance.[10] Bloom hadn't suggested that empathy was morally insignificant. He merely brought up some straightforward cases of moral decisions outside the personal realm. How should we distribute resources to geographically distant aggregates? What are our responsibilities to the environment? Empathy is obviously either insufficient or irrelevant as a moral compass for these kinds of questions. For philosophers, the point is so obvious as to be trivial. But, for a wider public, Bloom's attempt to cast small seeds of doubt on the power of empathy was deeply offensive. There was a long series of interviews with academic and nonacademic empathy experts from around the world, conducted by Edwin Rustch of the blog project The Center for Building a Culture of Empathy.[11] Expert commentators, like philosopher of mind and emotions Jesse Prinz, were widely dismissed for just not getting empathy or emotions. The case reflects, among other things, pushback against experts' attempts to influence wider social and cultural imaginaries.

There is a perceived crisis of valuation of emotions, characterized by a so-called empathy deficit. The first epigraph at the beginning of this section includes Obama's first use of the phrase, one he repeated throughout his campaign. The non-DSM-approved phrase "empathy deficit disorder" has been floating around pop psychology media since 2008 and has been popularized by psychology journalist and leading proponent of the emotional intelligence movement, Daniel Goleman.[12] A frequently and widely cited 2010 article by psychologist Sara Konrath argues that empathy has been in steady decline for the past 30 years.[13] It's based on a meta-analysis of 72 studies that measured empathy in college students—twentysomethings from rich Western countries—between 1979 and 2009.

At the risk of starting another backlash, I'll argue that talk of an empathy deficit is a tactic of generating artificial scarcity and in the process conferring epistemic value on emotions more generally. My skepticism about the apparent empathy deficit stems from one very underexamined fact: the concept of empathy is quite new, and the idea of its great value is even newer. There is no evidence that anyone thought of empathy as an enormously significant socio-moral phenomenon before there was an idea of a deficit. The first psychometric measure of empathy was introduced in the mid-1950s,[14] which means that the only thing Konrath's study shows is that empathy has been on the decline for at least half as long as people have been measuring it. Phrases such as "global empathic consciousness" imply that the value of empathy knows no bounds, but the idea that empathy is a socio-moral phenomenon emerged from a narrow range of Anglo-American contexts in the mid-20th century. And at its inception, empathy was not a socio-moral phenomenon.

The first instance of the English "empathy" is commonly attributed to Edward Titchener's 1909 *Lectures on the Experimental Psychology of the Thought-Processes.*[15] The word was a translation of the German *Einfühlung*, literally *in-feeling*. Titchener, who was born in England and had studied at

Oxford, trained in psychology in Germany with the founder of the first experimental psychology laboratory, Wilhelm Wundt. By the time he published the *Lectures,* Titchener held a post in the United States, at Cornell. Titchener's account of empathy was ambiguous and difficult to follow, but through a series of events unrelated to its content, it became influential. Titchener was the mentor of Edwin Boring, one of the first historians of psychology. The highlight of Boring's otherwise-unremarkable career was a very influential book on the history of experimental psychology, which focused heavily on (and arguably inflated the prominence of) Titchener's ideas, including his account of empathy.

Before Titchener's account of empathy, *Einfühlung* was used from the second half of the 18th century in German aesthetic psychology.[16] This usage marked a shift in focus from aesthetic objects—nature and works of art—to the spectator in theorizing aesthetic meaning. *Einfühlung* referred to a process by which the spectator imaginatively projects kinesthetic experience into an aesthetic object. As I approach a mountain, I might experience sensations of rising and expansion, and locate these feelings externally, in the mountain itself—a purely projective, anthropomorphic process.

The 19th-century German psychologist Theodor Lipps, an earlier student of Wundt, provided the most thorough account of *Einfühlung*.[17] Lipps was initially interested in optical illusions, but he extended *Einfühlung* to explain perception of the internal states of other people. For example, as I see you extend your arm, I might experience a sensation of striving and forward movement, yet locate that feeling in you. It's worth pointing out that Lipps was a translator and great fan of 18th-century Scottish philosopher David Hume, one of the most influential theorists of sympathy in the history of Western thought. Although Lipps's account of *Einfühlung* does not make overt use of Hume, it's hard to deny a connection. It is also worth noticing that, in Lipps, we still find a process of projection, rooted in the spectators' introspection of their own sensations.

Lipps's work on *Einfühlung* has been diversely interpreted and evaluated. Early 20th-century phenomenologists, Husserl, Scheler, and notably Stein, discussed *Einfühlung* to address the philosophical problem of solipsism. *Einfühlung* also played a role in the development of the hermeneutic tradition in the human sciences. In these and other examples, *Einfühlung,* while stimulating, has not escaped substantial criticism. There was no grand hope for *Einfühlung* as a solution to big problems.

Great hope for empathy, and the idea that knowing and connecting with others happens through emotions, emerged out of more recent Anglo-American psychology. Freud was a long and great admirer of Lipps, having initially discussed *Einfühlung* to explain the psychology of jokes.[18] Later, Freud came to view *Einfühlung* as central to rapport development in clinical contexts.[19] Freud's clinical interpretation of empathy became central in the

Anglo-American psychotherapeutic tradition, notably through the works of Carl Rogers since the 1930s[20] and Heinz Kohut since the 1960s.[21] Both use the English "empathy" to describe a crucial principle of relationships in which helpful response to emotional suffering is made possible. Since then, the idea of empathy as a positive socio-moral phenomenon that grounds our knowledge of and relations to others has grown significantly. It is the basis of the attachment theories that have come to define Anglo-American developmental psychology. In the early 2000s, the contentious discovery of the mirror neuron contributed considerably to popular attention to the idea of empathy, signaling if nothing else the commitment of researchers to generating evidence for an old idea through new methods.

Empathy has survived a relatively haphazard journey to socio-moral significance, and I suggest this reflects broader appeal to a psychotherapeutic reality—a world in which our knowledge of self and others is parsed through psychologistic discourses that focus on our inner emotional lives and realizing our true selves. Following a range of incisive critical thinking on the sciences of the mind, I hold that the rise of psychotherapeutic and, more generally, psychologizing discourses since World War II has fundamentally changed the way Western people see themselves.[22] A significant strand of this thinking suggests that, in the context of late capitalism, psychotherapeutic and psychological techniques and language have been widely co-opted by capital, first as managerial discourses in the service of producing more willingly compliant workers and then more broadly as marketing techniques of corporations.[23] These shifts transferred psychotherapeutic thinking and ways of speaking from private spheres of the psychotherapeutic encounter and other intimate relationships into the worlds of work and mass consumption. Another significant strand of thinking has demonstrated that the psychotherapeutic concept of self-realization is the basis of the rise of daytime talk shows, the immediate predecessors of reality TV. The psychotherapeutic reality I've described might be connected with what the cultural sociologist Eva Illouz has called "emotional capitalism."[24] We would do well now to consider its political consequences.

Demotic Reality

Youth now understand fame itself—as opposed to some traditional skill-based route to fame—as a viable career option. Although the situation is disturbing, we should appreciate that while ordinary celebrity is problematic on many levels, it is actually extremely difficult to accomplish and even more difficult to maintain. We should be generous enough to interrogate the contexts that could produce such aspirations.

One possibility is that, appearances of empathy deficits aside, resources to express emotion authentically are presented as available to everybody.

Although highly successful reality TV stars like the Kardashians and the cast of *Real Housewives* perform their emotions in ways that might be considered contrived, the performances mobilize familiar expressive resources and they operate largely within accessible spaces, like the Internet. A weakness of honest pedagogical attempts to communicate truth and facts is that they tend to highlight inequality of distribution of traditional epistemic resources. Widespread guerilla marketing of affect, feeling, and emotion seems to raise the property value of the self.

Another possibility is that ordinary fame capitalizes on the already-entrenched psychotherapeutic value of self-realization. Reality TV cast members often speak as though the genre is rooted in principles of self-improvement through emotional development and greater reflexive awareness. When an independently financially successful couple is asked why they chose to do a reality TV show, they say without hesitation that they realized that one party did not fully understand the other's experience of domestic violence, and thus it was the former's duty to take that journey. After being fired from *RHBH* and joining the cast of a different show, Brandi Glanville tells an interviewer that the new show is much better, because they really actually push the cast members to grow and become better versions of themselves, as opposed to just pretending to do that.

We now commonly use the word "democratize" to refer to situations that make something accessible to everyone. If we take this usage for granted, there is a sense in which the widespread legitimization of appeals to emotion, along with the circulation of emotion as epistemic currency, actually does democratize knowledge or something like it. But, while I have no qualms with semantic change, I would caution against this rendering of democratic. Cultural and media theorist Graeme Turner offers the very useful concept of "the demotic turn" to trace the use of ordinary people for media content since the early 2000s.[25] Turner has been centrally concerned with how this turn fails to guarantee material opportunities to reshape political landscapes, thus undermining the core motivations of democratization. He warns against trusting the tech optimists who promulgate association between new media and democracy, since their interests are too tightly intertwined with capital. I add that we should be wary of the conversion of affect into epistemic currency. Most obviously, the primary function of branded affect is to market consumer goods. However, I raise two other concerns, which strike me as understudied.

First, affect as epistemic currency may bind personal expression of self so tightly with public participation that the latter becomes depoliticized in undesirable ways. At the time of my writing this chapter, the Fall 2017 #metoo campaign to raise awareness over sexual assault, in the aftermath of the highly publicized Harvey Weinstein affair, is quite fresh. This campaign is notable for seeming to have at least some real political and material effects on institutional arrangements in Hollywood. It also serves highly confessional and psychotherapeutic purposes. The campaign provides a useful example of why we should not confuse psychotherapeutic value with political success. Since the initial success of the campaign, we have now discovered that the #metoo hashtag was originally mobilized by an unknown black woman, Tarana Burke, 10 years before the white, traditional celebrity actress Alyssa Milano mobilized it again with more success.[26] Commenting on the Weinstein affair, Anita Hill has argued that we can explain the unprecedented success of the second campaign by recognizing that this case is entirely built on highly atypical power dynamics: the women involved are high-status Hollywood celebrities—celebrities in the traditional sense of the term—who collectively and in some cases individually have more power than Weinstein himself.[27] The case of Burke makes clear that having access to infrastructures that enable and encourage us to make ourselves vulnerable and our emotional lives visible does not in fact guarantee any political or material consequences. The Fall 2017 #metoo campaign undoubtedly served many nonpolitical interests for many women, by offering a confessional or psychotherapeutic opportunity. While I do not begrudge anyone this kind of opportunity, I still think it is important not to confuse psychotherapeutic benefit to some individuals with political progress for all women.

Second, as we have seen in the case of reality TV, authentication strategies powerful enough to convert emotion into epistemic currency are modes of production, circulation, and distribution of branding and other marketing materials. I should emphasize that this is not an accusation of false consciousness about the authenticity of our emotional lives. I accept that affect qua epistemic currency is indeed authentic, as long as it reflects the way the concept of authenticity is being used. I also accept that self-branding and presenting one's affective life in ways that are convertible to epistemic currency is a certain contemporary mode of self-realization. My only suggestion is that we keep in mind that the main goal of these processes is to serve capitalist interests.

As I have suggested throughout this chapter, the complex and networked nature of the infrastructures of new media raises new and crucial questions about the relationship between form and content. Although this kind of relationship is more slippery and less salient in relation to emotions than it is in relation to truth and facts, we need to begin to better understand the former, if for no other reason than the fact that affect is now a significantly valued form of epistemic currency.

Conclusion

Most of us now have easy access to plentiful resources for emotional expression, as well as infrastructures to make this expression visible. That does not mean we are rich with opportunities to author or take ownership of our emotional lives. As we increasingly make use of widely available and recognized resources for emotional expression, we are increasingly likely to interpret our affective lives and ourselves through those resources. The language of emojis is determined by the Unicode Consortium, a group of volunteer representatives of high-powered tech companies. While the main goal of the consortium is to internationalize software standards and data, the apparently endless diversity of affective life constantly bumps up against the consortium's efforts to generate universal languages. For its part, the most significant factor in the approval of a new emoji is whether it is amenable to distinct graphic representation.

There is no emoji that communicates elation—that highly ephemeral, visceral feeling of buoyancy and lightness, accompanied by atmospheric brightness, that for a short time makes us exude a sense of peace. Technocrats can't get no respect, but neither can poets, or even postmodernists for that matter. The situation can on some level be attributed to the fact that our epistemic resources, including not only old fashioned forms of knowledge but feelings too, are being redirected by demotic systems, which are in turn being redirected by external interests, especially the interests of media companies. In this world of rapidly proliferating conceptual redundancy, perhaps it's best not to presume that much of anything is sacred.

Notes

1. See, for example, Sue Collins, "Making the Most of 15 Minutes: Reality TV's Dispensable Celebrity," *Television & New Media* 9, no. 2 (2008): 87–110; Chad Raphael, "The Political-Economic Origins of Reali-TV," S. Murray and L. Oullette, eds., *Reality TV: Remaking Television Culture* (New York: New York University Press, 2009), 123–40; Graeme Turner, "The Mass Production of Celebrity: Celetoids, Reality TV, and the 'Demotic Turn,'" *International Journal of Cultural Studies* 9, no. 2 (2006): 153–65.

2. Laura Grindstaff and Susan Murray, "Branded Celebrity: Branded Affect and the Emotion Economy," *Public Culture* 27, no. 1 (2015): 109–10.

3. Ibid., 111.

4. Ibid., 115.

5. See Laura Grindstaff, *The Money Shot: Trash, Class, and the Making of TV Talk* (Chicago: University of Chicago Press, 2002); Grindstaff and Murray, "Branded Celebrity," 125–26; John Saade and Joe Borgenicht, *The Reality TV Handbook* (Philadelphia: Quirk Books, 2004).

6. Alice Marwick and danah boyd, "It's Just Drama: Teen Perspectives on Conflict and Aggression in the Networked Era," *Journal of Youth Studies* 7, no. 9 (2014): 1–17.

7. Gary Fine, "Gossip," Thomas A. Green, ed., *Folkore: An Encyclopedia of Beliefs, Customs, Tales, Music, and Art* (Santa Barbara, CA: ABC-CLIO, 1997), pp. 422–23.

8. Barack Obama, "Convocation Speech at Northwestern University," 2006, http://www.northwestern.edu/newscenter/stories/2006/06/barack.html.

9. Jeremy Rifkin, *The Empathic Civilization: The Race to Global Consciousness in a World in Crisis* (Cambridge, UK: Polity, 2009).

10. Paul Bloom, "The Baby in the Well," *New Yorker,* May 20, 2013, https://www.newyorker.com/magazine/2013/05/20/the-baby-in-the-well. Bloom has since written a book on the same subject. See Paul Bloom, *Against Empathy: The Case for Rational Compassion* (London, UK: Penguin, 2016).

11. For a summary of the fallout of the publication of Bloom's *New Yorker* article, see the following from the Centre for Building a Culture of Empathy: http://cultureofempathy.com/References/Experts/Others/Paul-Bloom.htm.

12. See Daniel Goleman, *Emotional Intelligence* (New York: Bantam Books, 1995).

13. Sara Konrath, Edward H. O'Brien, and Courtney Hsing, "Changes in Dispositional Empathy in American College Students over Time: A Meta-Analysis," *Personality and Social Psychology Review* 15, no. 2 (2011): 180–98.

14. L. Cronbach, "Processes Affecting Scores on 'Understanding of Others' and 'Assumed Similarity,'" *Psychological Bulletin,* 52 (1955): 177–93.

15. E. B. Titchener, *Lectures on the Experimental Psychology of Thought-Processes* (New York: Macmillan, 1909).

16. See R. Vischer, "On the Optical Sense of Form: A Contribution to Aesthetics," *Empathy, Form, and Space,* eds. and trans., H. F. Mallgrave and Eleftherios Ikonomou (Santa Monica, CA: The Getty Center for the History of Art and the Humanities, 1994, originally published 1873), pp. 89–123.

17. See T. Lipps, "Einfühlung, Innere Nachahmung und Organempfindung," *Archiv für gesamte Psychologie* 1 (1903a): 465–519 (translated as "Empathy, Inner Imitation and Sense-Feelings," *A Modern Book of Esthetics,* 374–82 [New York: Holt, Rinehart and Winston, 1979]); 1903b. *Aesthetik,* vol. 1 (Hamburg: Voss Verlag, 1905); *Aesthetik,* vol. 2 (Hamburg: Voss Verlag, 1906); "Einfühlung und Ästhetischer Genuß," *Die Zukunft* 16 (1907): 100–114; "Das Wissen von Fremden Ichen," *Psychologische Untersuchungen* 1 (1912/1913): 694–722; "Zur Einfühlung," *Psychologische Untersuchungen* 2 (1912/1913): 111–491.

18. Sigmund Freud, *Jokes and Their Relations to the Unconscious* (New York: W. W. Norton & Company, 1960).

19. See George W. Pigman, "Freud and the History of Empathy," *International Journal of Psychoanalysis* 76 (1995): 237–56.

20. Although there are many relevant publications, a representative and highly cited example is Carl Rogers, "Empathic: An Unappreciated Way of Being," *The Counseling Psychologist* 5, no. 2 (1975): 2–10.

21. Heinz Kohut, "Introspection, Empathy, and Psychoanalysis: An Examination of the Relationship between Mode of Observation and Theory." *Journal of the American Psychoanalytic Association* 7, no. 3 (1959): 459–83.

22. See Nikolas Rose, *Inventing Our Selves: Psychology, Power, and Personhood* (Cambridge, UK: Cambridge University Press, 1998); also Philip Cushman, *Constructing the Self, Constructing America: A Cultural History of Psychotherapy* (Reading, MA: Addison-Wesley/Addison Wesley Longman, 1996).

23. See Eva Illouz, *Cold Intimacies: The Making of Emotional Capitalism* (London, UK: Polity, 2007); William Davies, *The Happiness Industry: How the Government and Big Business Sold us Well-Being* (New York: Verso Books, 2015).

24. Illouz, *Cold Intimacies.*

25. See Graeme Turner, *Ordinary People and the Media: The Demotic Turn* (Thousand Oaks, CA: Sage Publications, 2010), and "The Mass Production of Celebrity."

26. See "Meet Tarana Burke, Activist Who Started 'Me Too' Campaign to Ignite Conversation on Sexual Assault," October 17, 2017, https://www.democracynow.org/2017/10/17/meet_tarana_burke_the_activist_who.

27. See Jane Mayer, "Anita Hill on Weinstein, Trump, and Watershed Moment for Sexual Harassment Accusations," *New Yorker,* November 1, 2017, https://www.newyorker.com/news/news-desk/anita-hill-on-weinstein-trump-and-a-watershed-moment-for-sexual-harassment-accusations.

CHAPTER EIGHT

Truth and Trolling

Jason Hannan

In October 2017, Dr. Bandy Lee, a psychiatrist at Yale University, published an astonishing and historically unprecedented collection of essays entitled *The Dangerous Case of Donald Trump: 27 Psychiatrists and Mental Health Experts Assess a President*.[1] Featuring leading authorities in psychiatry and psychology, this collection represents a rare stance among thousands of mental health professionals who challenge the absolute nature of the so-called Goldwater Rule in psychiatry. According to the Goldwater Rule, it is unethical for psychiatrists to comment on the mental health of public figures who have not been formally diagnosed in person. Under exceptional circumstances, this collection argues, mental health professionals have a "duty to warn" fellow citizens when a public figure, owing to a severely compromised mental state, poses a grave threat to public safety and security. It is a telling moment indeed that the election of Donald Trump has proven to be just such an exceptional circumstance. Writing with an unusual combination of professional seriousness and a profound sense of alarm, the contributors to *The Dangerous Case of Donald Trump* argue that President Trump suffers from extreme hedonism, pathological narcissism, sociopathy, delusional disorder, and even madness. They consider the unique ethical challenges that Trump's presidency poses to mental health professionals, as well as its tragic psychological effects—the stress, anxiety, depression, and even trauma—upon the American public and even the rest of humanity.

That Trump suffers from mental health problems, however, is not difficult for nonprofessionals to see, as Lee and her fellow contributors acknowledge. His erratic behavior; his paranoia concerning everyone around him; his sheer viciousness toward those whom he regards as "enemies"; his pathetic obsession with the political legacy of Barack Obama; his bizarre, rambling, and incoherent speeches; his deranged, often inexplicable tweets at 5 a.m.; and his severely abusive and dysfunctional relationship with truth and reality are all signs of a mind suffering from severe problems. While it is certainly helpful for psychiatrists and psychologists to bolster this widely held public impression with their professional judgment, very little of Lee's otherwise-laudable and courageous book is especially revelatory. In fact, missing from the book is any mention of Trump as the one character type for which he has justifiably become notorious, a character type that demands greater analysis by mental health professionals, that of the troll.

Like countless anonymous users lurking in the shadows of social media, seeking to get their thrill from harassing others, President Donald Trump is an out-and-out troll. He contributes to the degradation of the public sphere through malicious comments that serve no purpose other than to sow discord and division. He has insulted, threatened, and lied about so many people, places, and things that it is literally impossible to keep track of it all. But the difference between Trump and his anonymous counterparts is that Trump does not hide behind the veil of anonymity. Quite to the contrary, he proudly and defiantly puts his vile personality on public display, using it to seek attention from his loyal base of supporters. And this key difference marks an extremely dangerous turning point in political history: the emergence of the troll as a mainstream character in the drama of liberal democracy.

How did this happen? How did trolling, a destructive form of sociopathic behavior originally confined to the obscure corners of the Internet, eventually become a mainstream political practice? The aim of this chapter is to answer this question. It draws from the work of one of the most prophetic critics of our bizarre and chaotic times: Neil Postman. Best known for his book *Amusing Ourselves to Death: Public Discourse in the Age of Show Business*,[2] Postman offers a trenchant analysis of the fragmentation of public discourse. This chapter builds on Postman's insights into the hopes of shedding light on the emergence of a figure that Postman had never anticipated: the troll. In what follows, I argue that the troll is the logical outcome of a culture of hyper-fragmentation, in which the false certainties of a black-and-white worldview offer greater existential comfort than the patient search for truth.

Postman on the Prehistory of Television

The 1980s was an era for some of the most iconic television shows in entertainment history: *Cheers, ALF, The A-Team, Dynasty, Family Ties, Knight Rider, Growing Pains,* and *MacGyver*. It was also the era of Ronald Reagan, Dr. Ruth Westheimer, Benny Hinn, Jimmy Swaggart, and the birth of *CNN* and *USA Today*. Of these two lists, it was the latter with which Postman was principally concerned. He took issue, not with entertainment per se, but rather with serious public figures and media content that took the form of entertainment. The problem as he saw it lay in a shared medium, namely, television. Although Ronald Reagan as president was no longer Ronald Reagan the Hollywood actor, and although CNN and *USA Today* were founded as news sources, they reflected the dominance of entertainment in public discourse. Entertainment, it turned out, had become the key to political persuasion. How did this come to be?

Postman was very much a fish out of water in 20th-century America. He belonged to the 18th century, an age he deeply romanticized and whose culture he very much wished to revive. It was not so much the morals and the politics of the 18th century as it was the intellectual environment for which he was so nostalgic. The name he gave to this period was Typographic America, and the distinctive feature he admired so much about this earlier America was a quasi-religious form of devotion to the printed word. Postman relates what are admittedly remarkable facts about Typographic America's limitless appetite for books. He recounts how books featured prominently in the earliest days of the American colonies. Books were included in the Mayflower. Bookstores and libraries were established almost as soon as the early colonists set foot in the New World. Because the Christian religion revolved around a book, Christian leaders of various denominations called for mandatory schooling so that laypersons could access the content of scripture. But beyond religious reasons, the call for mandatory public schooling was driven by the belief that only through the printed word could knowledge of any kind, whether religious or secular, be accessed. The ability to read was thus a religious, moral, and intellectual duty (2005, pp. 30–33).

This love of books was expressed in a certain pride among early Americans for the great size and incredible diversity of public and private libraries. It was expressed in a pride for an impressively high rate of literacy among (white) men and women. This high rate of literacy, moreover, cut across class (though not racial) lines, as attested by several proclamations celebrating the reading habits of the workingman.[3] This relatively high rate of literacy among free, white American citizens enabled truly astronomical book sales, even by contemporary standards. Thomas Paine occupies a special place in Postman's historical imagination. The uneducated son of a poor, working-class family, Paine would later go on to write popular works of political philosophy that rivaled Voltaire in their philosophical sophistication and played a critical role in igniting the American Revolution. Postman also takes care to note that Charles Dickens was treated like a modern-day rock star, a status that no author today, save perhaps J. K. Rowling, could realistically expect to enjoy (34–39).

What type of thinking, then, did the age of typography produce? Postman illustrates what he calls the "typographic mind" (2005, p. 44) through the example of the famed Lincoln-Douglas debates: nine-hour festivals in which two rival senatorial candidates performed astounding feats of political oratory and dialectical debate, with the aim of winning over the hearts and minds of the audience. Postman is careful not to overly romanticize such events, noting their sensational, even entertaining, character. Still, he insists, there is something to be said about whole families able and eager to sit through nine hours of political oratory, with sufficient critical attention to their logical and factual content, as well as to their highly nuanced stylistic features. By contrast, it is difficult to imagine a modern American family able to sit through even a fraction of such an event without getting painfully antsy. The typographic mind, then, was patient, analytical, discriminating, and discerning, with a cultivated, disciplined attention to propositional content—that is, to facts, claims, and inferences. The typographic mind was especially sensitive to, even offended by, logical inconsistency and incoherence. A mind shaped by the printed word was prone to careful, systematic evaluation of claims, to logical analysis of arguments, and to an examination of the evidence. Put simply, the typographic mind not only exhibited a profound respect for truth but also reflected a certain conception of truth, namely, as that to be discovered through slow, critical deliberation. Reactionary, unreflective gut instincts were anathema to the typographic mind (2005, pp. 62–63).

On Postman's historical reading, the first dents inflicted on the typographic mind occurred with the invention of the telegraph and then with the daguerreotype. For a book about television, Postman reserves some rather pointed criticisms of telegraphy and photography. He invokes Henry David Thoreau, whose philosophical meditations on nature positioned him to be a prophetic observer of the new media of his age. Thoreau had seen that the ability to communicate instantaneously would feed the desire to communicate about anything and everything, especially the trivial. Postman notes that the infinitely greater facility of communication was the catalyst to an overabundance of content. Freeing communication from the strictures of distance and time created new types of information, defined by the speed with which they were communicated. Immediacy became encoded into its meaning. One obvious impact of the telegraph was on newspapers. The new instantaneous medium of communication opened up a space for new genres of news and information and new metrics for assessing them. Metrics, Postman tells us, became an end in itself, an obsession with the number of words but not their content (2005, pp. 64–67).

Postman also observes the historical novelty of contextless information, collections of random facts for which the reader had to supply the context and story. This new type of news supposedly held some practical urgency but in fact had no practical bearing on the reader's life. In oral and typographic cultures, Postman says, the importance of information was tied to possibilities for action. The telegraph changed what Postman calls the "information-action ratio." Suddenly, the "potency" of information was lost, thereby "dignifying irrelevance and amplifying impotence." The outcome was a new type of discourse, one consisting of mere bits and pieces of information—a disjointed collection of stand-alone headlines, fragments of stories with no larger plot, each competing for attention in a new attention economy (2005, pp. 68–70).

According to Postman's historical reading, the invention of photography aided the emergence of this new public discourse. Photography has long been described as a language, one that not only captures a thousand words but that operates according to its own unique grammar. Postman finds this way of thinking about photography incredibly misleading. If we take seriously the lofty idea of photography as a language, then, he insists, it would appear to be a severely impoverished language indeed. Photographs are records of instances and particulars only, not of abstract concepts and universals. Photographs capture some slice of reality but at the cost of the surrounding context. A photograph is therefore quite unlike a propositional sentence, whose natural home is within a larger series of such sentences, which together tell a story. The closest linguistic parallel to photography is the headline, a fragment of information, a floating limb whose phantom body we have to imagine. Photographs, like headlines, are bits and pieces of information, raw data that could be part of any number of stories. If we take seriously the idea of photography as a language, then photographs are at best linguistically primitive utterances incapable of rising to the level of discourse. As Postman would have it, you cannot have a conversation through mere photographs, for they cannot do the hard work of words and sentences.

Of what consequence are telegraphy and photography, then, for public discourse? According to Postman, the countless fragments with which telegraphy and photography flooded our mental environment, the vast majority of which could never be synthesized into a relevant story with a practical bearing on the life of the reader, created the popular celebration of trivia—facts that serve no purpose other than to amuse. Postman finds in this early flood of useless information the seeds of what would later become popular pastimes such as crossword puzzles, radio quiz shows, trivial pursuit, television game shows, and even television news shows. On his reading, telegraphy and photography, more so than radio and film, set the discursive stage for the televisual revolution (pp. 75–80).

Postman on Television

This prehistory of television is the key to making sense of the televisual revolution, for television, as Postman points out, can be conceptualized in two different ways. First, it can be conceptualized as a technology, a screen that displays moving images (p. 84).[4] But it can also be understood as a medium, the purposes to which the technology is put. To help clarify the distinction, Postman differentiates between brains and minds. The first is a concept from human anatomy, the latter a concept from culture and philosophy. How we understand the mind will vary based on the cultural context. Similarly, how television is understood will vary based on the cultural context. In the context of American culture, the primary purpose of television is to amuse and entertain. Postman holds that a thorough understanding of the television as a medium requires an analysis of the type of discourse it promotes. The discourse of television is dramatically different from the discourse of the printed word. Television discourse features captivating, mesmerizing visual material that requires very little time and even less thought to digest. Everything about television, from the fragments of information to the rapid movement of one image to the next to the mind-numbing flashiness, is not conducive to the typographic mind but rather to its opposite: a passive, shallow, uncritical, and highly fragmented mind. Television discourse is not an arena for competing ideas but rather for stimuli competing for an increasingly short and fragmented attention span. On this view, entertainment can be understood as nonrational stimuli that keep the mind preoccupied.

Yet Postman did not take issue with television entertainment per se. Rather, his concern was for serious content that took the form of entertainment. Almost every topic of public discourse, from politics to religion to science and even economics and health, has been reinvented in light of television. In a mental environment defined by short and fleeting attention spans, conformity to the standards of the dominant medium is of the essence. In the age of television, those standards are the standards of entertainment. Hence, Postman argues that entertainment has become the "supra-ideology" of our time, the conceptual ground on which public discourse now proceeds. The consequence of submitting to the logic of entertainment is to treat public discourse the way we treat television shows. We expect to understand the content instantly. We expect it to be conveyed quickly. We expect no discomfort. Most important, we expect it to be amusing and entertaining. And if it fails these standards, we simply switch it off, the way we would a television show that fails to entertain us.

Postman illustrates the corrosive effects of television on public discourse through the example of an 80-minute debate on ABC in 1983. The topic was nuclear war. The guests were William F. Buckley, Henry Kissinger, Robert McNamara, Carl Sagan, Brent Scowcroft, and Elie Wiesel—all very serious intellectual figures, not entertainers. Yet, somehow, this 80-minute debate managed to produce very little substance at all. Each speaker was asked a question about really a very serious subject matter. Yet they were each given only two or three minutes to answer it. The forced brevity of their responses was matched by the forced superficiality. It was literally impossible to say anything meaningful and substantive in such a ludicrously small window. The guests were thus compelled to offer slogans and aphorisms, even lines of poetry, something quick and light, but no actual ideas that would leave a lasting intellectual impression in the viewers' minds. Before a guest could reach any depth on a given question, the moderator asked a different guest a different question. The end result was hardly a discussion. Rather, it was like a wild ride at an amusement park, a collection of disjointed comments that didn't fit into a coherent whole. Therefore, if this wasn't a debate, then what was it? According to Postman, it was the *performance* of a debate, a kind of theater in which the guests act out what serious thought and discussion might look like if the sound were off.

A more extreme version of this kind of non-debate can be found in the horrendous ritual of presidential debates during each election season. Here, political candidates competing for the most powerful position on earth perform the same empty, meaningless, insubstantial debates, offering catchy and witty talking points, often at the cost of sheer relevance to the question, in the hopes of being the catchiest and wittiest performer on stage. Presidential debates barely conceal their intention to amuse and entertain. While the candidates are expected to look presidential and speak presidentially, the point of a presidential debate is the same as that of a pro-wrestling match: to watch one candidate eviscerate the other. As Postman observes, the most memorable takeaway from a presidential debate is not a principled point of agreement or even a principled point of disagreement but rather an unprincipled, one-line zinger, a power-packed punch that leaves the weaker candidate bloodied and defeated.

But Postman's sharpest critique of television discourse concerns the words "Now . . . this," a kind of magical incantation that television newscasters recite to indicate breaking for a commercial. The function of "Now . . . this" is to provide a seamless transition from one self-contained moment to the next. "Now . . . this" creates the false semblance of continuity. In fact, it masks the radical discontinuity between individual segments, stringing them together like a never-ending necklace, but with one dramatic difference: uttering the words "Now . . . this" actually severs any logical link to the immediate past, instantly vanishing from memory whatever fleeting content was contained in the previous moment. "Now . . . this" is an assault on memory, one of the primary causes of fleeting attention spans in a televisual culture. What, then, passes for truth in a "Now . . . this" universe, which has no patience for systematic thought, no tolerance for nuance, no room for complexity, and no desire for substance, a universe in which fleeting thoughts are erased as fast as they are produced? What must politicians, newscasters, and talk show hosts do to prove their credibility, to convince the audience that they possess and embody the truth? According to Postman, the answer lies in their skills as performers, that is, as actors and entertainers. The more entertaining the performer, the more convincing, the more "truthful" they appear to the audience. What matters is not truth or truthfulness but rather the *performance* of truth and truthfulness. Put simply, the personality makes all the difference. Intellectual content matters far less than personal likeability. In a "Now . . . this" universe, the measure of truth is whether your audience would like to have a beer with you.

While books condition the mind to expect continuity of logic, subject matter, tone, and rhetorical style, the incessant ambush of "Now . . . this" on the mind effectively shatters that expectation. "Now . . . this" normalizes fragmentation, discontinuity, inconsistency, and even incoherence, to the point that they become the background of human thought, taken for granted much like the air we breathe. In a universe in which fragmentation has become so ingrained in our basic structure of expectations, the consequences for truth are severe. As Postman says, "I should go so far as to say that embedded in the surrealistic frame of a television news show is a theory of anti-communication, featuring a type of discourse that abandons logic, reason, sequence, and rules of contradiction" (2005, p. 105). The ease with which we move from one self-contained moment on television to the next, with no logical continuity between them, and to switch mental frames from news of mass killing to commercials for cereals and deodorants, creates a new type of collective mindset in which "contradiction is useless as a test of truth or merit, because contradiction no longer exists" (p. 110). According to Postman, the rapid spread of this new mindset into the general culture explains why Americans were not much bothered by Ronald Reagan's innumerable contradictions: they had grown insensitive to contradictions. Herein lie the seeds for what we might call our post-truth world.

Updating Postman: From Television to Social Media

If we are to apply Postman's thesis to political discourse today in the hopes of making sense of our post-truth world, then it is necessary to update that thesis in light of the new dominant media of our time. Television now competes with social media, which in many significant ways have redefined contemporary politics and public discourse. And just as we ask what type of discourse television creates, we ought to ask the same of social media.

The social media revolution began with the explosive rise of Facebook in the mid-2000s. Facebook was originally designed as a digital yearbook, a way to record memories, to share pictures, to express taste in music, movies, and television shows, and to capture all those quirks and idiosyncrasies that characterize the youthful personalities of high school life. But Facebook was different from print yearbooks in key respects: it was interactive and could be continuously updated with personal news, new pictures, and new preferences. Built into the design of Facebook was the spirit of high school, a popularity contest in which excellence is determined by social connections. The heart of Facebook was not entertainment but social popularity among friends and peers. Although the design of Facebook has undergone numerous revisions since its inception, it has retained this original structure and purpose.

Twitter was similarly designed as a social tool to be used between friends. The basic idea was that friends would let other friends know if they were at this coffee shop or that café, a way of keeping track of each other's latest happenings. Twitter took one component of Facebook, the status update, and made it into the sole feature. Like Facebook, the structural design of Twitter implicitly defined excellence quantitatively, by the number of followers, likes, and shares. Twitter has since been used for more than mere status updates between friends. It has become a critical tool for journalism, politics, education, and activism. But social popularity is, nonetheless, the primary logic of the medium. It does not matter, for example, how good a journalist one might be; the fewer followers, the less authority a journalist holds on Twitter.

Other social media, including Instagram, Vine, and Pinterest, were designed in a similar spirit: for young people to connect on the basis of shared tastes and preferences, and which also defined success in terms of followers, likes, shares, and comments. Like television, social media quickly succumbed to commercial influence and thus now also serve commercial purposes. But the heart of social media is, nonetheless, fundamentally different from that of television. The direct and interactive structure of social media, in which proactive users play a far greater role than passive television viewers, created a new communication paradigm. In a sense, the stage of showbiz has been replaced by bleachers of the high school.

From Social to Antisocial Media

In keeping with high school as a metaphor for contemporary politics, it is illustrative to compare the presidencies of Barack Obama and Donald Trump. While both have become known as social media presidents, Obama is the first Facebook president and Trump the first Twitter president. And while Facebook and Twitter are the two most popular social media, Facebook is the more social medium, while Twitter has undoubtedly become the more antisocial medium. The devolution from social to antisocial media can be tracked by a comparison of the two presidencies.

When Obama first emerged onto the national political scene in 2004 with his powerful speech at the Democratic National Convention (DNC), it was clear that he was unlike anyone else in American politics. The young, sharp, energetic, hyper-eloquent, and deeply charismatic senator from Illinois,

Barack Obama was the first black political figure since Jesse Jackson to captivate so many American hearts and minds. His command of the entire crowd at the DNC was a historic moment. He seemed to hit all the right notes, calling out injustice, while hammering home what would become his signature message of hope and his vision of America as inclusive and all-embracing. He had established a name and reputation for himself in national politics, setting the stage for his announcement in 2007 of his candidacy for president of the United States.

In the three years following Obama's historic DNC speech, Facebook rose from an obscure tool for students at Harvard to a worldwide social media powerhouse. From the start, Obama's communications team recognized the new media landscape and immediately capitalized on it. Obama's campaign website was modeled after social media, enabling users to connect with one another, organize local meetings, conduct outreach campaigns, and recruit volunteers for canvasing projects. The interactive features of the campaign website created a genuine sense of grassroots community and solidarity, and fueled the sense of hope that kindled in the hearts of Obama's supporters. On Facebook, YouTube, Twitter, and Instagram, he quickly amassed an enormous army of followers in the tens of millions.

Yet it was not merely Obama's strategic use of social media that set him apart from the competition. Obama's political style lent itself to the mentality and aesthetic of social media. Obama was very tuned in to popular culture in a way that was truly unprecedented. He shared with the public the musical artists on his iPod. He talked about his love of popular television shows like *The Wire,* even going so far as to offer commentary on the lead characters. He appeared on *Late Night with David Letterman* and participated in one of Letterman's popular Top Ten Lists. He understood hipster humor and irony, even exercising it better than hipsters themselves. He befriended Beyoncé and Jay-Z. He welcomed Bruce Springsteen at his political rallies. He danced on stage with Ellen DeGeneres. He and Michelle Obama shared a fist bump that got reported around the world. He appeared on *The Daily Show with Jon Stewart*. And he shared the stage with Oprah, one of his most enthusiastic supporters. All of these friendships lent themselves to glamorous news coverage that rapidly circulated on social media, feeding the buzz and excitement surrounding his historic candidacy. It was clear that Obama was no ordinary candidate. He wasn't simply the more likeable choice. He exuded sheer coolness and hipness in a way that left other politicians green with envy. Voting for Barack Obama was like voting for class president.

Obama's stunning victory effectively changed the rules for democratic politics. He demonstrated that politicians could no longer be the dull, lifeless zombies the American public had grown to loathe. Political candidates now not only had to challenge the standards of the status quo but also had to prove their cool factor by playing the social media game. This, however, turned out to be a curse for the Democratic Party. Obama was not just good at social media; he was too good, leaving his political party in a state of smugness and complacency. After Obama, the Democratic Party had falsely assumed that the game was oriented in their favor, that it only had to be played to be won, and that Republicans were a hopelessly clueless and technologically illiterate bunch who could scarcely navigate their way through the exotic world of social media.

Hillary Clinton's presidential campaign embodied all of these arrogant assumptions in the most extreme form. Clinton assumed that she, too, was the hipster candidate, the natural choice for liberal voters. She falsely banked on her gender as a settled case for victory, creating the #ImWithHer hashtag that narcissistically centered on her rather than an actual vision for the country. She thought she could endear herself to Latinos, one of the most powerful voting blocs, by presenting a list of things she "has in common with your abuela," a campaign that backfired spectacularly. She was roundly mocked on Twitter for the many ways in which she was not like anyone's abuela, including her massive wealth and her penchant for deporting child refugees to Central American countries torn apart by internal violence. She created precisely the kind of dull, lifeless, spiritless, and utterly uninspiring content for social media that the Obama generation despised, beginning with her bizarre announcement video, which was remarkable for its conspicuous lack of a message. When it became clear that she lacked a personality, she played the only card she knows: insisting she's not the other candidate. This turned out to be a losing strategy. Put simply, Clinton thought she could play social media like a guitar, when in fact she had no sense of melody. Her arrogance, combined with her social media ineptitude, only fed the parasitic monster who was eventually to defeat her in the general election, albeit with the help of the Electoral College: Donald Trump.

Trump is very much a Twitter president. He has come to embody everything for which Twitter is now so hated: incessant, paranoid, inarticulate, incoherent, ugly, venomous, harassing, and bullying tweets. Of all social media, Twitter is the favorite playground for trolls. The nature of the medium encourages trolling. While rational conversations are possible in theory, they only rarely occur in practice. This has everything to do with Twitter's 140-character limit. It is difficult to say anything meaningful, intelligent, complex, or profound in such an absurdly small space. The mental universe of Twitter presents a dramatic contrast to the typographic mind. Twitter disintegrates the mind far beyond what Postman could have imagined. Instead of "Now . . . this" cutting up mental content into separate and discrete units, the practice of scrolling down a literally endless and chaotic feed of tweets effectively shreds what remains of an extremely limited attention span. To a mind accustomed to habitual scrolling, even a television show can be difficult to sit through.

What type of conversations can one possibly have on Twitter? To compete on Twitter, to say something that will actually get recognized, Twitter users must strive to stand out from the vast and endless sea of tweets. An entire message and a clear pathos must be captured in the span of a single sentence. Witty humor is often the standard means of effective tweeting. But anger is another. Self-righteous anger, especially in reply to another tweet, comes more easily than patient dialogue. Twitter does not lend itself to nuance or to careful interpretation. It practically encourages instinctive, knee-jerk reactions, a common transaction in Twitter's discursive economy, creating an extremely tense and paranoid environment. Even the most benign tweets are easily misunderstood and therefore become the targets of malicious attacks, often forcing the tweets to be deleted. And since civility requires far more time and patience than Twitter affords, incivility becomes the ruling ethos. Twitter's official rules of conduct are enforced with appalling infrequency and inconsistency, allowing bullies to thrive unchecked. As if in a war zone ravaged by lawlessness, bullies often band together, like stray dogs who hunt in packs. They wait in the shadows for unsuspecting targets, alert each other at the smell of blood, and then viciously attack their prey at their weakest moment, unleashing the worst possible instincts: racism, misogyny, homophobia, xenophobia. Countless users have become casualties of Twitter bullies, deleting their accounts to preserve their psychological well-being. Borrowing somewhat misleadingly from Norse mythology, we have come to designate these bullies as trolls.

A recent study in the journal *Personality and Individual Differences* sought to understand the psychological motivations behind trolls.[5] The study looked for a link between trolling and what the authors called "the Dark Tetrad of personality": Machiavellianism, psychopathy, and sadism. The study found an overwhelming correlation between trolling and the Dark Tetrad, thereby confirming what had long been suspected: that trolls have severe personality disorders. Trolls disrupt conversations, not because they have a point to make but because they love disruption. They attack others, not because they have a principled objection but because they love attacking others. Reasoning with a troll is virtually impossible. Trolls thrive on the misery and suffering of others. They derive pleasure from watching their victims squirm in pain. While intended as an analysis of Internet trolls in general, the study turned out to be a stunningly accurate psychological profile of the president of the United States.

Trump was, of course, a sadist and a psychopath long before the rise of social media. But he found a natural home on Twitter, a medium perfectly suited to his extremely limited vocabulary, his even more limited attention span, and his uniquely immature personality. On Twitter, Trump is free to be Trump, an obnoxious jerk and power-tripping authoritarian who thoughtlessly passes judgment on anyone and anything he regards as even the slightest threat to his ego. According to a now-outdated report in the *New York Times,* Trump has attacked no less than 650 people, places, and things on Twitter alone. His targets have included individual citizens, fellow politicians, Mexicans, Muslims, feminists, athletes, celebrities, the liberal half of America, and the European Union. He has repeatedly attacked the press, calling journalists "dishonest," "Fake News," "phony," "sick," "DISTORTING DEMOCRACY in our country!" "highly slanted," with an "agenda of hate," "phony sources," "fabricated lies," and "the enemy of the American People." He has attacked Obamacare as "failing," "broken," "dead," a "disaster," "in a death spiral," "bad healthcare," "imploding fast," "a complete and total disaster," and "torturing the American People."[6] In 2016, Trump attacked Chuck Jones, the Indianapolis union leader who criticized Trump for falsely claiming to have saved 1,100 jobs at Carrier Corporation.[7] Following Trump's attacks on Twitter, Jones received death threats. Around the same time, Trump attacked Lauren Batchelder, a 19-year-old college student from New Hampshire, simply for asking a challenging question at a public forum. He took to Twitter to write, "The arrogant young woman who questioned me in such a nasty fashion at No Labels yesterday was a Jeb staffer! HOW CAN HE BEAT RUSSIA & CHINA?" This was followed by, "How can Jeb Bush expect to deal with China, Russia + Iran if he gets caught doing a 'plant' during my speech yesterday in NH?" The young woman, a college Republican, also received death threats. It is a remarkable point in the history of liberal democracies when the leader of the so-called greatest nation on earth directs the collective fury of an increasingly violent and irrational legion of reactionary conservatives against a teenager, threatening her with physical and sexual harm, and even death.[8]

Conclusion: The Medium Is the Menace

If we wish to understand why we now inhabit a post-truth world, and why a pathological liar and authoritarian personality has managed to come to power in a liberal democracy, we should carefully examine the role of social media on politics and public discourse. In *Understanding Media: The Extensions of Man,* Marshall McLuhan provocatively held that "the medium is the message." He argued that the keys to unlocking a culture lie in the dominant media of the age. On this view, the medium is more significant than the content, carrying greater meaning and power. While this insight has been taken up in different ways, Neil Postman's greatest contribution has been to apply that insight to the study of political culture and public discourse. Through a penchant analysis of the effects of television on thought and speech, Postman made a compelling case that the nature of democracy was transformed, perhaps irrevocably, by the advent of the screen. Although the formal institutional structure of American democracy had remained the same, the content had radically morphed from the sober and systematic thought of the age of typography to the silly entertainment of the age of television, culminating in Postman's time with the election of a Hollywood actor, Ronald Reagan. If only Postman could have lived to witness the presidency of Donald Trump.

In the spirit of both McLuhan and Postman, we ought to take seriously the radical consequences of social media on our culture and politics. Social media are no longer an innocent tool for connecting with friends and competing for popularity. Facebook and Twitter have so thoroughly colonized our collective psyche that we now think and communicate according to their logics. We now inhabit a political environment perpetually on edge, in which even offline we anticipate the kind of reactionary criticisms we have come to expect online. It is becoming more and more common to hear stories of friendships being torn apart and entire Thanksgiving and Christmas dinners ruined by this toxic atmosphere. But beyond the effects on social and family relations, social media have transformed political style and practice. It is now commonplace for politicians to troll each other online and even troll ordinary citizens. The great benefit of social media—enabling everyone to connect with each other more easily and directly than ever before—has turned out to be their greatest curse. Whatever benefit social media offer through instantaneous communication, they destroy by breeding incivility. It is not easy to turn the other cheek after being slapped for no reason by a troll. Even the most civilized users will feel the urge to fight back in the face of repeated trolling.

The genius of Donald Trump, if one can call it that, is to have injected himself into this toxic atmosphere, poisoning it further and playing the trolling game better than anyone else. Trump has changed American politics by elevating trolling, both online and off, into mainstream political practice. Whether he trolls his "enemies" or gets trolled in turn, Trump wins precisely because everyone loses. To confront Trump with truth and logic is to leave him perfectly unscathed. To confront him with insults, the only language he knows how to speak, is to reinforce his sordid mentality and to drag everyone, along with American democracy itself, into the dark and filthy abyss in which Trump has made his home. It is impossible to win an argument against a man who will defend the size of his penis in public debate. It is impossible to win an argument against a man who resorts to childish name-calling, such as "Crooked Hillary," "Pocahontas," and "Rocket Man." Perhaps most dishearteningly, it is impossible to win an argument against a man who lacks principle, who does not stand for anything other than his own ego, and whose every thought and deed revolves around the magnification of his personal glory. That such a disgusting personality should become the most powerful man on earth is a testament, not to his political savvy but rather to the power of social media to redefine the nature of democratic politics.

Notes

1. Bandy Lee, ed., *The Dangerous Case of Donald Trump: 27 Psychiatrists and Mental Health Experts Assess a President* (New York: Thomas Dunne Books, 2017).

2. Neil Postman, *Amusing Ourselves to Death: Public Discourse in the Age of Show Business* (New York: Penguin, 2005).

3. Postman's nostalgia for the old days, including his admiration for the lack of a "literary aristocracy" (p. 34) unfortunately left him all but blind to the near universal illiteracy among slaves, who were denied an education as a matter of principle. Had he considered the wretched condition of slaves, his picture of the 18th century might not have been so glowing.

4. The transition of television from television sets to websites like Netflix, which can be viewed on technologies other than television (e.g., laptops, tablets, and cell phones), illustrates why the technological definition of television is so limited. Many of us watch television today without actually owning a television.

5. Erin E. Buckels, Paul D. Trapnell, and Delroy L. Paulhus, "Trolls Just Want to Have Fun," *Personality and Individual Differences* 67 (2014): 97–102.

6. Kevin Queely, "Trump Is on Track to Insult 650 People, Places and Things on Twitter by the End of His First Term," *New York Times,* July 26, 2017, https://www.nytimes.com/interactive/2017/07/26/upshot/president-trumps-newest-focus-discrediting-the-news-media-obamacare.html.

7. Abigail Tracy, "Union Boss Who Criticized Carrier Deal Gets Death Threats after Trump Blasts Him on Twitter," *Vanity Fair,* December 8, 2016, https://www.vanityfair.com/news/2016/12/donald-trump-chuck-jones-carrier.

8. Jenna Johnson, "This Is What Happens When Donald Trump Attacks a Private Citizen on Twitter," *Washington Post,* December 8, 2016, https://www.washingtonpost.com/politics/this-is-what-happens-when-donald-trump-attacks-a-private-citizen-on-twitter/2016/12/08/a1380ece-bd62-11e6-91ee-1adddfe36cbe_story.html?utm_term=.9df39e1c33c6.

CHAPTER NINE

Truth, Post-Truth, and Subscriptions: Consensus, Truth, and Social Norms in Algorithmic Media

Alex Leitch

Sometime in mid-2016, I noticed that none of my friends seemed to be taking photos of their lunch anymore. This was the middle of the U.S. election, and I was spending more time on social media than was strictly appropriate. In another place and time, maybe I would not have noticed so quickly, but spending every day on social media meant I noticed the missing meals. Instagram had rolled out a change to their time line, effectively hiding the photos that previously defined the service. The neutral design language of Instagram hid the change by minimizing timestamps into illegibility.

Instagram's business model is to imply that everything a user sees is happening in the moment, or very recently, so the change was difficult to spot. The result was that one day on lunch break, there were no photos of anyone else's meals. I checked for them, and eventually the photos reappeared, buried many pages deep and many refreshes into the time line. In place of the lunch photos were photos of bigger things, with more "likes": art events, staged shots of vacations, people at parties, new people, important people, a lot of people. Accounts held by people more important, more public, more popular than my friends and me. Their photos were great, well staged, properly composed, nicely lit. These are nice people; they're successful and popular; they smile a lot. In theory, this should have brought more warmth to the service. In practice, their photos were all from places I wasn't and couldn't have been, and replaced something familiar with the sinking sensation of missing out, which I never used to feel when I was looking at pictures of my friend's lunch.

On the surface, this change is innocuous, only a business update, but in a connected world it is not so simple. Three months after the change, I was talking to a friend about their projects and how I never saw them again. This friend moved to the South for work, and I figured she was maybe busy and happy and didn't care to tell her old friends about her crafts anymore, maybe wasn't on the service. The sinking feeling hit when this friend, a good friend, a close friend, a friend whom I don't see often, said, "I don't know what you're talking about, I put up photos of my crochet every day." I'd misunderstood: the friend had not stopped posting photos. Instagram had decided that crochet photos, like lunch photos, weren't so important as other images, and so they disappeared. The service had decided that in a busy world crochet didn't count as things going on and consequently misplaced a regular friendly interaction with photos of conferences from near-strangers.

Regular, friendly interactions are a way of sustaining social ties, which in turn set the social norms. Replacing crochet or lunch with elite conference attendance changes a norm, and with it the perception of truth. Sharing a small thing had become abnormal. The truth of what I was seeing had changed. When the new truth in my online world became high achievement, it took Instagram from a comforting thing on a sleepless night to the cause of insomnia. It also removed any trace of instant interaction from the service, and with it the sense of spending time together with people in an invisible world.

When a service is synchronous, more information is available to users. As an example, if someone likes an older photo, it means that he or she must have gone looking for it. This set of consistent behaviors is how we know what is rude or polite, warm or cold. It is a key to feeling close to people. Now that attention to older content is enforced, the subtleties of timed interaction that bring friends closer together are much harder to manage. Users are forced to pay more attention to what the service thinks they will enjoy or deems important, and that devalues a personal preference while making it more difficult to establish social norms within a group of friends or peers.

Instagram is not alone in changing to the viral-chasing attention model. In the mid-2010s, all the major social media services—Facebook first, but Twitter quickly followed—replaced their chronological, ordered time lines with "news" and interactions prioritized by popularity. The new feeds have generated a world of competitive misinformation, a post-truth attention economy based on engagement metrics, rather than on humanity, or synchronous experience. Once upon an Internet, communities were formed from knowing when things were happening, where, and feeling connected—or disconnected, if no one else was awake. In such limited communities, it was possible to form social norms and preferences that, while separate from the normal world, still held a sense of their own values.

A sense of shared values and social connection is still prevalent in some areas of the Internet, with regular meetups and consistent time zones, but in the large social media companies and platforms, the importance of community as defined by shared time has been downgraded. Rather than a sense of everyone in it together, the default feeds of Facebook and Twitter provide an unreliable narrative, coupled with a false sense of urgency brought on by many moving pieces—someone "liked" this, but when? Two days ago? Eight hours? What's happening *now* has been deprivileged and made unreliable. This loss brings questions about truth and post-truth forward: without knowing when something happened, how can we decide what happened?

This move to the values of the crowd is fundamental in a way that design language purposefully obscures. Crowd values are different than personal values: the values of a one-way broadcast might be yelled at, but when the crowd is closer, a more likely option is to be silent, to stop using the service, or to stop using it as though it were actually personal. A top-down model is the model of the broadcast news service, less interactive and vocal than peer-to-peer interaction. The value proposition of old broadcast media is not dozens of small interactions by many with many but rather many listening to one. A huge audience for one big viral story, or attention on auto-playing videos which are not so different from television—this is not the same interaction as people sharing a lot of very small things quickly. Put another way, mass culture and popular culture smooth things out and replace small, localized true things with things true for a larger group. This larger group might be distracting, but it is unlikely to be socially engaging, and a lack of conversation does not necessarily help with fear, loneliness, and the shock of the new.

The feeling of loss in a missing set of time lines is personal. Facebook is the strongest example purely by scale, although the asynchronous time lines are widely disliked wherever they show up.[1] Facebook's original metaphor is the "wall," intended as a digital door to a college dorm room, where friends leave messages while you're out. Better than voicemail because it's semipublic, a crowded wall can signal popularity, a recognition that they'd missed you. The more friends near your wall, the busier the service. The metaphor of the wall worked until Facebook opened the circle of trust to the public, causing context collapse by allowing noncollege students to sign up. Parents joined the service, then grandparents, and then, abruptly, employers. When employers landed, the service became wholly public: image mattered more than closeness or memories, and it became more important to be able to remove yourself from photos than to keep them up. The perception of the service shifted from a small group of connected friends to a user base of more than two billion accounts. The sheer variety of things considered to be true, and important, within that group of people is almost too much to think about, much less program.

What social service can hope to fairly cover two billion users of up to seven generations' age difference at once? Facebook tries, but the news means different things to those people depending on what they bring to the party. All that history, and all those contexts collapsing, leads to a nebulous sense of what's real and true and factual, much less what's in good taste. The racism of an uncle at a party looks very different when all the racist uncles can come together on one platform. Unfortunately, racist uncles are great users of the Internet, and the metrics of the social media services insist this represents success. It couldn't be further from the small-scale communication of a dorm-room door.

If someone wrote hate speech on your door at college, that person would be rightly given the boot for harassment. Facebook's goal, to host an enormous, advertisement-ready user base for data mining, has driven the company to have one of the most accessible platforms in the world. The ease of use has opened up who can spend time online. Facebook has gone so far as to kick off "digital colonialism" fights by offering free Facebook bundled with phones in non-North American countries.[2] Its enthusiasm for eyeballs on the service has greatly changed the nature of interacting with the platform. Used all over the world, Facebook has the power to meaningfully influence who sees what—and if advertising works, it then may be presumed to have the power to help influence who thinks what. This is the core of the question of post-truth in the Internet age: how much influence does what you think your peers think have on what you believe is real?

When first opened, the social media attention markets were driven by intimate sharing over distance with established peer groups. People shared important life events, as they do now, but services skewed young: more breakups than divorces, more hookups than babies, but also intensely personal jokes with friends, things embarrassing for a parent—the original surveillance state—to see. These jokes were important because they represented real intimacy, vulnerability, and risk, sort of risk that might make someone trust someone else a little bit more. This type of bonding was possible because the service was not yet truly public. The jokes might be edgy, but a population of largely similar people did not have to face the cost of context collapse, which is: different things are true at once all the time, and figuring out which of the many real realities is an emotionally expensive and time-consuming process. Sometimes, what is really real can change in front of you. The process of sorting out which reality is most plausible is more challenging when digital image manipulation is added to the mix.

There is a video circulating on the Internet of Barack Obama speaking fluent Chinese. American history has made Obama a favored target of video manipulation demonstrations. Putting words in the mouth of the finest public speaker America has seen in the 21st century is a good game. Though there is no solid evidence for Obama's fluency in either Mandarin or Cantonese, there he is, up on screen, apparently speaking the language like a Beijinger born and bred. The video seems to promise a future of news that has little to do with the truth, a future even less reliable than the present. Technology for video and photo manipulation is improving and could make it more and more challenging to decide what really happened, and this seems to undermine its status as a reliable proxy for truth. The status of images and video as real or unreal is important to public discourse, but the most recent debates about it have started in the realm of the personal, where complaints about what could be treated as "real" appeared on a mass scale almost as soon as Instagram launched. The most common complaint about Instagram is the photos young women post of themselves—the selfie—but a quick follow-up, used to this day, is the phrase "no-one cares about your lunch," which may be true for some but patently is not for others.

Instagram is split into accounts that depict impossibly good lives and the more familiar accounts that depict the lives of everyone else, which includes a lot of photos of staged food or staged friends. The complaints about staged images are familiar: that no one's meal or life could be so perfect every day, that selfies are pure vanity, that filters removed the skill needed to make a quality photograph. Technology stages the shot for you, cleans it up, and provides the lighting. The cleaned-up photo, beautifully lit, serves to attract attention, and attention, even negative attention, is referred to as "engagement." Attention is what Instagram measures.

Engagement is a metric that the old broadcast media are very familiar with. The Nielsen rating system has been in place since the 1930s, leading to "sweeps" special episodes four times a year in a feat more reliable than the turning of the seasons. A sweeps episode, full of special guest stars or major plot events, is the direct precursor to the algorithmic feed picking the most-liked photo or video and popping it into view, surrounded by ads, designed to grab your attention. This is not, strictly, truthful: sometimes these episodes contribute to the canon of what has happened in the plot of the show, and sometimes they do not. They are specifically misrepresenting what has happened in that specific story in order to drive attention: a form of post-truth within a fictional universe. The primary differences here are that the sweeps are passive works of fiction. They are one-way broadcasts, and the ratings system is a blunt instrument compared to the fine knife of the "Like" button. The "Like" button trains Facebook to know what its audience wants in real time, and to serve up more of it, to drive more engagement.

All major social media services are driven by engagement metrics. In the case of Instagram, bought by Facebook, this engagement is shown by a double-tap, which grants a photo a heart. In the case of Facebook, which is large and alarming and good at knowing where people are looking, the like can be a like—a thumbs-up—or several other values, which change seasonally. The "Like" button generated user insight only Google had ever had a chance to come close to before, insight used to target advertising, and this advertising is used, as ever, to change what en masse people interpret as good or interesting or true. The metrics for advertising exist only while the audience continues to click, and therefore, the attention economy of social media is dedicated not to those things which are most sociable but instead to those which are most sticky, which keep people in place the longest. An engagement metric is a flypaper for human attention, and like a flypaper, it does not particularly care what is happening to the people locked in place.

When Facebook mainly focused on synchronous time lines and genuine, low-level interactions with friends, there were occasional breakouts of viral attention to one person or another, but mainly, people engaged with one another. The recent focus on sharing articles from outside the service covers for a separate problem.

Boredom

Very little is happening on any given day in a usual human life. When social media services were perceived as semiprivate, this boredom was addressed by multiple posts a day, or conversations with other bored friends. Now the platform is public, and people largely know better than to hang out there sharing on a sick day. Facebook's shrinking personal-share metric[3] is a measure of this problem, which, in turn, drives up the amount of engagement that needs to be generated by news articles real and imagined. This, in turn, encourages articles with a less-than-earnest slant on the news to produce more material, because attention to articles drives money from advertisements, while, in turn, giving the impression that nothing is happening in the user's immediate vicinity, even if other users are logging in as often as once or twice a week to share updates and check in. The cycle leads to attention-grabbing artificiality as the biggest available distraction. Social-norm-reinforcing views of the banal are reduced and may disappear entirely.

When the only views available are loud news, and the small pieces go missing, it's easy to lose track of the social glue that holds diverse groups together. Into this gap fall pieces of un-truth, to fill in the space where normally a photo of someone's lunch would go.

A short digression: the inventor of Facebook's "Like" button has pointed out, publicly, that no one cared about likes until the notification counter turned from blue to red.[4] Drawing attention to attention being paid helped keep people involved in the service, but attention is only so elastic, and the notifications panel of the service has gone from tracking only conversations to every kind of update imaginable in the time that Facebook has been running. Small conversations used to be the absolute norm of the service but now have moved to being less usual; reaction buttons have taken their place and then been doctored to show a compiled number of likes per share rather than a chain. These are tiny user experience alterations, but as we have seen, small user experience choices can impact what people see and, through that, what can be believed. Seeing people's everyday lives, the very piece that Facebook is losing, is what helps with social bonds and trust.

There is a lot of value in little groups of people who know other small groups of people and can vouch for them reliably. This is the original value of the Internet, all the weirdos in a room together, sharing ideas and dreams outside their small towns, but the value of people talking to one another in small groups has until now been hard to export or quantify. It would usually stay mainly in the group, in the sense of bonds strengthened and values established, and from there can turn into favors done and owed—the social debts that let people trust one another. Take that and put it online, and sometimes you get little groups of people over vast areas of space, which was intended as a feature, not a bug. The social media engines we have now are able to quantify those conversations and turn them into advertising categories, which is not the most tempting persuasion to have more of those conversations on those services. Indeed, the translation of small things into alarmingly specific, frequently racist advertising categories[5] seems like a good reason to stop talking at all.

The original intent of the social services was to facilitate closeness at scale, a sort of invisible, omnipresent local bar. Foursquare promised more "coincidental" meetings with friends, where Twitter, as represented in Brad Colbow's comic "The Long Slow Death of Twitter," was once a local pub where one could meet friends and has turned into cable news and an ongoing bar fight. Instagram and Twitter both let people eat together in passing at vast remove—so vast that one party might be having dinner and the other lunch or breakfast. This was not enough engagement to keep the metrics up, and so the social media services have replaced the cocktail party metaphor with a new one: the slot machine.

The pull-down-to-refresh metric comes straight from Vegas, delivering content promoted on the basis of preexisting attention. The design metaphor is identical to a slot machine demanding a pull to see if you've won big, and the research is in: slot machines put people in a flow state, disappearing time and money while binding attention—news, for example, or entertaining videos, or pictures but from three weeks ago. The emphasis on viral content keeps attention half-focused on the service, sticky and stressful, with a sense that something is going on just around the corner. The whole point of an asynchronous time line is that every time a user refreshes his or her feed, there will be something new in it—a post with preexisting high engagement or a fresh ad, even if nothing new has been posted by the people they follow. The stress of engaging is part of the addictive service design. More users stuck in the service means more money from advertisers and promoters, without even making the users themselves spend that money directly.

The effort within a social media service now is to promote content that will trap attention on the service. Conspiracy theories, post-truth by any other name, are an easy match to that algorithm. Sticky and tempting, a conspiracy theory is the sweeps episode of social media: something that is just true *enough* to keep you going, while the rest of reality, tedious, threatening, full of taxes, and generally difficult, rolls along around it. It would be nice to believe that someone is in charge and that the world is small and close to a dorm-room door, and therefore these stories crop up, making post-truth more tempting while collapsing social context—or, worse, only occasionally collapsing context.

The reason for sticky attention is pretty simple: only so many people in the casino spend enough money to keep the place in business. Commonly called "high rollers" or "whales," they can afford to lose and lose and lose again. Social media services do not have whales—they have "influencers" instead, people who can drive attention to the service. All social media services run at a tremendous cost, and their return on investment per user is very low. They, therefore, rely on ever-increasing user bases and engagement in order to stay in business. The promise of user engagement and account numbers is that these services can grow forever, but this is untrue: "everyone" is never who is implicitly invited to the party. There are always limits, based on manners, on common interests, on geography and politics, and when everyone is really for real invited, the party gets weird, because some sets of beliefs are compatible and other sets are purposefully not. The familiar made suddenly strange is the fundamental unit of the uncanny.

This is what context collapse does—it brings the uncanny home. On a social media service, primed for engagement, an encounter with the uncanny might induce rage, or a rabbit hole. The uncanny is always a thing out of place, a moment when something certain becomes uncertain, and that space is the space of change. It cannot happen in an environment composed of solid truths—it takes root in the home of maybe.

Maybe, however, is not good for user engagement. This is what makes it worthwhile to tune newsfeed algorithms not just for engagement but to ensure that users do not encounter beliefs inimical to their own. Any given group can then believe any given thing, and the context collapse will only happen by chance. Context collapse is bad for business, and so Facebook is committed to never presenting an offensive view to any of its two billion users. An example of this is the red-feed blue-feed experiment by J. Keegan for the *Wall Street Journal*.[6] A "filter bubble" is a newsfeed that has been carefully stripped of divergent opinions to ensure a user is not offended by his or her engagement with a service. The filtration, in turn, keeps users on a service for longer, generating higher engagement metrics but reducing the apparent diversity of opinion shown to any given user or group of users. Politically, this seems to generate more extremes of opinion, because rather than seeing a mix of thought, users begin to see only that which they find appealing.

A given user's filter bubble may or may not have an impact on that person or the greater world, but what will have an impact is many bubbles put together. In this respect, social media strongly resembles the character No Face from Studio Ghibli's fable Spirited Away: asynchronous, tuned social media take on the characteristics of the people who have used it and can offer them only more and more of the same as it rampages through their lives. The supposedly neutral becomes villainous the way all things do: by supplying too much of a good thing to one person at a time. One does not even need to work to find engagement groups on the service, because they are suggested in the search function. The service claims to be neutral, so people can join any group they like, and the conspiracy theory groups are among the stickiest. To the service, this is all to the good: any interest a user expresses is good for getting him or her to spend more time on the service, which is good for both serving ads and, if they have an ad-blocker enabled, telling advertisers there is a large audience available to serve. Pre-Facebook, the conspiracy theories were there, but they simply didn't have the reach.

The conspiracy theories have the reach now. What used to be contained on 4chan or Something Awful—ugly sites with ugly reputations—seems now to be everywhere. The mix of engagement metrics and user experience mechanics tuned to keep people on the service has also made things that were once too ugly for the mainstream a popular conversation and the only way to reliably kill time. The least fact-checked tabloids made grabby and interactive and up all night the way no one's friends are. Prioritized at the expense of normal socializing, because these services are not private from the people we care about, it is difficult to persuade someone of the truth of something. We need to have small conversations about small things to build trust before we are able to have large conversations about risky ideas. A circle of trust and confidence in our peers, from bad jokes at cemeteries to good ones on any given Wednesday, is what lets us know who to talk to when things are more challenging. The sense of safety lets us investigate new ideas that could be bad without fear of losing our social circles. Present someone with too much information that contradicts what he or she already believes, and a person will retreat further into his or her beliefs, an interaction known as the backfire effect.[7] Challenged too much, and we will decide that we were right all along, that our opinion has never been more correct, and this, too, promotes an opening for post-truth anti-factual news to take over.

This is a problem in a social media universe always busy with nothing going on. The Internet, at its best, is a powerful tool against isolation and fear. The sense that there is always someone to talk to, even in the middle of the night, can be a real balm for loneliness. The cure is only as good as the company, though, and people can and will leave if they are too uncomfortable. Facebook, slowly losing personal sharing as it increases the proportion of public news, is running a risk: the audience can always find a new place to hang out. The consequence is a service motivated to provide a superposition of can't-miss major life events—the sort of hatch-match-dispatch announcements you once would hear from your family about your cousin—and news that may or may not be real. Users stay on the service, share less than ever, and gain a pervasive sense that something is always happening, reinforcing the loop even as there is less intimacy to be found. This results in dozens of user groups sharing semipublic opinions without sharing much, if anything, about their more human selves. Eventually, they go somewhere else, to where the people are: Reddit, a private chat channel, anywhere.

Private channels have tighter social norms, and often more people posting more things, but they are also distant from the mainstream service's encouragement of personal sharing between disparate groups. While it is likely that one might encounter a high school classmate or a cousin on the larger services, the odds vanish to impossibility on the smaller ones. What is true reverts to being tested against the norms of the group, which often means the norms of the loudest and most regular users of that space. This is regulated in physical spaces with harassment policies, to varied effect, but physical spaces have upward limits on the number of people they can encompass. This is less true of the digital world, where content moderation costs time and money. An incomplete yet appealing truth can go far within a small set of interconnected social crews before rumbling up into the mainstream, and yet before connected platforms gave flight to these incomplete truths, the issue of private rules and ideologies was not so much a problem as it is now.

Post-truth and fake news are a symptom of visibility. Social media promotion and engagement metrics have made distinct groups large enough to find each other and establish antithetical social norms. What is true for one group is untrue for another. The first place people look for what is normal or true is their own community, and a small Internet community may develop its own norms and truths. These may or may not correspond to apparently popular norms and truths. In hindsight, the ability of a service like Instagram to connect disparate people around small, normal, consistent interactions was a pretty big deal, precisely because lunch photos are not that interesting. Valuable, but not interesting, not sticky—people will close a tab on the banal details of another person's life, up until they love that person, and the banal details of their life become the most important thing.

It is this sense of investment in another person's story that gives us community, which can be rooted in place but is sourced in time. Time spent together with people we at least tolerate, if not enjoy, is how we build groups with strong enough connections to trust in risky ideas, to have confidence in a world revealed as entirely uncertain. Our social norms, from "in this family we eat dinner together" to "we hang out on Tuesdays at the garage" to "Caturday," can and do carry outward to "in this community we do not believe in top-down leadership, but rather in conversation" or "everyone in this social circle believes their friends should vote," and can persuade unconvinced friends in a new direction.

A social norm is a specific type of habit, that automatic piece of how a person goes about his or her day. A habit is a way to engage the world that does not cost extra energy: it just lets you move along on a set of rules you believe to be true and inoffensive, because they are supported by the people with whom you interact. Asynchronous feeds have worked, technically, to undermine our ability to socially determine what is true, because they have replaced our social support systems we had come to rely on with an unreliable narrative, which is the friend who is never quite there.

A corporation selecting something to publish is the norm for most news before 1994 and for the vast majority of news after: what has changed is the reach and intimacy of the experience. It is easy and lonely now, to read the news and share. There never was a great big bright moment when the truth was publicly agreed on, but for a while, there was a chance to talk to absent friends, and so to escape the feeling no one cared, the source of loneliness. There is no sign that the corporations involved wish to restore chronological time, or make it harder to find groups that hate the world and love the Internet. There is no reason for these companies to take responsibility for the worlds they govern while the current model turns the most profit, and this is why there are many smaller and more private worlds popping up. Private worlds have private laws, and they will continue to make private truths visible while these broadcast platforms choose to maximize engagement over meaning and attention over intent.

A community is where one goes to share time with people, often the same people, again and again. It is a place we go to decide what should be true, in small ways, in our small lives. Everyone should have access to this power, the power to be un-lonely, the power to not feel small. Whether that power remains accessible is an open question, but it is unfair to treat truth as a new question. The new issue is how we figure out who to listen to and to whom we are allowed to listen.

Notes

1. J. D. Biersdorfer, "Putting Your Twitter Feed Back in Chronological Order," *New York Times,* March 21, 2016, https://www.nytimes.com/2016/03/22/tech nology/personaltech/putting-your-twitter-feed-back-in-chronological-order.html.

2. A. LaFrance, "Facebook and the New Colonialism," *Atlantic,* February 11, 2016, https://www.theatlantic.com/technology/archive/2016/02/facebook-and-the-new-colonialism/462393/.

3. E. Griffith, "Facebook Users Are Sharing Fewer Personal Updates and It's a Big Problem," April 7, 2016, http://fortune.com/2016/04/07/facebook-sharing-decline/.

4. P. Lewis, "'Our Minds Can Be Hijacked': The Tech Insiders Who Fear a Smartphone Dystopia," *Guardian,* October 6, 2017, https://www.theguardian .com/technology/2017/oct/05/smartphone-addiction-silicon-valley-dystopia.

5. S. Stevenson, "Google and Facebook Face Criticism for Ads Targeting Racist Sentiments," *Nytimes.com,* 2017, https://www.nytimes.com/2017/09/15/busi ness/facebook-advertising-anti-semitism.html.

6. J. Keegan, "Blue Feed, Red Feed," May 16, 2016, http://graphics.wsj.com/blue-feed-red-feed/.

7. B. Nyhan and J. Reifler, "When Connections Fail: The Persistence of Political Misperceptions," *Political Behavior* 32, no. 2 (2010): 303–330, https://doi.org/10.1007/s11109-010-9112-2.

CHAPTER TEN

Lords of Mendacity

Paul Fairfield

There is a steamroller passing over us. It assumes many forms and is known by many names, not all of which are fit for print; post-truth, sophistry, and nonsense are a few. Time and again the idea is that the weaker argument is being made to appear the stronger as credulous minds are being hoodwinked by cunning and sinister forces, most of whom are politicians who themselves are little more than puppets of the privileged and the affluent. The discourse of democracy, we increasingly hear, has been co-opted by the mendacious and the self-serving, while values of impartial justice and truth itself are sacrificed to corporate greed, ethno-nationalism, populism, or some similar entity. If most of the commentary is directed toward politicians, the commentators themselves most often are members of the journalistic profession, those disinterested speakers of the truth to power whose business is not to proselytize but to inform, to report on what is happening without undue bias or the insertion of merely personal opinion on what the consumers of such information might wish to conclude. More than a little bad faith may be seen here; however, the claims I wish to advance in what follows are not quite what one hears today in the press, be it mainstream, "alt," or "fake." My first claim concerns democratic politicians and can be summarized briefly: it was always thus, and nothing we have seen in recent years—including in American presidential politics—is unprecedented or surprising. My second claim concerns the lion's share of contemporary political journalism: the self-image of many in this profession as neutral reporter, vetter of facts, and guardian of political veracity not only defies credulity but is a primary instance—is indeed the primary instance—of the phenomenon of which so many are now speaking. The true lords of mendacity are not the politicians whose antics are both largely transparent and as old as democracy but the disinterested watchdogs who report on them in the daily press.

What is most intriguing about the post-truth phenomenon, as it has come to be called, is not what we hear from journalists but something more insidious and that is implicit to contemporary media themselves. First, however, let us hear from some of the journalists who are analyzing the phenomenon. No less than three books appeared in 2017 that bear the title *Post-Truth,* all of which are written by journalists and all of which take a very similar line. What is post-truth, as they understand it, and how did it come to pass? Where is it located and who are its main exponents, if one can be said to be an exponent of such a thing—perpetrators perhaps? James Ball speaks of post-truth and a colorful synonym as "a catch-all word to cover misrepresentation, half-truths and outrageous lies alike." One who engages in it "will say what works to get the outcome they want, and care little whether it's true or not. To many (this author included), this serves as a relatively fair description of many modern political campaigns."[1] Evan Davis notes that the term "post-truth" arose out of a deep frustration with the political events of 2016 and "came to refer to a number of different things; the liberals' use of the phrase was obviously fueled by Donald Trump's election campaign, but that was just a small part of it. In the United Kingdom's EU referendum campaign, both sides were said to have used extreme exaggeration or direct falsehood in order to draw attention to the issues that favored their side of the argument."[2] Matthew d'Ancona similarly remarks that post-truth politics constitutes "the triumph of the visceral over the rational, the deceptively simple over the honestly complex."[3] It is a discourse in which thoughtful inquiry into public policy questions is replaced by statements that are strategically oriented, often knowingly false, and calculated to capture attention.

By far the main example of the phenomenon each of these authors notes is rhetoric from politicians, while also mentioning corporate-funded research, marketing material, and the pseudo-connections of social media. Much lower on the list is media spin and bombast—which they quickly justify on the grounds that news organizations must do this to get attention. Sober reflection does not draw viewers or sell newspapers, and traditional outlets are struggling to compete in the current environment. Journalism is not the problem but the solution—if it is allowed to uphold its ideals. Davis, for instance, maintains that "the much-maligned mainstream media" is a victim of post-truth rather than a perpetrator and ought to react to the onslaught by "simply do[ing] its job with the usual rigour and set out the facts as it always would." When it commits factual errors, "as it inevitably will from time to time," it should simply admit its mistake and not be intimidated by politicians.[4] Ball echoes the sentiment, albeit on a less optimistic note: "Earnest media outlets . . . simply cannot keep up with the onslaught, especially given their bone-deep habit of trying to give a hearing to both sides of a political argument."[5] Journalism's commitment to fair-mindedness and balanced reporting, he worries, is now hampering its ability to vet politicians' statements. D'Ancona strikes a more optimistic note while echoing the view that journalism is the solution and not the problem. Where the aim of populist politicians is to simplify and mislead, "the task of journalism is to reveal the complexity, nuance and paradox of public life, as well as to ferret out wrongdoing and, most important of all, to water the roots of democracy with a steady supply of reliable news." The same author maintains that the roots of the post-truth phenomenon lie in neither journalism nor even politics but in philosophy, and postmodern thought in particular: "No less than any other age, the Post-Truth era has its own intellectual geology—a basis in the postmodern philosophy of the late twentieth century, often abstruse and impenetrable, that has been popularized and distilled to the point that it is recognizable—albeit without attribution—in many features of contemporary culture. As esoteric as much of it may seem, it is worth persevering with this line of inquiry. It is impossible to fight Post-Truth without an understanding of its deepest roots."[6] There follows a section of four and a half pages in which d'Ancona trots out several standard misconceptions of postmodern philosophy and exhibits no understanding whatever of the thinkers he briefly cites.

While it is not my intention to reject this analysis in its entirety, the journalists I have cited have missed a few points that pertain to the implication of this profession as well as the technology on which it relies in the phenomenon of which they are speaking. There is a long-standing tendency among political reporters in particular to don a vestment of neutrality, a dedication to a "just the facts" approach to whatever story they are covering and a good-faith openness to hear and report on whatever the relevant parties are doing without deteriorating into partisanship, be it overt or covert. It is inscribed in their expressions and carefully watched over by editors and producers ever anxious to avoid the dreaded accusation of activism, manipulation, or, worst of all, indoctrination. Equal time for liberals, conservatives, and any other group that claims a sizable portion of the electorate is a basic principle, and if at times it resembles a fig leaf, then other journalists will quickly intervene in a display of professional integrity and often some sanctimony. Think of how Fox News, to take an obvious example, is regularly castigated for conservative partisanship by its network competitors. How do matters stand with the latter? The following is anecdotal but not atypical: as I write this, the website of CNN features approximately 90 headlines on its main page, covering everything from politics to world events, entertainment, sports, and so on, 37 of which pertain directly or indirectly to the current president of the United States and nearly all of which mention him by name. I do not have time on this day, or any other, to read the 37 stories. I have, however, read the headlines, and of the 37, those that intimate in no uncertain terms that their authors would have very much preferred that the candidate of the other party had won the last presidential election number precisely 37, a matter that may be confirmed by tuning into this network at any time of the day or night since the election just mentioned and indeed for several months prior. It is not letting the cat out of the bag to say that those pulling the strings at CNN were not pleased with the election result of November 2016.

Why the fig leaf? Is some vestige of positivism still exercising a hold on mainstream journalism, a commitment to at least the appearance of value neutrality, even if it is belied in nearly every instance? The liberal and conservative press both do this, and the exceptions are few and getting fewer. This is not simply an American phenomenon. The situation is much the same in other Western nations, including my own. In Canada, the CBC has long insisted that it is politically neutral and, of course, it is nothing of the kind and never has been. It has long inclined toward the moderate left, and while it is owned by the federal government, its journalists invariably employ that great term of derision, "state-owned," whenever referencing broadcasters in authoritarian regimes. North Korea's KCNA is perhaps the most notorious of this lot at present, enjoying no journalistic autonomy whatever and being beholden to a party line. Does MSNBC have a party line? It is not state-owned, it is true, but does it matter if what one cares about is reporting that is factual, unbiased, or, if this is too much to ask, fair-minded?

It takes no great hermeneut of suspicion to see that there is more than a little untruth at work here, of which the veneer of nonpartisanship is only one clear instance. It is curious that the aforementioned journalists do not mention this except in passing. It appears to be a triviality to their way of thinking. Post-truth is a phenomenon involving politicians, corporations, and any number of others, not the news media. Should one ask, why so much suspicion over here and so little over there? one will receive no answer but for the following: readers and viewers of the news both know and accept that journalists are political advocates of a kind, but this is nothing to worry about so long as it is restrained and balanced with equal time for the other side.

Bad faith is the lie one tells not to others but to oneself, and what the journalistic profession or a sizable portion of it has been telling itself for decades is that this breed of professionals is above the fray of partisanship and that whatever political content its utterances may contain is in the usual course of things limited to reporting and analyzing information with no attempt at anything resembling activism. Serious journalism deals with facts, not values. It tows no party line. Anyone who believes this is invited to spend five minutes reading a newspaper or watching virtually any political news program on virtually any television network while actually paying attention. To say that much of it is biased is more than an understatement. It is a lie, but what is curious about it is how many journalists themselves appear to believe it. When I was a student in Catholic schools, the priests and nuns would sometimes teach us about other religions; their intention, they said, was to inform. Of course, their intention was nothing of the kind, and as best I can recall all the students knew it. It was to mind their flock, and I am reminded of this every time I open a newspaper or watch some panel of experts analyze the daily news. Some are given the title of commentator, others reporter, anchor, moderator, or what have you, but these are distinctions without a difference. If truth is what one has tuned in to see, one had better turn to the sports channel.

What political journalism, or the lion's share of it, is implicated in is not only advocacy but something still more insidious. This is an order of discourse in which information, entertainment, advertising, gossip, persuasion, stimulation, and manipulation are elided entirely and which often go by the name of "perception," a term that when spoken of by the press typically means appearance with an intimation of falsity. Perceptions may be accurate or inaccurate, but when journalists say they are in the perception business they mean that what matters is how things appear ("optics") rather than how they are. If one is clever, one can make just about anything appear any way one wishes. If one wishes to portray a politician as racist, for instance, one may—or the opposite, as one likes—and competent journalists fully understand this. It is they who decide how a public figure will be perceived, where this means both known and judged. The perennial wisdom has long been that it is suicidal for politicians to speak ill of the press since the latter always has the last word in the business of public perception and perhaps is even entitled to this. The palpable indignation President Trump's electoral victory inspired among journalists is, I suspect, due far less to anything this man has done than to the possibility that for the first time in recent memory American voters appear beyond the command of media opinion-makers and despite efforts that can deteriorate into the extreme. (As I write this, for example—and the examples are far too plentiful to document—a major American network is standing by with reporters and a camera crew outside a venue where their president is giving a speech. They are there, as they have done many times in the past, to cover not the speech—to this they appear perfectly indifferent—but any street fights that might erupt between protesters and supporters of this president. To their evident frustration, they did not.)

It is well known that changes in communication technology have meant that many voters now receive information and ideas from a larger variety of sources than in the days of Walter Cronkite, and traditional news outlets are seeing their hold on the public mind diminishing, a phenomenon that in itself is likely to the good. In response, and ever mindful of their bottom line, traditional news has shaded ever more into entertainment, sensationalism, and uncivility on the premise that shouting draws more attention than reflection, as it surely does. It is now commonplace, for instance, for some incident, however commonplace, to be deemed newsworthy for the sole reason that it is accompanied by camera footage that is visually compelling and preferably shocking. Unparliamentary language makes headlines while carefully reasoned argumentation is deemed unnewsworthy. Loud protests to the contrary notwithstanding, the primary aim of this business is not to inform but to compete for attention amid the general cacophony, and an attention that has been increasingly monetized. Once something is monetized—virtually anything, from information to education and democracy itself—it is corrupted, downgraded to a means where formerly it was at least potentially an end. Political journalism and quite possibly politics itself now stand in this condition, clinging to ideals of old, disingenuously for the most part, while transforming into the opposite. Shock journalism, infotainment, and what a former American president called "the politics of personal destruction" now hold center stage, and if honest reporting of the old school still exists, it is far from the norm.

To describe mainstream political news coverage as fake is simplistic. What appears to be taking place, and ever more so, is not that plain deception has replaced truthfulness but something far more subtle. There is no need to attribute bad intentions to the great majority of journalists. Bad faith is a form of untruth, but there is more self-deception at work here than any overt lying to an audience. Journalists are citizens, political beings whose values and opinions cannot be bracketed from their interpretations. Expecting complete value neutrality is pointless for the simple reason that it is impossible to bracket one's personal convictions entirely in analyzing or even describing the events of the day. A liberal will not only judge but recount what the government is doing from the standpoint of what a liberal cares about and notices. The capacity for attention itself is highly selective, and what any of us attends to reflects what one believes and values. The issue lies not here but in the pretense of objectivity and neutrality. News organizations try to ensure that their coverage is palatable to a general audience. There are exceptions to this, of course, but the more reputable and mainstream television networks and newspapers routinely claim that they are beholden to no political party or special interest, and this claim is manifestly untrue. If it is a breach of the journalist's code to confess any outright political affiliation, their methods of indirect communication make this a moot point.

The purpose of the reporting here is not to report but to bring the audience around to the journalists' or their employer's opinions, as much of their viewership knows, while feigning professional neutrality. It is emphatically not to provide information for their viewers' reflection or even to do their thinking for them but to provide a substitute for reflection. To stimulate, entertain, bombard, gain, and hold attention is the name of the game while mobilizing action. By the middle of the 20th century, French existentialist

Gabriel Marcel was already commenting on "this state of partial insensibil-ity," which new technology of mass communication was ushering onto the scene. As he remarked, "Seeking to avoid any rash generalizations, I think we can nevertheless say this about our contemporary world. There are to-day [1952] an increasing number of people whose awareness is, in the strict sense of the phrase, without a focus; and the techniques which have transformed the framework of daily life for such people at such a prodigious pace—I am thinking particularly of the cinema and the radio—are making a most pow-erful contribution towards this defocalizing process." If the capacity of awareness had long acquired its basic orientation in intimate proximity to particular objects and persons, as Marcel believed, "this feeling of intimacy," which under normal conditions "tends to create a focus for human aware-ness," had begun to dissolve in the rage for technique that was sweeping the world. The steamroller that was passing over us, it seemed to him (as to a great many other existential phenomenologists), was technology itself, of which the news media was but one manifestation. His denunciation of the popular press was grounded on what he saw as a pronounced and inevitable "bias against reflection, against reflection of every type." The pseudo-reflection that is "reporting" to a mass audience via mass technology amounts to a purely "mechanical method of diffusing thought which almost inevitably degrades whatever message men are seeking to diffuse."[7] The medium "is" not the message but cheapens it by creating an atmosphere that is antitheti-cal to thinking, that pushes us along in the interim between commercials in a direction that is determined in advance.

The concept of propaganda here comes to the fore. It seemed to Marcel that "there is a close kinship between propaganda and . . . techniques of deg-radation," where what was being degraded was not only ideas but freedom and nothing less than our humanity itself. His diagnosis was startling and exaggerated in places, but that a text like *Man against Mass Society* was alive to a phenomenon both centuries in the making and utterly contemporary is undeniable. To someone lacking historical knowledge, post-truth is new, unprecedented, and analyzable without relation to what is happening in the culture in a larger sense. It no more appeared from out of the blue than the mid-20th-century propaganda of which Marcel was speaking. Both are signs of the times, and to speak of them as two is already inaccurate. Propaganda, as he spoke of it, is a technology of ideas, "a method not of persuasion but of seduction," whether for money, power, or both, the "manipulation of opin-ion" that the mass media effect is made possible by technology while also being its natural consequence.[8] How might a serious political thinker articu-late an idea of even minor complexity on Twitter? The reply that should be obvious, but may no longer be, is that he or she cannot, that what the tech-nology calls forth and allows are micro-thoughts only, trivialities one might say, but trivialities that become a cacophony and a monopoly. Today a

"Twitter storm" is hard news and is treated by news organizations with the same seriousness as a State of the Union Address likely because it is immediate and instantly consumable and calls for little to no thought by journalists and audience alike. Unlike a text such as the present volume, it may be digested in the time it takes to eat a peanut and is about as difficult. Peanuts have their place in a balanced diet, but fine dining they are not, and an exclusive diet of them is unhealthy. The same is true of the great majority of news stories that command, hold, or even allow concentrated attention for an instant before passing on to what else there is. This "what else" phenomenon of our time can look like curiosity but is its opposite. It is a kind of pseudo-reflection that is more psychological than intellectual and that effectively banishes the latter. Many who now think themselves politically astute, journalists included, know what the president tweeted five minutes ago and have never heard of Rousseau or Mill.

Let me take this opportunity to express no opinion whatsoever on either Brexit or President Trump. On both I shall take a pass. My topic is post-truth in the news media, and my hypothesis is that putting members of this profession, however well intentioned they may be, in charge of political truth, as many claim as a kind of right, may be compared to putting a coyote in charge of a henhouse. It is imprudent, for much the same reasons, and we can say this without casting aspersions on coyotes or their motives. They too must eat, and to their credit they appear to do so without a hint of bad faith and without even uttering the word "truth." Journalists have a job to do, which involves pleasing superiors, courting advertisers, forming perceptions, leading the horse to water, and being selectively accurate. Let us not overstate matters: they are not con artists or plain liars, and attributing bad intentions is in the majority of instances out of order. What can be said is that the American election campaign of 2016 saw journalists from all or nearly all major news organizations practicing a covert—sometimes overt—activism, largely on behalf of a candidate who did not win, that since that time they have daily castigated voters and their president while exercising the full extent of their power to ensure a different result next time, and that this phenomenon is unusual only in its level of transparency. The fig leaf usually stays on.

Seduction is not a lie, or not usually. Even when it crosses boundaries of ethics or professionalism, it works not by being fake but by being selectively true, and where the principle of selection is whatever is effective in bringing an audience into a particular state of belief and, better, emotion, one that is likely to mobilize action in a desired direction. It is a manipulation that does not know itself as such since the lie it tells is both a partial presentation of the truth and an example of bad faith far more than simple deception. It is mendacity with a clear conscience, a crusader in its mind for what is good and true, and that usually imagines it is resisting an enemy. Short on subtlety, "effective propaganda," as Marcel further noted, "is a matter of reconnoitering and exploiting as skillfully as possible the weaknesses of the enemy's position, while at the same time as little as possible giving the enemy the feeling that he is an enemy, that one is fighting him."[9] The press is not fighting President Trump, they tell us; they are investigating, vetting claims, fact-checking, and speaking the truth to power. Every reporter is a Woodward and a Bernstein, and every politician (or most of them) a Nixon.

Shortly following the publication of Marcel's *Man against Mass Society* came Jacques Ellul's *The Technological Society* (1954) and *Propaganda* (1965), both of which continue a similar line of thought the contemporary relevance of which is plain to see. Ellul's analysis of propaganda is especially germane here. While writing in the context of the Cold War, he pointed out that propaganda "has become a very general phenomenon in the modern world. Differences in political regimes matter little." It is not only authoritarian states, or states of any kind, that engage in it. "Whatever the diversity of countries and methods, they have one characteristic in common: concern with effectiveness. Propaganda is made, first of all, because of a will to action, for the purpose of effectively arming policy and giving irresistible power to its decisions. Whoever handles this instrument can be concerned solely with effectiveness. This is the supreme law. . . . This instrument belongs to the technological universe, shares its characteristics, and is indissolubly linked to it." Propaganda must be grasped together not with any particular ideology but with technology, and indeed it is a technology. It is a technique of mobilizing populations to act as the controllers of the instrument desire, not merely manipulating minds but doing so with an end in view. "The aim of modern propaganda is no longer to modify ideas, but to provoke action. It is no longer to change adherence to a doctrine, but to make the individual cling irrationally to a process of action. It is no longer to lead to a choice, but to loosen the reflexes. It is no longer to transform an opinion, but to arouse an active and mythical belief."[10]

Key to his analysis is a distinction Ellul drew between vertical and horizontal propaganda, where the former connotes a technique of psychological manipulation on the part of an agency of one kind or another. Vertical propaganda "comes from above" and conforms to the popular conception of the word as something exercised by leaders, usually the state, who abuse their authority by pulling, or attempting to pull, the wool down over the eyes of the masses. Classical Soviet and Fascist propaganda come to mind here. It seeks a monopoly on ideas and centralizes and controls information to the full extent of its power. To work it requires a collective passivity of both action and thought.

Propaganda of the second kind is more insidious and "can be called horizontal because it is made *inside* the group (not from the top), where, in principle, all individuals are equal and there is no leader. The individual makes contact with others at his own level rather than with a leader; such propaganda therefore always seeks 'conscious adherence.' Its content is presented in didactic fashion and addressed to the intelligence. The leader, the propagandist, is there only as a sort of *animator* or discussion leader; sometimes his presence and his identity are not even known." It is a group phenomenon in which the continuing adherence of the individual is gained through constant reassurance that the world he or she seeks requires a conformity of mind which does not call itself conformity but some iteration of the chosen. Every person is mobilized to keep watch over his or her peers and to spread the word, remain vigilant, and not lose sight of an enemy that is always at the gate. The party line that sets in is nothing to worry about for the only alternative is the devil in one of his cunning disguises. "The individual participates actively in the life of this group, in a genuine and living dialogue. . . . Only in speaking will the individual gradually discover his own convictions (which also will be those of the group), become irrevocably involved, and help others to form their opinions (which are identical). . . . Progress is slow; there must be many meetings . . . so that a common experience can be shared."[11]

Horizontal propaganda is far more pervasive in our time than vertical and is a commonplace of political journalism as of politics generally, including in the universities where it is better concealed but no less prevalent. The "meticulous encirclement of everybody" that it brings about "is peculiarly a system that seems to coincide perfectly with egalitarian societies claiming to be based on the will of the people and calling themselves democratic." It bears an intimate relation to information, which it does not withhold but selects and interprets with an eye to repetition and reassurance that what we believed yesterday remains true today. It not only imparts information but bombards us with an endless supply of it, all prepackaged for ready consumption. Such facts do not call for reflection or even allow for it. The aim is not to inform (or not as an end) but to encircle, reassure, and mobilize action. As Ellul noted, one "must not be allowed a moment of meditation or reflection in which to see himself vis-à-vis the propagandist, as happens when the propaganda is not continuous. At that moment the individual emerges from the grip of propaganda. Instead, successful propaganda will occupy every moment of the individual's life. . . . The individual must not be allowed to recover, to collect himself, to remain untouched by propaganda during any relatively long period, for propaganda is . . . based on slow, constant impregnation."[12]

The relevance of this to news media was not lost on Ellul. "Without the mass media there can be no modern propaganda," he maintained, and it is particularly effective when centralized in as few hands as possible. Group allegiance is enforced by means of technology of information and communication that has the effect of minding the flock, maintaining boundaries of inside and outside, and creating a mass mentality. The readership of a newspaper comes to resemble the membership of a party or the congregation of a church, and the daily ritual of reading its stories and editorials provides reassurance about what is happening and that our side knows the truth. "Those who read the press of their group and listen to the radio of their group are constantly reinforced in their allegiance. They learn more and more that their group is right, that its actions are justified; thus their beliefs are strengthened. At the same time, such propaganda contains elements of criticism and refutation of other groups, which will never be read or heard by a member of another group."[13] Liberals no more watch Fox News than conservatives watch CNN or Buddhists attend church. News organizations compete by playing on existing divisions within a population, deepening and monetizing them more effectively than any political party, and often while lamenting the very divisions that they foster. The general tone of alarm, indignation, and recrimination on which they rely as a marketing tool becomes inseparable from the information they impart, and ostensible distinctions between hard news, editorials, commentaries, and advertisements are an illusion.

For Ellul, information and communication technology was but one manifestation of the steamroller that is modern technique, by which he meant "the *totality of methods rationally arrived at and having absolute efficiency* . . . in *every* field of human activity." No respite is permitted from a technology the watchwords of which are efficiency, effectiveness, adaptation, outcomes, procedures, and order. "Technical activity automatically eliminates every nontechnical activity or transforms it into a technical activity," and the news media are no exception.[14] The content of communication is not fake but is inseparable from the form, and the form is determined by requirements of efficiency and profitability.

Any journalist, perhaps anyone else, who has read this chapter to the end is likely to suspect its author of being a closet supporter of President Trump given the line of critique I have advanced and other critiques that I have not advanced. Let me change my mind, then, and declare on the record that I am not now, nor have I ever been, a member of the Republican Party, the "alt right," or a Trump supporter. Being Canadian, I do not get a vote in American elections, am pleased to be living in the land of Trudeau (even if The Younger), and have come to regard political extremes of all kinds as about equally dangerous. I incline toward a form of individualism but do not care for politicians who make the same claim; I suspect they are trying to sell me on a religion, or guns. The center lane may be uninspired, but after a few centuries of experimentation in democracy or what has passed for it, it would appear that inspiration is a value best sought in private life and that any politics that quickens the pulse also meets a bad end. The center prizes civility over ideology, compromise over hyperpartisanship, and is despised by the doctrinaire of both the left and the right. It speaks slowly, if at all, of political truth and finds it in a democratic discourse that is negotiated, rhetorical, agonistic, multifarious, partisan, interpretive, at times imaginative, and always inseparable from "perception" and the will to power. It is not a rationalist's tea party. From its ancient inception, democracy in its numerous iterations has never lacked a shadow of which both ancient and modern political theorists have been well aware. A politics that holds out a promise of equal freedom invariably includes no little sophistry, alienation, resentment, and self-seeking and has from the beginning. Understanding democracy requires grasping together two ideas that are contradictory in principle and inseparable in practice, the struggle between which is fundamental to our form of democracy and every other: truth and untruth, rationality and irrationality existing side by side. Struggle is of the essence of politics, and democratic politicians from the best to the worst have always been strategically oriented far more than they are truth seekers. The same is now true of the great majority of political journalists.

Notes

1. James Ball, *Post-Truth: How Bullshit Conquered the World* (London: Biteback Publishing, 2017), Kindle edition, no page numbers.

2. Evan Davis, *Post-Truth: Why We Have Reached Peak Bullshit and What We Can Do about It* (London: Little, Brown Book Group, 2017), p. xii.

3. Matthew d'Ancona, *Post-Truth: The New War on Truth and How to Fight Back* (London: Ebury Press, 2017), p. 20.

4. Davis, *Post-Truth,* 289–90.

5. Ball, *Post-Truth.*

6. d'Ancona, *Post-Truth,* pp. 40, 91.

7. Gabriel Marcel, *Man against Mass Society,* trans. G. S. Fraser (South Bend, IN: St. Augustine's Press, 2008), pp. 40, 109, 119.

8. Ibid., 36, 39.

9. Ibid., 38.

10. Jacques Ellul, *Propaganda: The Formation of Men's Attitudes,* trans. K. Kellen and J. Lerner (New York: Vintage Books, 1973), pp. ix–x, 25.

11. Ibid., 80, 81.

12. Ibid., 17, 84.

13. Ibid., 102, 213.

14. Jacques Ellul, *The Technological Society,* trans. J. Wilkinson (New York: Vintage Books, 1964), pp. xxv, 83.

CHAPTER ELEVEN

Losing the Feel for Truth in Post-Truth "Democracies": When Macro Data Harvesting and Micro-Targeting Befuddle Democratic Thought

Chris Beeman

Truth has historically been something we develop a feel for or skill in, that we get good at knowing, and the feeling of what is true and what is not is something we come to know over time. But when the stuff of which we are made of is known better by computer algorithms than by ourselves, our grip on what is true becomes more tenuous; if we cannot check truth against the world and against our own better sense, where can it be found? When the "we" that is ourselves is "understood" better by sophisticated programs that can compare, say, a change in predilection for soccer over football over a 10-year period of our lives, then the computer has a kind of privileged insight into what is true for us. While we might, if asked, still endorse football, the information available through our likes, our browsing history, and our tweets say otherwise. In this case, the latent past, and perhaps its subtle effect on the present, is better comprehended in the *now* that we know by programs that can simultaneously know the *then*. The truth we feel at present is only a moment in time; if the previous truths we knew can be compared—and used—against this one, in ways that we humans cannot possibly understand, then we become vulnerable to manipulation by sophisticated algorithms that stretch and weave latent preferences to offer tapestries of the future that seem to us, well, surprisingly attractive: almost as if we had designed them ourselves. And, of course, we have. We just don't store that kind of information and we therefore do not know we designed them. And because we don't, we are vulnerable to those, and those *its,* that do.

What Is True?

In a chapter to do with post-truth—normally defined as assertions that feel true but that have no basis in fact—a little broad background on truth is apropos. This definition, after all, presupposes that we do know what facts are. Generally, when most people think of truth, we mean something like what philosophers refer to as a correspondence theory of truth. By this is meant, broadly, that what we think about the world corresponds to the way the world actually is. Something is true when the world and our beliefs about it are in agreement. So, to say "it is true that the grass I see outside my window is green" is to make a claim about the correspondence between my observation and a quality of the grass I see. In the 18th century, Immanuel Kant disrupted this prima facie straightforward notion by pointing out that both what we thought about it and what we observed going on in it were governed by our perceptions: my cognizing what is true and my cognizing the object about which my cognizing is true are both products of my thinking. Kant's criticism retains its force today: that if this theory alone is employed, we are using the same means to check for correspondence as we were employing to come up with theories about it.

Recent minimalist or deflationary theories around truth have pointed out that truth has historically been treated as a quality or an ideal. They suggest that it is more accurately thought of as a kind of stamp that reinforces the statement made in the claim. In this sense, claiming something is true does not add anything new to a claim. It just restates the claim more emphatically and draws attention to the fact that a claim is being made. In the aforementioned case, it would be simpler to say that the grass I see outside my window is green, so I might as well just say so. If I happened to mention the green grass during an August drought, this might be an example of post-truth. And, of course, the most well-known figure in a post-truth world is Donald Trump, whose modus operandi is to not merely state post-truths but exaggerate them, making, as it were, post-post-truths of them.

To this end, recent theories around truth have also invoked the significance of language around correspondence claims, pointing out that language, as the vehicle for communicating ideas about truth, to some extent must shape truth. Yet, whatever might be the influence of language, correspondence theories about truth also must presuppose something about the world: that there is some objectively knowable thing out there about which claims can be made.

Later theorists, such as the American pragmatists Peirce, Dewey, and James, suggested that truth be approached, not by aiming for perfect correspondence with the world, which would be impossible, but with something like an attempt to establish progressively more accurate reliability tested over time. For Peirce, what was true was what people would find out about something if the inquiry were to go as far as it could, within limits of usefulness. This idea tended to move the emphasis of the idea of truth as something like a quality inherent or not in things to something like a process of interpretation of the world that involved both perceiver and perception. Still later, Michel Foucault attempted not to use the term at all, preferring instead "Regimes of Truth," which emphasized the power structures within which truth operated. Others think of truth as something like a shorthand to show preference for one view over another. But in all cases noted, there is something being considered that has to do with the way the world is and one's beliefs about it.

There is clearly some value in being able to perceive something going on in the world in ways that correspond to what is going on in the world. My ability to know that the wildebeest is here and not there, and to predict its next position at exactly the moment when the atlatl-tossed spear will be there, might make the difference between dinner and emptiness. And my ability to spot the scant and slightly decayed surface leaf signifying the liquid-containing *bi! bulb* plant, while traveling in San territory, may mean life or death in such a desert environment. For other beings, the same principle of discerning what is from what is not applies. This is perhaps a lesser sense of truth, but the point is that there is a practical and useful element knowing roughly the difference between the two is probably linked to a species' survival.

There is also so much that is not agreed on around what is true. For the purpose of this chapter, I will be speaking about what is true in the everyday, correspondence sense. That is, that for something to be true, there has to be a correspondence between what we think about the world and what is going on in the world. While this might seem antiquated, it turns out that even professional philosophers still mostly adhere to correspondence theories of truth. In a 2009 survey of professional philosophers, 45 percent of respondents (3,226 total, including 1,803 philosophy faculty members and/or PhDs and 829 philosophy graduate students) accept or lean toward correspondence theories, 21 percent toward deflationary, and 14 percent toward epistemic.[1]

And surely this kind of meaning of truth is at the heart of what is at stake in a post-truth world. When we are simply living our lives, it matters whether there actually are weapons of mass destruction being stored for use under an unpredictable dictatorship. The narratives around this are also important because of what these say about power relations and how relationships can affect, say, the *use* of these weapons. But knowledge about whether destructive weapons actually are in the world is important—as much in the case of what have hitherto been regarded as "safe" states and those not—and this is one sense of truth that appears to be going missing in a post-truth world.

Chilling CPUs

This idea was brought home to me recently when I read an article reprinted in the *Guardian Weekly,* originally printed in the *Observer.* It was Carole Cadwalladr's work, entitled "Did Big Data Tip It for Brexit?"[2] Cadwalladr's research traces how big data and micro-targeting of individual electors played a role in Trump's campaign and election in 2016 and in the Brexit referendum (to determine if the United Kingdom would continue its membership in the European Union) in 2017. Cadwalladr's concern is the immediate threat to democracy. I share this concern. But I think the danger goes deeper than this and has to do with human identity and the central role that something like a feel for truth can play in that identity. A little summary of Cadwalladr's story is needed to set the stage for this bigger claim.

According to Cadwalladr, a firm called Cambridge Analytica (previously SCL Elections), based in London, is at the heart of concerns over both the "yes" vote in the Brexit referendum and Trump's election. She interviews several people connected with the firm. One describes its use of psychological warfare techniques, or psychological operations, *psyops* for short, in its work in the Brexit campaign and in the American presidential election of 2016. These are the same methods used to effect mass change of sentiment in civilian populations by military interests. Cadwalladr's source claims that Cambridge Analytica has used these techniques in many countries of the global south. But this firm used the same patterns of effecting sentiment change and applied them in the United Kingdom, on its own citizens. Expertise in psyops was coupled with the use of big data, made possible through its legal sale by companies like Facebook. Cadwalladr goes to some length to show the interconnection between major world players, including the U.S. billionaire Mercer, and others in what appears to be an attempt to influence the ways in which democracies function. Two investigations on the illegal use of information and the possible breaking of UK electoral laws are under way. But the big three strands to the story from Cadwalladr's perspective are as follows:

How the foundations of an authoritarian surveillance state are being laid in the US. How British democracy was subverted through a covert, far-reaching plan of coordination enabled by a US billionaire. And how we are in the midst of a massive land grab for power by billionaires via our data. Data which is being silently amassed, harvested and stored. Whoever owns this data owns the future.[3]

While the scope of this movement is made clear by the interests of major players in it, what most interests me in this chapter is the last point: the very pressing interest of billionaires in our data. After all, why should they be so interested? And if a citizen has done nothing wrong, why should they be concerned with its use? After all, they are just going to use this information to target us with a few products, aren't they?

As it turns out, Cadwalladr links the first two points, and especially, of the two, the second—the subversion of British democracy—to the third. That is, the problem with the amassing of data is how it can be used. The bet these billionaire investors are making is likely to be a good one. There is no reason to think that they, who have been so successful in past investments in the Web, computer, data, and knowledge-based businesses, are wrong. The problem with the amassing data—and then using it back on the very people who gave it up in the first place, but in new and creative ways—is that we citizens lose our capacity to choose a candidate, using reason. We lose this, because what allows us to have some confidence in the true-ness of our ideas—in philosophical terms, the accuracy of our propositions—has been compromised. And this is because the mass accumulation of big data, combined with the micro-targeting (at the level of the individual voter) of information at precisely the right instant, is a more powerful influence on us than our reason alone.

Allow me to give a more precise explanation of the process, which is the pattern that Cadwalladr traces: in the case at hand, Cambridge Analytica legally buys information from Facebook. (Groundbreaking work was done at the University of Cambridge a few years ago that showed how simple Facebook "likes" about apparently unrelated issues could be used to correctly discern voter preferences, such as sexuality.) Cambridge Analytica then matches profiles—presumably including things about persons that they do not know themselves, made up of untold billions of bits of information about millions of prospective voters—to individuals and to their contact information. (David Carroll, professor at the Parsons School in New York City, in an interview with the CBC's *Day 6,* just as this is going to press, has suggested that the key to the effectiveness of this technique in psychological manipulation is to link data about consumer and personal information to data about existing voting preference.)[4] In the few days before a presidential election vote—or perhaps a referendum on Brexit—individuals are targeted with multiple advertisements on different platforms, based on their profile. As one of Cadwalladr's sources says, "The goal is to capture every single aspect of a voter's information environment. . . . And the personality data enabled Cambridge Analytica to craft individual messages."[5]

This is the method used to infiltrate democratic processes by what has been called "disinformation."[6] This is at the heart of psyops. But now psyops has a new and powerful ally: big data. The particular way in which an individual voter will be targeted is reliably determined by that voter's completely accessible profile, made up of almost infinitely many bits of information, provided at low cost through the Web. A central principle of psyops is that the person to be manipulated has vulnerabilities, and these can be easily discerned from what the person provides through Facebook, Twitter, and other social media. As Tamsin Shaw, associate professor of philosophy at New York University, quoted in Cadwalladr's article says,

> The capacity for this science to be used to manipulate emotions is very well established. This is military-funded technology that has been harnessed by a global plutocracy and is being used to sway elections in ways that people can't even see, don't even realize is happening to them. . . . It's about exploiting existing phenomenon like nationalism and then using it to manipulate people at the margins.[7]

From an academic perspective, the research shows that psyops works. But what about from the perspective of the billionaire actors in this scenario? One ex-employee of Cambridge Analytica claims:

> It's not a political consultancy. . . . You have to understand this is not a normal company in any way. I don't think Mercer even cares if it ever makes any money. It's the product of a billionaire spending huge amounts of money to build his own experimental science lab, to test what works, to find tiny slivers of influence that can tip an election. . . . This is one of the smartest computer scientists in the world. He is not going to splash $15m on bullshit.[8]

Let us assume that this billionaire is, with very savvy judgment indeed, investing his money. He does not want to make immediate profit. What he wants is to own the information that runs the show, where the show is the ways in which individual and large-scale decisions are made, not just by governments but by individual citizens. If this multiplicity of codes is broken, if the ways in which decisions are made, and the bases for these are known, then the need to sell post-truths is not an issue: post-truths will be the only thing that seem true to such a citizen.

And here is the key, as I see it, and the relevance to the idea of truth. The idea that we are always reasoning beings, operating in reasonable ways, is so far from accurate that we are vulnerable to the misuse of the truth that actually surrounds this myth. If something could know, simply by examining the residue of who we are as evidenced by the trail of information we leave behind us thousands of times a day as we update profiles, post tweets, visit preferred sites, and express likes and dislikes, then we are known better than we know ourselves. It is akin to the scent a wolf leaves in each of its prints on a trail, to alert others of its presence. Only, it knows it is doing this.

There is a well-known phenomenon that occurs when people fill out questionnaires. It is called "social desirability bias." The term means that we try to portray ourselves in a favorable light, in any given context. Therefore, the stories we tell about ourselves tend to be ones that make us better than we are. Oftentimes, we ourselves do not even know that we are lying when we do so. (That is why more sophisticated surveys include questions, the most likely answers to which for persons simply trying to improve their image are mutually contradictory.) But if something did know when we were lying, then it would know us better than we knew ourselves. And if it did so, we could be vulnerable to being controlled in ways we could little imagine and much less understand.

And Where's the Love?

Imagine that a very smart program is developed that will choose your ideal mate. I do not mean one using the algorithms that are now in play; I mean one that actually will choose your ideal mate with a far greater likelihood of success than you or any other person could. Everything that is knowable that you know about yourself and everything that is knowable that you do not know about yourself will be brought into the equation. And let's say you go along with this: you agree to be part of this procedure. You come to know the eight finalists. You spend time with each of them and the computer algorithm further refines its choices. But when the final call is made, the person chosen for you is not the one you had expected or intended, or indeed hoped for. How you felt you got along with this person is never the same as how you got along, true. But even taking this into account, the person you chose, and not the one the algorithm did, really felt like the person was by far the best choice for you.

The question is, what are you going to do about it? If the kind of truth that is experienced in a decision like this one is in part based on your perceptions at the moment of decision, which are not able to be included in a program like the one proposed, then your decision ought to predominate. Therefore, what you are going to do is to act contrary to the choice of the algorithm. But, ah, I forgot to tell you. The rules are that you are permitted either to accept the computer's choice or not to be with any of the other prospective partners considered.

Most of us would find the rules too onerous. And that is the point. Preference in ballots, as in love, is able to be changed and sometimes has to be changed, last minute, often in response to factors we do not understand or, perhaps, even know. And this ability to choose something and to change one's mind, based on one's moment-by-moment change of perceptions around truth, is what is at the heart of democracies. If this were not guaranteed, we citizens would quickly revolt.

Besides, somehow this grates most of us the wrong way: we want to be wrong sometimes and to have control of our own wrong decision. The person we were that chose the wrong person is the "real" person we are. To give over this authority to a program is to abrogate responsibility in a democracy. This much is clear. But I think it is more than this: it is to also leave over decision-making to something that certainly is more capable than humans of knowing a history of our individual being, but which is ultimately out of touch with what is true for us now. Most people would recoil at the notion of a program choosing suitable partners, whatever claims corporations may make related to the efficacy of their algorithms.

And more significantly, it is the imprecision around choosing that is at the heart of democracy. That power, *-kratia,* is in the hands of the people, *demos,* to do with what they would like, is certainly dangerous—Trump was, after all, elected. That is to say, the preference we feel for good reasons at the moment of decision is not the same as the one we feel as polls are being collected. We would feel justifiably trespassed if we had to decide on a candidate for good reasons and could not change that decision because of the unfortunate wording of a rebuttal on an issue of, say, race relations, on the night before the election. So much is said in so little time.

Thus, at the heart of what constitutes democracy is also its point of vulnerability. This is the right of citizens to participate in decisions around policies and to elect representatives who will actually represent their views. This is also the point at which the delicate—and sometimes blunt force—of psyops is at work. As Cadwalladr writes:

> This is not just a story about social psychology and data analytics. It has to be understood in terms of a military contractor using military strategies on a civilian population. David Miller, a professor of sociology at Bath University and an authority in psyops and propaganda, says it is "an extraordinary scandal that this should be anywhere near a democracy. It should be clear to voters where information is coming from, and if it's not transparent or open where it's coming from, it raises the question of whether we are actually living in a democracy or not."[9]

The question that is critical here is, why, for the condition of democracy to obtain, is it necessary for information to be transparent: for us to know "where information is coming from"? I think this is where the idea of truth most emphatically enters this equation, and the argument goes thus.

If we know where information is coming from, we have some chance to account for its effect on us. We are often aware of circumstances in which we are vulnerable and know we are, because it has happened before to us, say to be influenced by outside forces that may alter our normal good sense. For example, let's say that I am capable of making informed decisions about many things in my life in a reason-based manner. But my partner—that one I married after the computer algorithm described earlier said she would be just my second best choice (I broke the rules)—knows that I am much more likely to say "yes" to an idea I would otherwise be reluctant to agree to, after a good game of chess. And even though I know this is coming, even though I know and regret that I have been put in this position before, even though I think this thought at the moment the chess board comes out, and even though I say this to my partner, I am still vulnerable to being manipulated once that chess game is done. (I really should have gone with the number one choice of that algorithm.) In this case, it is not just that I am easy to manipulate: that option is covered by the fact that I know this is coming. It is that I am in a different position and that I receive information differently and accede to requests differently after a chess game.

But once this has happened many times, I might just say "no" in advance to any request made after a chess game. This means that even if I am targeted in ways over which I have virtually no control, I may still be protected from harm. I am, as it were, accounting for my own biases and vulnerabilities by using self-knowledge to protect me, knowing that there are ways I can be manipulated over which I have no control—in the moment of manipulation. In other words, when I understand where information comes from, in my determination of what is true in that moment, I am able to account for my own vulnerabilities and to get closer to the heart of what is true than what is not. Recall the pragmatist preoccupation, not with absolute truth, but with ever-more-accurate approximations in an always "good enough" understanding.

It is the same with the micro-targeting of the enormous bathtub-sized vessels of facts at the disposal of the manipulators of what had hitherto been democratic elections. Pulling out embarrassing facts relevant to politicians is nothing new to American-style politics. But the targeting of individual voters with what exactly corresponds in their case to the most vulnerable points of manipulation—because that knowledge is often invisible to the voters themselves, using psychological warfare techniques—the moment after my game of chess is done, as it were—is new. And it is precisely that these moments of non-reason-based decision carry so much weight in things like elections that such manipulation may pose a threat to democracy. How many people who are bigoted think of themselves as bigots?

And Back to Truth

Let us go back to some of those earlier ideas on truth. If most of us operate with a correspondence theory of truth, which is to say that we check what we think of against what the world appears to be sending us, then, as Kant rightly

showed in the 18th century, we are vulnerable at the point at which cognizing takes place. And this governs both my perception of my own thinking
and what the world appears to be presenting me. With this in mind, suppose
it is clear from the data harvesting done around my tweets and Facebook
likes that I am most concerned about the issue of safety, which is not the
response I would give, if asked. I would prefer to think myself far more an
egalitarian idealist. An election rolls around. The true thing I am looking for
is which candidate will be most likely to assure me of safety. I do not remember or even know that this is the most significant thing I am looking for in a
candidate. But the algorithm checking my likes and browsing preferences
does, and at exactly the right instant, just before the election, I am presented
with multiple versions of the same two advertisements. The first emphasizes
the secure, reliable, and time-tested record of the candidate that I am desired
to vote for on the kinds of safety that I value. The second shows the unreliable, varied, and flighty responses of the other. And none of this information
is presented in ways that I can consciously reason through. Perhaps it is
through images of people being assaulted. Or, if my concern over safety is
actually about traffic safety, my newsfeed suddenly features scores of articles
on recent collision in my locale. Thus, when I try to decide on what is true,
either in a conscious or unconscious way, I am forced into a certain position.
The news stories themselves are all factual. But they are arranged and orchestrated to give an impression that will, in a subconscious way, affect my choice.

And, Predictably, to Trump

Thus, the apparent inconsistent ravings of President Donald Trump could
be taken at face value as evidence of the impoverishment of democracy in the
United States. But they could also be understood as a clever tactic in a
longue-duree war against reasoned argument. In this interpretation, if Trump
and his ilk make claims that are patently untrue, but which "ring true" in the
sense of being both *factistic* (resembling what other facts appear to be) and
appealing to the prejudices of a certain body of electors, then the electorate
may get used to being fed the food that they prefer. But it is more dangerous
than this. Once they prefer the food of falsehood—easily checked but clearly
no longer necessary in the safe space of a secure democracy like America—they
come to rely on this diet. *Just tell me what you want me to think, and I will think
it. All I demand is that my worst biases and prejudices be acted out, with you as the
central dramatist, in public.*

And, of course, the benefit in coming to control a larger population is that
the kind of "being true" that is hard fought and requires substantial effort to
bring to light and to prove only counts as another opinion. *You have your
opinion; Trump has his; I have mine. We might as well just pick one. Let me see, who
is the most famous? And who is the most entertaining. I'll pick his.*

In other words, when the skill of reasoned argument is lost and entertainment replaces it, it is hard to remember what it feels like to prove something to be likely true. Ad hominem arguments are a good test of this: until only recently in Canada, ad hominems (literally, "toward the person," i.e., personal slurs) were considered bad form. Perhaps Mulroney's "You had an option, sir," an accusation made in the Canadian Federal election of 1984 against opponent John Turner and spoken with such a scathing tone that an ad hominem attack was made, brought these back into fashion.

But ad hominems are used as the primary form of argumentation in American political debate now. Somehow this is coming to be seen as a legitimate style of argumentation. And the satisfaction for a hateful electorate when hearing their opponents slammed may perhaps give a similar internal feeling to the kind of aesthetic appeal that John Dewey (that same pragmatist) described in his version of the scientific method. Both could be "felt" as true. If we lose the skill of discernment between the two, we lose the aesthetic sense that can tell us if we are on a right track or an incorrect one. Trump regularly silences reasoned argument with threats and insults. In doing so, he is schooling a portion of an electorate to think that insults that are disconnected from the point at hand are good reasons for finding the point at hand to be lacking.

The Feel of Truth

And here we are brought to the crux. If truth is something that has a feel, that we develop a skill in knowing, and that we get good at knowing, to what extent is our approaching of it—and skill at forming it—a construct of the society that we live in? After all, rhetoric was taught as a subject in ancient Rome, and an imitation of this practice was continued in England's finest universities until recently. The form of an argument could cause it to be more persuasive than the facts arranged and presented otherwise might be.

For truthfulness surely has a feel to it. When a bell *really* rings true, it does so with a clarity and deeply felt resonance that can move the spirit. This is unlike the superficial kind of ringing true that happens when a little indulgence, like a prejudice that we wish to have reaffirmed, is meted out. And truth likewise rings true. But it is this very poetic and nonmechanistic aspect to it that perhaps makes it possible for it to be subverted. If we are fed the calorie-rich but nutrient-poor diet of false truths long enough, we may forget the deep satisfaction of a simple carrot.

There is a glimmer of hope for the revivification of another kind of truth that may survive a post-truth world. The victim of post-truth in a correspondence theory will always be, by definition, truth itself. But if truth were sometime different than this, a different result might occur. In other words, while most of us still operate with a correspondence theory of truth, perhaps a change in what constitutes truth may protect us from the worst effects of post-truth.

Heidegger's *Aletheia,* usually translated from the Greek as "unconceal-ment," derives from an earlier notion of truth that was later displaced by our current proclivity for checking an idea against facts in the world. In this notion of truth, what had previously been unknown is brought into the realm of the known. Nothing is ever fully reliable, but new and more satisfy-ing (through their accuracy) views of the world may be uncovered—discovered—as they are brought into being. While this view sounds to be just a poetic version of correspondence, its emphasis is quite otherwise: the force here is in discovery through deeper inquiry of what is already there but perhaps overlooked. Heidegger's image of a clearing in a forest, a place of clarity of vision amid more dim vistas, seems to rest more on the feeling of truth than its ability to be checked. And it rests more on the constant new-ness of ideas, and draws attention to how these must be, in each moment, revisited.

In other words, this view of truth may enable us to take the weak point of vulnerability in democracies—that something has to feel true to us for us to decide on it—and turn it into a strength, by requiring us to be conscious of its feeling and need for constant rebirth more than we would otherwise. Once we think of truth as something that we have to work at to feel accu-rately, and to bring into being in each moment, we may be less vulnerable to the superficial feelings of truths presented to us in a post-truth context.

Notes

1. "The PhilPapers Surveys—Preliminary Survey Results," The PhilPapers Surveys, Philpapers.org.

2. Carole Cadwalladr, "Did Big Data Tip It for Brexit?" *Guardian Weekly,* May 19–26, 2017, 26–30.

3. Ibid., 27.

4. David Carroll, interviewed by Brent Bambury, host, *Day 6, CBC.* Broadcast October 14, 2017, http://www.cbc.ca/radio/day6/episode-359-harvey-weinstein-a-stock-market-for-sneakers-trump-s-data-mining-the-curious-incident-more-1.434 8278/data-mining-firm-behind-trump-election-built-psychological-profiles-of-nearly-every-american-voter-1.4348283.

5. Cadwalladr, "Did Big Data Tip It for Brexit?," 28.

6. Ibid.

7. Ibid.

8. Ibid.

9. Ibid.

References

Cadwalladr, Carole. "Did Big Data Tip It for Brexit?" *Guardian Weekly*, May 19–25, 2017, pp. 26–30.

Day 6, CBC. Broadcast October 14, 2017. http://www.cbc.ca/radio/day6/episode-359-harvey-weinstein-a-stock-market-for-sneakers-trump-s-data-mining-the-curious-incident-more-1.4348278/data-mining-firm-behind-trump-election-built-psychological-profiles-of-nearly-every-american-voter-1.4348283.

"The PhilPapers Surveys—Preliminary Survey Results," The PhilPapers Surveys, https://philpapers.org/.

CHAPTER TWELVE

Brazen New World: A Peircean Approach to Post-Truth

Mark Migotti

Public opinion—private laziness.

—Friedrich Nietzsche

"Post-truth," "alternative facts," "fake news"; oh dear! Philosophy is in the press, on the airwaves, all over the World Wide Web, but not in a good way. In my view, popular media promote philosophy well when they present philosophically rich ideas, problems, conundra, and so forth in an accessible, thought-provoking fashion with the aim of inciting readers and listeners to think more about them on their own. The BBC has long done this well, and podcasts such as *The Partially Examined Life* are following suit.

But to have to confront philosophical issues that sprout unbidden from the soil of public life in the confines of newspaper columns and other media is to be put in an awkward position indeed. And when you're confronting "post-truth," the difficulties multiply. For one thing, no reflective person can be in favor of post-truth. Unlike postmodernism, postcolonialism, post-Christianity, post-Kuhnian philosophy of science, or whatever, post-truth (as far as I can see) isn't something about which reasonable people can disagree; it's a malaise that needs to be diagnosed and deposited in the dustbin of history, not a new "controversial" way of thinking that needs to be judiciously examined "from both sides." And this means that the intellectual sangfroid needed to do good philosophy is easily compromised on this topic. As

Santayana so excellently observes, "In philosophy, partisanship is treason";[1] and the incapacity of post-truth to defend itself heightens the risk of mistaking well-meaning polemic against its manifest dangers and absurdities for substantial insight into the phenomenon.[2]

A further barrier to making philosophical headway with post-truth is the dense tangle of issues that make up the phenomenon: in post-truth the personal and the political, the empirical and the conceptual, the descriptive and the normative intertwine in very complicated ways. To take just one example which I won't have time to pursue, a great deal of writing about post-truth treats independence of mind and independence of the press as if they were much more tightly interconnected than they in fact are. While there are doubtless important connections between these two things, they are fundamentally distinct achievements, the one age-old and individual and the other only a few centuries old and social. To be sure, in the modern world, a responsible, independent press plays a crucial role in sustaining a public intellectual environment in which independent thought can thrive. But what relations there may be between thinking for yourself and being well informed about current events is something that, so far as I know, remains to be explored.[3] In any case, I take it that an age of post-truth must, if it is on us, be something different from an age of "post-established, authoritative news media," post-Walter Cronkite, as it were.

As I've just suggested, one family of philosophical questions raised by post-truth so understood has a Nietzschean accent: how are we to rank values, how are we to determine which ones are better and worse, and how, specifically, are we to rate the claims of truth and knowledge should these require us to sacrifice other good things? As my title indicates, however, in this chapter, I'm going to use Charles Sanders Peirce as my philosophical guide. Taking his "Fixation of Belief," published in 1878, as my main text, I aim to shed light on the philosophical roots and ramifications of post-truth by triangulating between this classic essay and Serbian American playwright Steve Tesich's lament for the sorry state of American public opinion, articulated in his "A Government of Lies" (1992), in which he used the locution "post-truth" for the first time in print, and Elizabeth Renzetti's comments on the frightening success President Trump seems to be having in his campaign to "set fire to the very notion of truth and observed reality" in a column that appeared in August 2017 in the Toronto *Globe and Mail*.

When I read the headline to Ms. Renzetti's column, "Is Donald Trump Winning His War on Reality?" I was baffled to the point of annoyance: "How can they print such arrant nonsense?" I muttered to myself? But a poll of grad students and colleagues in my department lounge revealed that my reaction was far from unanimous. Some thought that the headline suggested that Trump was engaged in a propaganda war, against everything he finds objectionable. But propaganda, as its etymology testifies, is in the first instance about propagating things, not attacking them. Granted, if the things propagated are false, then I suppose reality, or a sense of reality, could be said to be a casualty but more in the way of collateral damage than express target. Moreover, Renzetti, grants that "all politicians try to reach voters directly without the pesky interference of news outlets" but opines that what is "on the loose now is a different beast, one that seeks to destroy."

In fact, we're probably dealing not with a single beast but an unruly pack or an incongruous menagerie. And what, if anything, is really new about it all is a good question.

To wage a metaphorical war against the reality of this or that, parapsychology, astrology, palmistry, graphology, whatever, presumably is to call into question the credibility of the target item. Debunking of this sort is the stock in trade of the *Skeptical Inquirer* and other myth busters. It is carried out in the service of truth and depends on a robust opposition between what's real and what's not. But what's troubling the more reflective wing of the commentariat these days, what the *Globe and Mail*'s headline writer probably meant to invoke, and what prompts the present volume is the prospect that precisely this contrast between myth and reality is being wittingly put in peril, that the very distinction between fact and fabrication—said to have been derided by Karl Rove as a foolish prejudice of out-of-touch naïfs living in antiquated "reality-based communities"[4]—is falling into desuetude.

Fair enough, but there's a serious question into how much desuetude a distinction as fundamental as this one can fall. Can a functioning society, or a functioning human being, get away with *no* regard for truth, fact, and reality? Probably not, but as Peirce points out, they can try.

In Peirce's terms, to try to dispense with the contrast between fact and fabrication is to try to adhere to the tenacious method of fixing belief, the first of four ordered methods he considers in "The Fixation." Setting out the elements of what has come to be known as the doubt-belief model of inquiry, Peirce notes that doubt and belief differ along conceptual, psychological, and behavioral dimensions. Conceptually, doubt is vouchsafed in questions, belief in judgments and assertions; psychologically, doubt is a dissatisfied state of mind from which we naturally seek escape, belief a satisfied state which we are naturally inclined to sustain; and behaviorally, "our beliefs guide our desires and shape our actions, . . . [while] doubt never has such an effect."[5]

When we are in doubt about something, we are moved to "struggle to attain belief," and Peirce dubs this struggle "inquiry," though he admits that "this is sometimes not a very apt designation" (§374). But "if the settlement of opinion is the sole object of inquiry, and if belief is of the nature of a habit," Peirce wonders why we shouldn't "attain the desired end by taking any answer to a question which we may fancy" (§377)? Those who adopt this method of inquiry (or "inquiry") will, the moment doubt insinuates itself, seize on some belief or other which quells it, and then "constantly reiterate[e]" this chosen opinion to themselves, "dwelling on all which may conduce to [it] and learning to turn with contempt and hatred from anything which might disturb it." Followers of this method of fixing belief adopt a policy of make-believe in the precise sense of *making* themselves believe; Peirce calls it "the method of tenacity."

Peirce's account of the method of tenacity reads today like prophecy. Internet sites and social media are dominated by people loudly pronouncing the answers to questions "which they fancy"? They sure are; such individuals "constantly reiterate to themselves" the beliefs with which they are comfortable and dwell, in their "echo chambers," on all that conduces to them? They sure do; they "turn with contempt and hatred" from anything which might disturb them in these beliefs? Just listen to the rants, if you can!

The method of tenacity, Peirce writes, is often adopted "out of an instinctive dislike of an undecided state of mind, exaggerated into a vague dread of doubt [that] makes men cling spasmodically to the views they already take"; and again, we are struck by the superabundance of confirmation to be found in the baying, bawling, and brawling of the ethersphere. The guiding principle of the method of tenacity is that "a steady and immovable faith yields great peace of mind," and Peirce grants that this is so. While those who adopt this method may expose themselves to "inconveniences"—as, for example, would someone who "should resolutely continue to believe that fire would not burn him, or that he would be eternally damned if he received his *ingesta* otherwise than through a stomach pump"—they "will not allow that its inconveniences are greater than its advantages." "I hold steadfastly to the truth," they will say, "and the truth is always wholesome."

Sometimes, Peirce maintains, the method of tenacity is employed deliberately and urged expressly as a prophylactic against error. "I remember," he writes,

> being entreated not to read a certain newspaper lest it change my opinion upon free-trade. "Lest I might be entrapped by its fallacies and misstatements" was the form of expression. "You are not," my friend said, "a special student of political economy. You might, therefore, easily be deceived by fallacious arguments upon the subject. You might, then, if you read this paper, be led to believe in protection. But you admit that free-trade is the true doctrine; and you do not wish to believe what is not true."

In the time of POTUS 45 and masses of angry Americans, untainted by economic theory, but immovably convinced that free trade is costing them jobs, the aptness of this case in point is remarkable. Take a step back, however, and it looks like plus ça change; meet the new beast, the same as the old beast. Haven't people been clinging tenaciously to dearly held beliefs and

wallowing in "selection bias" since forever? In a journalism class in my fresh-
man year of university, the latter concept was illustrated with a memorably
insouciant response of George Wallace's to a request for his reaction to a
withering *New York Times*: editorial about his campaign for president in
1968: "Anyone that would think of voting for me," Wallace replied, "doesn't
read the *New York Times*."

Certainly, people will believe what they will, and what some will believe is
jaw-droppingly incredible; and they'll spout much nonsense, some of which
they truly believe, some of which they would like to believe (or believe that
they believe), and some of which they don't believe at all.[6] What may be new
is the tenacious method of fixing belief's receiving an unprecedented lease on
life and the level of dangerous nonsense in political discourse becoming
lethal. For reasons I will get to in a minute, Peirce believes that the method of
tenacity "will not hold its ground in practice." But maybe that's just because
he hadn't been exposed to the Internet, the problem with which, as journalist
John Diamond wrote in 1995, is that "everything written on it is true."

Peirce likens the rationale of the method of tenacity to that of the ostrich
that buries its head in the sand in response to signs of danger. In so doing,
Peirce writes, the unfortunate bird "very likely takes the happiest course. It
hides the danger, and then calmly says there is no danger; and if it feels perfectly sure there is none, why should it raise its head to see?"[7] If, with this in
mind, we turn to the article in which the term "post-truth" first appeared in
print, we will again be struck by Peirce's powers of foresight, for Steve Tesich
introduced his now-notorious locution in the course of lamenting a willful
ignorance on the part of the American public whose explanation (he, in
effect, suggested) was that the members of that public were fleeing en masse
into ostrichism motivated by precisely a desire to take that bird's proverbially
self-deluded "happiest course" in the face of unpleasant facts.

The burden of Tesich's essay is that in the aftermath of the Watergate
hearings and the resignation of President Nixon, more specifically in the
aftermath of disgust at the character of this traumatic episode, and the subsequent self-congratulation on the ability of America to allow truth to prevail
and democracy to triumph, "something totally unforeseen occurred [;] . . .
we began to shy away from the truth." As a case in point, Tesich argued that
the George H. W. Bush administration's decision to declassify telegrams of
July 1990 in which then ambassador to Iraq April Gillespie recounts her conversations with Saddam Hussein regarding Iraq's border dispute with Kuwait,
information that Tesich thinks proves beyond a doubt that the ostensible
grounds for the 1991 Gulf War with Iraq were entirely spurious, reveals that
the administration was "no longer afraid of the truth" because it could be
confident that "the truth will have little impact on us."

In Tesich's view, the Bush administration's blithe indifference to letting its
own mendacity become public knowledge testified to its arrogant contempt

for the American people. "We've given you a glorious victory," it was saying, "and we've given you back your self-esteem. Now here's the truth. Which do you prefer?" And instead of rising up in umbrage at the outrageous suggestion that respect for truth and respect for yourself are mutually exclusive, as opposed to mutually reinforcing, the public showed itself to be worthy of its government's scorn, a pliable intellectual mass in the hands of its rulers. "We are," Tesich warns, "rapidly becoming prototypes of a people that totalitarian monsters could only drool about in their dreams." Whereas "up to now [dictators] have had to work hard at suppressing the truth, we are saying that this is no longer necessary, that we have acquired a spiritual mechanism that can denude truth of any significance." And then the prescient coinage: "In a very fundamental way we, as a free people, have freely decided that we want to live in some post-truth world." Since we can't handle the truth, let's believe something more pleasing.

If our syndrome is post-truth, Peirce's method of tenacity is an instance of pre-truth. In the method of tenacity, "the conception of truth as something public is not yet developed." It's not that tenacious believers are unfamiliar with the words "true" or "truth"; as we've just heard, if challenged to defend a belief that seems to have many "inconveniences" attendant on acting on it, the tenacious believer will insist that he cleaves to the truth, which is always wholesome. But being able to use a word competently is no guarantee of any real understanding of what it signifies: "Merely to have such an acquaintance with [an] idea as to have become familiar with it, and to have lost all hesitancy in recognizing it in ordinary cases . . . only amounts to a subjective feeling of mastery which may be entirely mistaken."

Moreover, however you arrive at a belief and whatever sustains you in it, if you believe something, you take it to be true; that's what distinguishes believing something from considering it, hoping for it, and so on: "We think each one of our beliefs to be true and, indeed, it is a mere tautology to say so." But when tenacious believers say "I hold steadfastly to the truth and the truth is always wholesome," they can mean no more than "I hold steadfastly to what I believe and what I believe is always wholesome." If asked whether there is an important difference between what it is for something to be true and what it is for something to be believed by them, and if willing to give thought to what it is they are asked to pronounce on, tenacious believers may even give the correct answer, that there's all the difference in the world between these two things. But their actions belie their words; their intellectual habits reveal that this distinction means nothing to them.

According to Peirce the method of tenacity cannot sustain itself in practice because "the social impulse is against it," and this impulse is "too strong in man to be suppressed, without danger of destroying the human species." With post-truth on our minds, we may demur on the grounds that today, so far from destabilizing tenacious belief, an unholy nexus of social forces is currently allowing it a weird and frighteningly effective foothold. But if we did this, we'd be missing something important, the force of which can be brought into view by moving to the second of Peirce's methods of fixing belief, the method of authority.

"Unless we become hermits," then, "we shall necessarily influence each other's opinions," and this means that "the problem becomes how to fix belief, not in the individual merely, but in the community."

> Let the will of the state act, then, instead of that of the individual. Let an institution be created which shall have for its object to keep correct doctrines before the attention of the people, to reiterate them perpetually and to teach them to the young; having at the same time power to prevent contrary doctrines from being taught, advocated or expressed. Let all possible causes of a change of mind be removed from men's apprehensions. Let them be kept ignorant, lest they should learn of some reason to think otherwise than they do. Let their passions be enlisted, so that they may regard private and unusual opinions with hatred and horror.

Where Tesich speaks of old-school dictators as having to work hard at suppressing the truth, Peirce's point is that the first business of authoritarian regimes is the suppression of independent thought. In the preceding passage, he signals first the authoritarian regime's need to indoctrinate the young, second its need to banish public dissent, and third the importance of enlisting the passions of the populace on behalf of the tried and true, such that the public "regard private and unusual opinions with hatred and horror."

To the objection that the dogmatisms of mutually warring ideological factions that surround us tell against Peirce's confidence that the tenacity method of fixing belief will be unable to resist the pressure of "the social impulse" in humankind, we now see that the response is to point out that these "echo chambers" of mutually reinforcing incredibility are better described as instances of the authority method writ small than as examples of the method of *individual* tenacity. Peirce's method of authority is a method of sustaining communal belief by socially engineered entrenchment, as opposed to the method of sustaining individual belief by sheer force of will.

Still, when Peirce assures us that "the man who adopts [the method of individual tenacity] will find that other men think differently from him, and it will be apt to occur to him, in some saner moment, that their opinions are quite as good as his own, and this will shake his confidence in his belief," we may still want to reply: "But no, that is exactly what's so troubling about the whole post-truth thing; people don't seem to have these 'saner moments' in which grant that people who think differently from them have opinions 'quite as good as their own.'" Indeed, it may be thought that a signal problem with post-truth is precisely that it leads to the unpromising view that, to quote Prado, "no opinion expressed by a given individual can be judged superior or inferior to any other."[8]

With this, we arrive at an important difference between Peirce's pre-truth method of tenacity and the culture of post-truth. For the "can" in Prado's rendition of a post-truth credo is normative, and the credo is general. The idea is that *no one* is *entitled* to judge any given opinion to be inferior or superior to conflicting opinions on the same subject. On this understanding, post-truth involves a ruthless and ridiculously rigorous egalitarianism of opinion. What Peirce has in mind by the "the conception that [someone else's] thought or sentiment may be equivalent to one's own" is something different. His idea is that if we're not hermits, we'll talk to each other; and when we talk to each other, we'll be forced to realize that we each have our own opinions, which opens up the possibility of agreement, or disagreement, between us.

If we discover that we disagree about something, neither of us will continue to enjoy the unchallenged confidence in the truth of the relevant beliefs that we had before the disagreement came to light. It's not just that our confidence *should* be affected but that *unchallenged* confidence has been made impossible. This is why Peirce thinks that learning that the thought or sentiment of someone else may be equivalent to my own is a "distinctly new [and highly important] step" in the development of a full-blooded understanding of truth. It is also, of course, why practitioners of the authority method of fixing belief need to ensure strict uniformity of opinion. As long as you and I are of the same opinion, I can acknowledge that your thought is equivalent to my own without disturbance, and so, mutatis mutandis, can you.

In both the method of individual tenacity and the method of authority, it is the desire to feel confident about things that sustains belief in them: when feeling and opinion trump facts and evidence, beliefs are motivated by the "impulse to believe," not by anything to do with what is believed. Socially engineered authority differs from individual tenacity in that, if the social engineering is carried out effectively, the authority method of fixing belief can, by one measure anyway, hold its ground in practice over long periods of time: "Except the geological epochs, there are no periods of time so vast as those which are measured by some of these organized faiths [which exemplify the authority method of fixing belief]." How long will it be before the present Tower of Babel of the alt-right, doctrinaire left, crackpot conspiracy theorists, and so on topples is anybody's guess.

"If we scrutinize the matter closely," Peirce continues, "we shall find that there has not been one of [the] creeds [of these organized faiths] which has remained always the same; yet the change is so slow as to be imperceptible during one person's life, so that individual belief remains sensibly fixed." And then, a chilling pronouncement: "For the mass of mankind, then, there is perhaps no better method than this [the method of authority]. If it is their highest impulse to be intellectual slaves, then slaves they ought to remain."

More precisely, people with no inclination to think for themselves about difficult, important topics, politics and religion chief among them, may as well adhere to the dictates of some authority or other. On many other, less momentous subjects, all of us need to form our own opinions. For "no institution can undertake to regulate opinions upon every subject. Only the most important ones can be attended to, and on the rest men's minds must be left to the action of natural causes."

In the present context, and that of "The Fixation," two "natural causes" of belief stand out: sense experience and elementary principles of inference. If we couldn't rely on the evidence of our senses to provide us with generally true beliefs about our environment, we wouldn't be here to discuss the matter, and the same goes for our ability to reason logically, in the broadest sense of the term. As Peirce puts it, "We are doubtless in the main logic animals," since "logicality in regard to practical matters (if this be understood . . . as consisting in a wise union of security with fruitfulness of reasoning) is the most useful quality an animal can possess." In Quine's nice apothegm, "Creatures inveterately wrong in their inductions have a pathetic but praise-worthy tendency to die before reproducing their kind."[9]

When survival depends on getting it right, then utter disregard for truth and reality isn't an option. And when we reflect on the more egregious examples of brazening it out in the face of contrary evidence that have had us shaking our heads over the past year or so—the relative size of the crowd at Obama's first inaugural and at Trump's, whether Trump did or didn't call the White House "a real dump" during a round of golf (the August 2017 tempest in a teapot which provided Renzetti with the occasion for her "war on reality" column), and so on—we notice that they are basically free of palpable cost on the part of the those who are brazening it out. No loss of life or limb; no bridges collapsing; no harm, no foul.

Until recently you might have thought that the price of looking like a fool on a large stage would have been steep enough to prevent presidents and press secretaries from testifying to the truth of known falsehoods in public, but in this we may indeed be living in a new era. Adherents of the battling microcultures I've so often mentioned don't seem to care what anyone else thinks of them. As long as things are good between the opinion makers in the group, their base, all is well; the rest of the world can go to hell. And as long as we're not dealing with matters of life and limb, groups of this sort may be able to sustain themselves indefinitely. As Peirce remarks, immediately after emphasizing that logicality in *practical* matters may be the most useful quality an animal can possess, "outside of these it is probably of more advantage to the animal to have his mind filled with pleasing and encouraging visions, independently of their truth" (p. 5.371).

Not wanting to end on an exclusively gloomy note, I observe that while post-truth may be rampant, opposition to it is robust; the present volume being a fine case in point. And just when "post-truth" is deemed the word of the year, Einstein's extraordinary prediction of gravity waves is borne out by experimental evidence; a victory for truth and the human ability to fathom the universe if ever there was one. As a political culture, we may not be faring so well right now. But as a species, we may do all right in the longer term.

Notes

1. George Santayana, *The Life of Reason, Vol. 1: Reason in Common Sense* (Cambridge, MA: MIT Pess, 2011 [1910]), p. 68.

2. To adapt a maxim about morality of which Schopenhauer was fond of—preaching morality is easy, grounding it is hard—it's a lot easier to decry post-truth than to understand it.

3. For his part, Nietzsche thought that the political detritus of the day was inimical to productive philosophical thinking. "That which Heraclitus avoided . . . is still the same as that which *we* shun today: the noise and democratic chatter of the Ephesians, their politics, their latest news of the 'Empire' (the Persian you understand), their market business of 'today'—for we philosophers need to be spared one thing above all: everything to do with 'today'" (*Genealogy of Morals,* trans. Walter Kaufmann [New York: Vintage Books, 1969], III §8, 109).

4. Not only is it not, so far as I have been able to establish, a documented fact that it was Rove who coined the phrase "reality-based community," but the relevant passage in the article that introduced this form of words to the world is not obviously about post-truth at all. In the piece in question, in *New York Times Magazine,* Ron Suskind attributed the expression to an unnamed aide in the George W. Bush administration, who is quoted as having said that "guys like me were in what we call 'the reality-based community,' which he defined as people who 'believe that solutions emerge from your judicious study of discernible reality.' . . . 'That's not the way the world really works anymore,' he continued. 'We're an empire now, and when we act, we create our own reality. And while you're studying that reality—judiciously, as you will—we'll act again, creating other new realities, which you can study too, and that's how things will sort out. We're history's actors . . . and you, all of you, will be left to just study what we do'" (*New York Times Magazine,* October 17, 2004). This seems to me a mixture of truisms: political action is different from political analysis, and posturing: "We're an empire now." The truism is true but not alarming; the posturing is scary but has no obvious bearing on the plausibility of the view that solutions to political problems may require, or at least be helped by, the "judicious study of discernible reality."

5. Charles Sanders Peirce, "The Fixation of Belief," Charles Hartshone and Paul Weiss, eds., *Collected Papers* (CP) (Cambridge, MA: Harvard University

Press, 1931–1958), p. 5.371. Further citations from "The Fixation" will be identi-fied in the text by paragraph number of CP Volume 5 in brackets.

6. As our editor puts it, "The making of assertions that feel true to those mak-ing them, regardless of the facts, is a practice as old as linguistic interaction itself and nothing is likely to change it."

7. In fact, there seems to be no evidence that ostriches do respond to impend-ing danger in this proverbially and comically futile fashion. See, for example, the discussion of the subject at https://www.scienceworld.ca/blog/do-ostriches-really-bury-their-heads-sand.

8. Prado, in his proposal to contributors to this collection.

9. W.V.O. Quine, "Natural Kinds," *Ontological Relativity and Other Essays* (New York: Columbia University Press, 1969), p. 126.

CHAPTER THIRTEEN

The Fallacy of Post-Truth

Lawrie McFarlane

It has become commonplace to say that we live in a "post-truth" world; that one person's opinion is as good as another's; and that when we come right down to it, everything is subjective.

Writing in the online blog supported by the prestigious journal *Scientific American,* a British scholar, Julia Shaw, carried this notion to its ultimate limit: "I'm a factual relativist. I abandoned the idea of facts and 'the truth' some time last year . . . Why? Because much like Santa Claus and unicorns, facts don't actually exist."[1]

Let's set aside the not inconsiderable problem that Shaw is stating, as a fact, that there are no facts. Shaw's argument is that science is the basis of all knowledge, and since scientists never finally prove anything, facts are merely suppositions that may later be overturned. Over the course of history, there have been numerous attempts to advance this argument. For simplicity's sake, they can be sorted into three varieties, one contemporary and based in politics, one relatively modern and based on a category mistake, the other as old as the hills—the hills of Athens to be precise.

None of these arguments succeed, but let's begin with the contemporary, political variety. It has become routine over the past decade and a half to hear politicians accused of, and accusing each other of, statements that amount to the fabrication of "fake news." Circulation of fake news is very likely the most sociopolitically ominous aspect of professional and popular acceptance of post-truth, of the new tolerance of, and indeed, preference for subjectivity.

Arguably, an early version of fake news appeared in the September 15, 2004, edition of the *New York Times.* A few days previously, on September 8,

2004, a CBS news-show had featured memos which purported to show that then president George W. Bush, who was running for reelection, received preferential treatment during his service with the Texas Air National Guard. Under scrutiny, the memos, and their provenance, quickly fell apart, and both Dan Rather, the show's anchor man, and his producer were fired by CBS.

Nevertheless, the *New York Times,* in its September 15 edition, ran a news story intended to suggest that even if the memos were not genuine, their contents nevertheless coincided with the truth. The story was headlined, "Bush memos are fake, but accurate, typist says." It's always dangerous to identify the precise occasion on which a new phenomenon arose, but it is safe to say that the *New York Times* headline entered public discourse as an apparently novel sort of claim: that a document could be both fake and accurate.

We can dispense quickly with this specific instance of fake news. The *New York Times* wasn't really introducing a new form of epistemological assertion. It was trying to keep alive a story the basic truth of which it believed, namely, that Bush had received preferential treatment, while admitting that the documents at hand could not be verified as to who had authored them (supposedly Bush's commanding officer). Had the *New York Times* headline run something like this "Bush memos are fake, but the assertions contained in them actually are true," the problem would disappear. In short, this is merely shoddy headline writing. The *New York Times* could have made its point just as well using uncontroversial language that would have avoided the unfortunate application of both "fake" and "accurate" to the Bush memos. The memos were not both fake and accurate. The memos were fake, but the assertions made in them may well have been true.

However, there is a more problematic form of the notion of fake news and its emergence on the scene. We now frequently read media stories accusing politicians of creating fake news. The idea is to imply that certain politicians hold views so systematically divorced from a firm factual grounding that, in some important sense, they don't know truth from falsity. Of course, the allegation that a given politician has "misspoken himself," or just plain lied, is commonplace. But the suggestion here goes further. It is that some politicians are living in an alternate reality, one in which they may very well believe what they say is true, even when others know it is not. If this isn't exactly a new kind of epistemological assertion, it comes close to one by permitting the possibility that someone can be quite mistaken across a wide range of experiences and yet fail to realize it. Moreover, we're not talking here about a schizophrenic suffering delusions or an uneducated individual who simply lacks the grasp of basic facts we normally take for granted that adults understand. We are talking, rather, about someone in a position of power, or potentially about to be so, from whom we have a right to expect a minimal level of informed understanding. When we find a politician who does not appear to meet this qualification, we now assign to his statements the normative term "fake news."

This is a more complex claim than the "fake but accurate" usage, because it isn't mere sloppy writing. Nevertheless, it can, in fact, be dismissed. Part of the reason fake news emerged as a way to categorize some types of political assertion is that it can be easy to misunderstand, or misrepresent, what a politician actually meant to say. I recall on numerous occasions, as a deputy minister in both the Saskatchewan and British Columbia governments, hearing my minister or a colleague say something that could not be literally true or even close to it. And yet they were neither misinformed nor attempting to dissemble. I recall many other times attending cabinet meetings as an official and not understanding what decision had been reached, even though all of the ministers did. And it was my unfortunate duty to write the minutes for some of those meetings.

What happens around cabinet tables is that a form of abbreviated "poli-speech" develops, as ministers come to know each other, and the issues, well. Call it a form of shorthand. Partly, it is used to move things along when everybody agrees; partly, its purpose is to avoid confronting a dissenter with a too-obvious, and hence needlessly embarrassing, rebuff. Useful as this shorthand is, however, it can give rise to general confusion if used in public or in media interviews. Here are two examples: I remember a minister of mine, when asked if the rumor was true that his government was about to close a hospital in Regina, saying, "We're shutting that down." Those were, literally, his instructions from the premier: go out there and shut this rumor down. But by merely repeating words that rang in his head, he misled the reporters who heard him, leading them to think it was the hospital that was to be shut down. A second example occurred during the run-up to the D-Day landings, when Prime Minister Winston Churchill told a group of senior American officers, "I'm hardening on this." Churchill was referring to the D-Day landings. But his audience was horrified. Planning had been under way for two years, there were mere days left, and the prime minister was only "hardening" on the plan? Inadvertently, Churchill rekindled long-held suspicions on the American side that he had never wanted to attack northern France at all, preferring an assault through Turkey and the Balkans, which, to American minds, reflected British imperialist sentiments. But what apparently happened was that Churchill had used this phrase several times with his colleagues, some of whom, like him, feared a repeat of the trench warfare prevalent during World War I. This was language many around his cabinet table understood but in no way implied a lack of resolution on Churchill's part to go ahead with the landings. Nevertheless, by blurting out a careless phrase to an already-suspicious audience, he created a minor diplomatic crisis and undermined his standing with Britain's closest ally.

There is a second, equally innocent, cause of the rise of the term "fake news." It frequently falls to politicians to explain complex matters in simple language. Those who can do this with ease are sometimes called good "retail politicians." No matter how difficult the issue, they can reduce it to terms the ordinary man or woman in the street can understand. But not everyone has this gift. Prime Minister Jean Chrétien, for all his broken English, had it. His successors, Paul Martin and Stephen Harper, did not. Yet, no matter how inept a politician may be at reducing the complex to the simple, it is a job that must be done. And the results are often ammunition for opponents and news agencies. For example, while campaigning for the U.S. presidency, Donald Trump called then president Barack Obama "the founder of ISIS." This was seized on as a good example of fake news, an instance of a politician whose worldview was so distorted that he could come up with such a ridiculous allegation. But Trump didn't literally mean that Obama went off to the Middle East, met with various terrorist groups, and proposed the formation of ISIS. What he meant was that Obama's foreign policy, by creating a vacuum in that region, had created the conditions that enabled ISIS to emerge. Poor choice of words? Perhaps. But consider that it is common to read that the Versailles Treaty, by its one-sided terms, brought about World War II. No one suggests that David Lloyd George, British prime minister at the time, intentionally instigated a war. The proposition is simply that a poorly designed treaty made possible the backlash in Germany that led to the rise of Hitlerism.

I suggest then that the introduction of the term "fake news" is based either on political shorthand that often fails in conveying its message or on unfortunate human frailties that do not justify what I believe is a very damaging practice. The news media share some of the blame here. Fake news at times appears as little more than a rhetorical device for dismissing opinions or claims with which journalists personally disagree. And this is not done just by opinion-column writers. News reporters increasingly employ this strategy.

The harm here comes from conflating two incompatible terms: "fake" and "news." If something is fake, it is not news in the sense implied. But by running the two together in this manner, our news media have helped generate the impression that there are several competing versions of the news, some of which are more credible than the others. This does an immense disservice to the whole concept of news. In any self-respecting media outlet, there is only one version of the news, namely, the version that has been fact-checked and which the editors stand behind. But a generation of young people have been introduced to the idea that news itself is a malleable commodity. This is a retrograde step that undermines the very organizations that make use of it.

And it has an unfortunate concomitant. We now see newspapers and network news shows rushing allegations into print that turn out to be poorly sourced, inadequately fact-checked, and in some cases just plain false. Of course, human error is ever with us. Recall the headline in the *Chicago Daily Tribune* on November 3, 1948, "Dewey defeats Truman." Oops. But it does appear, of late, that the editors of our news agencies are employing increasingly lax standards. In June 2017, CNN ran several stories, each of which had to be retracted within days. On June 7 the news agency made the claim that James Comey, recently dismissed from his post as director of the FBI, would testify before Congress that he had not told Donald Trump, on three occasions, that Trump was not under investigation. Trump had said that Comey did tell him this. The story was based on an anonymous source. The next day Comey released a copy of his prepared remarks for Congress, in which he noted that he had indeed given three such assurances to Trump.

Shortly after that, on June 26, the news station reported that a confidant of Donald Trump, Anthony Scaramucci, was under investigation by the U.S. Senate for potentially improper involvement with a Russian investment fund. That led to the resignation of three of CNN's most highly regarded journalists, one of them a Pulitzer Prize winner, when it became known the story was not true. At the same time a CNN producer, John Bonifield, was caught on tape admitting that the network's Trump-Russia narrative was "mostly bullshit" and that CNN was pursuing this issue because it was good for ratings and revenues.

But rather than conduct soul searching, some journalists are now arguing that the whole idea of objectivity is passé. Here is Mitchell Stephens, writing in the June 26, 2017, edition of the online magazine *Politico*: "The big news is that many of our best journalists seem, in news coverage, not just opinion pieces, to be moving away from balance and nonpartisanship. Is this the end of all that is good and decent in American journalism? Nah. I say good for them. An abandonment of the pretense to 'objectivity'—in many ways a return to American journalism's roots—is long overdue." Similar claims are becoming increasingly common, as some reporters appear willing to abandon objectivity as an outmoded value. It is difficult to avoid the conclusion that this will not end well.

Let us turn then to the second argument that we live in a post-truth world, that one can say what *feels* true to oneself, and that facts do not exist. It is frequently pointed out in support of this argument, as Julia Shaw does, that scientific claims made at one point in time are disproven or withdrawn in a later era. Thus, the belief that the sun revolves around our planet, held true in the Middle Ages, has now been discarded. Likewise, the idea that the Earth is flat fell out of favor centuries ago.

We've seen the same revisionism in other scientific fields, such as medicine and dietary science. We now know the germ theory of infection is correct. But as late as the mid-19th century, physicians were ridiculed for suggesting it, and one, Ignaz Semmelweiss, was committed to a lunatic asylum—to use the then-current term—where he committed suicide after enduring beatings by the guards for making the radical proposal that doctors attending childbirth should first wash their hands.

In addition, a number of dietary warnings issued as recently as 50 years ago are now in doubt. Thus, for example, it is no longer believed that foods such as eggs, cream, and cheese, which are rich in dietary cholesterol, represent as much of a threat to heart health as was once thought true. Apparently dietary cholesterol does not enter the blood stream to the extent previously believed.

This argument is also encountered in nonscientific fields. Perhaps the most pronounced manifestation of this view is the claim that there are no such things as historical facts. Thus, we are reminded, for instance, that the indigenous peoples of North America, historically viewed by colonial settlers as backward and inferior, are now accorded their due dignity and rights. Again the fire-bombing of Dresden during World War II was believed at the time by most citizens of the allied countries to be just retribution for other horrors inflicted by Germany. The same might be said of the nuclear attacks on Hiroshima and Nagasaki. Indeed, it was held by some that U.S. president Harry Truman would have been impeached had he refused to authorize the attack, and this fact had subsequently become known.

Today, we are not so sure. Japan was already on its knees, with conventional bombing having created as much damage as nuclear bombs. And Dresden was hardly a significant enough military target to warrant complete destruction.

In short, the substance of this first attempt to argue that there are no facts rests on demonstrations of circumstances in which apparently settled understandings were later revised or altered. In simple terms, things often are not as they appear. Before we turn to upending this argument, it is worth noting a development in the entertainment industry that may have played a role in weakening our confidence in facts. This is the emergence of highly realistic, but nevertheless manufactured scenes on television and in movies. Computer-generated imagery is now almost indistinguishable from the real thing. Who can tell where virtual reality ends and the genuine article takes over?

This is a difficult notion to tie down. How exactly the construct we call reality is influenced and shaped is not at all clear. Yet we do know, from the work of philosophers like Michel Foucault, that our sense of self, and how we see the world, is heavily influenced by consciousness-shaping forces. Might not the emergence of virtual reality have played a part in loosening our grasp on what is real and what is not?

Very well, then. There appear to be a wealth of historical circumstances and current-day experiences that might call in question the idea that absolute facts exist. Therefore, is Julia Shaw right after all? No. First of all, there very definitely are facts in our world and plenty of them. For instance, it is a fact that the current prime minister of Canada is Justin Trudeau. Again, it is a fact that President John F. Kennedy was assassinated. And it is a fact that Japan attacked Pearl Harbor on December 7, 1941.

These are not theories that future evidence might disprove. They are plain, unequivocal facts. Hundreds of people witnessed Kennedy's assassination in person. Hundreds of millions more saw it replayed on television. There are the medical logs at Parkland Memorial Hospital where Kennedy was treated and died. There is the testimony of dozens of doctors, nurses, and pathologists. There is Jackie Kennedy's blood-spattered dress, Lyndon Johnson being sworn in aboard Air Force One, French president Charles de Gaulle striding, grim faced, behind Kennedy's funeral cortege.

So yes, there indeed are facts in our world. Here is the error that Shaw and others who share her viewpoint commit: there is a world of difference between statements of fact—that is, assertions that something is true—and judgments or theses. The claim that the sun revolves around the Earth was a scientific thesis; it was an attempt to account for observations at a time when no alternative theory was supported by evidence then available. Likewise, the claim made 300 years ago that indigenous North Americans were backward and primitive was a judgment, not a fact. So too were the contemporary beliefs that the attacks on Dresden, and on Hiroshima and Nagasaki, were fully justified. Some now take a different view of these matters because our scale of values has changed. In short, it is not facts that are mutable but theories and judgments. And science, as Shaw does correctly observe, is a collection of theories, not facts. This second argument against the existence of facts, then, rests on a category error: the error of mistaking judgments or theories for factual statements.

Now, I would expect to face the following challenge. You say facts and theories are different, and that may be so. But how are we to tell one from the other? For if the two are, in practical circumstances, indistinguishable, then what validity is there in your line of thought? And here we encounter the third, and much older, category of arguments to the effect that there are no indisputable facts.

Plato, in *The Republic,* imagines a cave in which a number of individuals are chained together facing a wall. Behind them a fire is lit, and as other inhabitants walk to and fro in front of the fire, their shadows are cast on the wall. Those chained in place never see the real people behind them, they see only the shadows, and for them, this shadow world is their entire reality. Their world is, in this sense, an illusion, but they have no way of discovering that. Illusion, for them, becomes reality. This idea became one of the precursors of an entire school of ancient Greek philosophy: skepticism. The original skeptics did not necessarily dismiss all knowledge as flawed and unprovable, but they counseled against overconfidence in claiming knowledge. Theirs was, in a sense, a form of pragmatism. They believed they had discovered systemic weaknesses in the way humans arrive at knowledge. But, on the other hand, they also accepted the impracticality of employing this doctrine in everyday life. Therefore, they counseled wariness rather than outright rejection of factual knowledge.

In the 17th century, the French philosopher René Descartes carried this line of thought a step further. In his *Discourse on the Method* and later in his *Principles of Philosophy,* Descartes describes a thought experiment. One by one, he examines the sources of his knowledge of the external world. Sensory evidence is suspect, he declares, because our senses so often mislead us. A simple example: collect three bowls, fill one with hot water, one with cold water, and one with lukewarm water. Place one hand in the hot water and one in the cold. Then after a minute or two, place both in the lukewarm bowl. To the hand that was in the hot water, the lukewarm water will feel cold. But to the hand that was in cold water, the lukewarm water will feel hot. Yet a single bowl of water cannot be both hot and cold at the same time. Clearly our sense of touch is unreliable. The similar criticism can be leveled at our other senses. People frequently mistake what they think they saw, hence all those "Bigfoot" sightings. Gunshots are frequently mistaken for cars backfiring. How something smells, cologne or food, often depends on what strong odors we have been exposed to previously.

Descartes then turns to his inner thoughts. Might these not also be other than they seem? For instance, while he is sitting in a darkened room conducting this thought experiment, is it not possible that instead he is dreaming? And what about hallucinations? The Nobel Prize–winning mathematician, John Nash, whose story is told in the movie *A Beautiful Mind,* believed aliens had appointed him emperor of the Antarctic. When he was in his late twenties, Nash turned down a prestigious university appointment because he claimed he was "busy forming a world government." The point, though, is that Nash was a bright guy. You would think he would realize the intrinsic impossibility of these ideas. But he did not. When asked why, he answered that it was because he got them from the same place he got all his wonderful mathematical insights. In short, he could not tell illusion from reality.

Descartes's conclusion is that on a purely rational basis, he was obliged to dismiss as unreliable almost everything he thought he knew:

> Thus, because our senses sometimes deceive us, I wished to suppose that nothing is just as they cause us to imagine it to be; and because there are men who deceive themselves in their reasoning and fall into paralogisms, even concerning the simplest matters of geometry, and judging that I was as subject to error as was any other, I rejected as false all the reasons formerly accepted by me as demonstrations. And since all the same thoughts and conceptions which we have while awake may also come to us in sleep, without any of them being at that time true, I resolved to assume that

everything that entered into my mind was no more true than the illusions
of my dreams.[2]

Descartes rescues one point of certainty:

> But immediately afterwards I noticed that whilst I thus wished to think all
> things false, it was absolutely essential that the "I" who thought this should
> be somewhat, and remarking that this truth "*I think, therefore I am*" [empha-
> sis mine] was so certain and so assured that all the most extravagant sup-
> positions brought forward by the sceptics were incapable of shaking it.[3]

And that, so far as human thought and perception is concerned, is all we
can claim to know. Descartes does go on to pull a fast one that has made him
a favorite of first-year, philosophy-course teachers everywhere. He asserts as
a matter of faith that there is an all-powerful God and that by His nature, He
would not permit us to be deluded. Therefore, while our mortal sources of
knowledge are not in themselves reliable, we have God's word for it that they
can be taken at face value. A skeptic or an atheist might wonder why this
belief is any better founded than the others Descartes dispenses with.

Here, then, in summary, is the third argument against the view that we do
indeed possess factual knowledge of the world. Much, if not virtually all, of
that knowledge comes to us via our senses and through our powers of
thought and reasoning. But as experience shows, these mental faculties are
open to numerous distorting influences and, in some circumstances, are
quite frail. Yet the claim to know something entails far more than a statement
of belief or inner conviction. It entails, by definition, a degree of accompany-
ing proof or justification that is robust beyond dispute. And such certainty
lies outside our reach.

Therefore, let us see if we can dispose of this line of reasoning. First, as
noted at the outset, there is a certain unseemliness in claiming, as a fact, that
there are no facts. And this is more than a mere rhetorical maneuver. The
term "fact" has meaning only if there are degrees of certainty, from vague and
unsubstantiated beliefs at one end through well-supported opinions to justified claims of knowledge at the other end. The very idea that there are facts
depends on these distinctions. Just as there cannot be an up without a down,
or a right without a wrong, so there cannot be error without truth or falsity
without facticity.

Consider the offside rule in soccer. Now, there need be no such rule. Its
existence is purely a matter of convention. But so long as the rule applies,
offside exists, as, by necessity, does onside. You cannot have one without the
other. The same can be said of facts. This term also derives its meaning from
a rule book, the book of language. It is possible to imagine a language that

made no use of such terms as "truth" or "fact," but it is not possible to imagine such a language in which "false" or "mere opinion" still had meaning. There is a logical interconnectedness between them. Hence, when Julia Shaw says, "I am a factual relativist," on what imagined distinction is she trading? What could it mean to be a relativist, if it were not also possible to be an objectivist?

What can be said is that standards for truth vary from circumstance to circumstance. An astronomer who claims to have detected alien life is making a very large claim. And large claims demand an equally large body of evidence. But if I get up in the morning and the ground is white, I'm entitled to say it snowed during the night. Yes, a Hollywood special-effects team could have come by and sprayed my yard with fake snow, but the chances of that are remote. That is to say, it takes a larger body of evidence to support the claim that alien life exists than to support the observation that it snowed last night. There are other fields that employ their own standards of proof. In our court system, for example, prosecutors must satisfy jurors "beyond a reasonable doubt."

This is the crux of the matter. In daily life, we do not require mathematical certainty. The evidence conditions required for everyday observations vary considerably from those required to support scientific theses. Shaw may be right that scientists never finally prove anything, though it is hard to imagine, for instance, how the heliocentric theory regarding our solar system could ever be disproved. But she errs entirely in extending that claim to the assertion that we live in a post-fact world and that facts, like unicorns, do not actually exist.

Does any of this matter? Yes, it does. Notions like fact and truth are among the most important signposts that guide us through our lives. They are not merely options. Discard them in favor of some woolly relativism or, worse still, the subjectivism that underlies use of post-truth worldviews, and anything goes. We read frequently of a "war on science." In truth, that has been going on since the 15th century (and arguably longer). Concepts like truth and reason have not come easily to our species. Perhaps our history of fallibility—and not just fallibility but disastrous, potentially life-ending fallibility (the Cuban missile crisis, North Korea's mad pursuit of weapons of mass destruction, two world wars)—has taught us a lesson. We are not just capable of error. Computers are capable of error, robots are capable of error, albeit not often to such an extent.

But humans have an additional weakness: we can not only screw up, but we may be willing to deny it right to the bitter end. It's not just a matter of ego, though egos certainly count. It's a matter of inner conviction. We can hold to our story as God's honest truth, long after the facts went out with the tide. Once we become attached to a narrative, it has a way of altering our perception, or recollection, of events. This, of course, was Descartes's point—that our inner compass is fallible and, more to the point, alarmingly self-justifying, even in the face of what should count as indisputable evidence to the contrary.

Therefore, here is the quandary. That humans are fallible no one would deny. Yet our lives are founded on a basis of knowledge that cannot be disturbed—in the main—without wrecking the very distinction that supports not only the concepts of truth and facticity but, just as important, the contrary notions of falsity and fake knowledge. There is no eluding this reality. Even to try would invite superstition, willful ignorance, and hapless credulity. There's a term for that: "medievalism." And as things stand, that's where we are headed. So much for the Age of Reason.

Notes

1. Julia Shaw, "I'm a Scientist, and I Don't Believe in Facts," 2016, https://blogs.scientificamerican.com/mind-guest-blog/im-a-scientist-and-i-dont-believe-in-facts/.

2. René Descartes, *Discourse on Method and Meditations,* trans. Elizabeth Haldane and G.R.T. Ross (Mineola, NY: Dover Publications, 2003 [1637]), *Discourse,* Part IV, p. 65.

3. Ibid.

About the Editor and Contributors

Editor

C. G. Prado, PhD, is emeritus professor of philosophy, Queen's University, and a fellow of the Royal Society and listed in *Who's Who in Canada*. He has authored, coauthored, and edited 19 books on religion, Descartes, Michel Foucault, assisted suicide, and social media. His most recent are *Coping with Choices to Die* (Cambridge) and *Social Media and Your Brain* (Praeger). He has also contributed to a number of edited collections and published numerous journal articles (see www.cgprado.com).

Contributors

Chris Beeman, PhD, is assistant professor of education at Brandon University. His research includes long-term friendships and research relationships with Teme Augama Anishinaabe and other aboriginal elders in exploring the connection between human beings and their physical locale through the growing and gathering of food.

Juan Pablo Bermúdez, PhD, teaches philosophy at the Universidad Externado de Colombia. His work bridges the classical Greek tradition of Plato and Aristotle and contemporary issues at the intersection of philosophy and psychology. His current focus is on deciphering the philosophical implications of empirical research on the human mind and what we can learn from them to lead more autonomous and authentic lives. He has written and lectured on topics such as the nature of automatic behavior, the limitations of our decision-making capacities, and what we can do to overcome them.

Khadija Coxon is a Toronto writer and editor, currently living in Kingston, Ontario. With degrees in English and philosophy, she has written about a variety of topics involving big questions, including emotions, food, social media, and expertise. She has worked on the journal *Social Studies of Science,* is a founding member of its companion blog *Transmissions,* and currently is an acquisitions editor for McGill-Queen's University Press.

Paul Fairfield, PhD, is professor of philosophy at Queen's University. He is the author of several books on hermeneutics, existential phenomenology, and the philosophy of education, including *Teachability and Learnability, Death: A Philosophical Inquiry, Philosophical Hermeneutics Reinterpreted,* and *Education after Dewey* (www.paulfairfield.com).

Jason Hannan, PhD, is associate professor in the Department of Rhetoric and Communications at the University of Winnipeg. He is the editor of *Philosophical Profiles in the Theory of Communication* (2012) and of *Truth in the Public Sphere* (2016).

Greg Kelly, DPhil (Oxon.), is executive producer of the CBC Radio program *Ideas.* His work in CBC Radio and Television has won over two dozen national and international awards. His TV documentaries *Deadline Iraq* (2003) and *Beyond Words: Photographers of War* (2005) won several awards and were screened before live audiences in Bangkok, London, Moscow, New York, Paris, Toronto, and Vancouver. The éminence grise of photojournalism, John G. Morris described *Beyond Words* as "the most important documentary ever made about photojournalism." In 2006, Greg left the CBC to create and run the NPR daily current affairs program, *The Story.* He later moved to Radio Netherlands Worldwide, where he led the internationally acclaimed program, *The State We're In.* In 2013, he returned to Canada and assumed the helm of *Ideas,* heard by over a million listeners every week.

Mark Kingwell, MLitt, MPhil, PhD, DFA, is professor of philosophy at the University of Toronto and a contributing editor of *Harper's Magazine* in New York. He is the author or coauthor of 18 books of political, cultural, and aesthetic theory. In addition to many scholarly articles, his writing have appeared in more than 40 mainstream magazines and newspapers. His recent books are the essay collections *Unruly Voices* (2012) and *Measure Yourself against the Earth* (2015), and the monograph *Fail Better: Why Baseball Matters* (2017).

Alex Leitch, BA(Hons), MDes, is a writer and game designer living in Toronto, Ontario. She has written and produced many incentive-driven applications and games, most recently Hothouse, a Toronto Arts Council–sponsored installation of large-scale robotic flowers at *Come Up to My Room,* 2017, at the Gladstone Hotel. Alex teaches game design at OCAD University when not running artifact.digital, an interaction design consultancy.

Lawrie McFarlane, PhD, served as secretary of the Treasury Board, deputy minister of advanced education and manpower, deputy minister of education, and president and CEO of the Saskatoon Regional Health Board in Saskatchewan; and deputy minister of health, Treasury Board secretary, and deputy minister, Crown Corporations Secretariat, in British Columbia. He presently writes editorials for the *Victoria Times Colonist.* He is coauthor of *The Best Laid Plans: Health Care's Problems and Prospects* and has written editorials in the *Canadian Medical Association Journal.*

Mark Migotti, MPhil, PhD, is professor of philosophy at the University of Calgary. He has published on Schopenhauer, Nietzsche, Charles Sanders Peirce, and the nature of promising and penalties. With Richard Sanger, he is the author of *Hannah's Turn,* a play about Arendt's love affair with Heidegger, that was produced to wide acclaim at the Summerworks Festival in Toronto. His current projects include an interpretation of Nietzsche's *On the Genealogy of Morals* with the working title *Ethics and the Life of the Mind,* and a Socratic investigation into what it is to have sex that draws on ideas from H. P. Grice and Simone de Beauvoir.

Lisa Portmess, PhD, is Bittinger chair of philosophy at Gettysburg College. Her research focuses on philosophy of technology, applied ethics, and social philosophy. Her recent work has examined issues of Big Data and its linguistic representation, UN peacekeeping ethics, the moral ambiguity of cyber war, and MOOCs and postcolonial knowledge export. She served as a professor at the American University of Beirut, an American Philosophical Association congressional fellow, a resident fellow at the Centre for Philosophy and Public Affairs at the University of St. Andrews, and a Fulbright scholar at the American University in Cairo.

Sergio Sismondo, PhD, teaches in the departments of philosophy and of sociology at Queen's University. His current project is on the political economy of pharmaceutical knowledge, looking at relations between research and marketing in areas from clinical trials through medical education. He is the author of *An Introduction to Science and Technology Studies* and a number of other general and philosophical works in science and technology studies. He is also editor of the journal *Social Studies of Science.*

Index